Assessing Adolescents
with the MACI

Assessing Adolescents with the MACI

Using the Millon Adolescent Clinical Inventory

Joseph T. McCann

John Wiley & Sons, Inc.

New York • Chichester • Weinheim • Brisbane • Singapore • Toronto

ISBN 0-471-32619-4

Printed in the United States of America.

10 9 8 7 6 5 4 3 2 1

To my parents,
Mom and Hank;
Dad;
Mary and (the memory of) Joe.

Foreword

THE HISTORY of adolescent personality assessment is only of recent origin. We know that early interest in child guidance was stimulated by the work of Lightner Witmer, who created the first psychology clinic about 100 years ago. Despite his focus on young children and teenagers, clinicians did not seriously explore the adolescent realm insofar as enduring traits were concerned. The attention of adolescent psychologists, well into the mid-1930s, centered on appraising features such as intelligence, achievement, interest, and aptitude, rather than notions such as adolescent personality styles and psychopathology. Although it is not the first mental test to be used with troubled teenagers, the *Millon Adolescent Personality Inventory* (MAPI), initially distributed in 1974, sought to illuminate a wide range of psychological features that might increase our understanding of the clinical difficulties of young people.

The progenitor of the MAPI was the MCMI (*Millon Clinical Multiaxial Inventory*). This latter instrument was developed in the early 1970s in an effort to counteract the tendency of both instructors and students to develop their own methods to "operationalize" theoretical concepts that were first published in my 1969 *Modern Psychopathology* text. I became concerned about the quality of these diverse representations of the theory, and I protectively decided to organize an effort to construct an instrument myself that could be used by all investigators of my work. Not only would it add a degree of operational uniformity among researchers, but it would ensure, at least, a modicum of psychometric quality. Although the University of Illinois research group that I supervised in the early 1970s took on the responsibility of searching for an extant psychological instrument that might be employed to interpret the personality styles generated by the theoretical model, we found nothing that could serve that function effectively. Hence, we began constructing the MCMI, a new self-report inventory. After spending more than 6 years on this research project, we brought out the first of the three forms of the instrument in 1977.

During the years in which we developed the MCMI, several of my associates, both psychologists and psychiatrists, began to discuss the possibility of our constructing a "psychiatric test," not only for patients in mental health settings, but also for adolescents and for patients seen primarily for medical treatment. They not only encouraged, but contributed significantly to the development of what was then called the MAPI, the *Millon Adolescent Personality Inventory*, as well as the MBHI, the *Millon Behavioral Health Inventory*.

Some years after the publication of the MAPI, I noted that users of the instrument were primarily interested in matters of clinical significance. Well over 85% of those who used the MAPI preferred to employ it as a clinical tool. As a result of this awareness, we began to plan and undertake a series of modifications of the MAPI, producing changes that would prove of particular value to practicing clinicians who worked with adolescents. Notable among these changes was the inclusion of several clinical syndrome scales geared to such problematic concerns as depression, drug abuse, and anxiety. Also, the range of the personality styles/disorder scales were increased so they would accord more closely to the new *Diagnostic and Statistical Manual of Mental Disorders* (DSM-IV, APA, 1994). The product of these efforts, published in 1993, was designated the *Millon Adolescent Clinical Inventory*, also known as the MACI.

Joseph McCann, author of this first full text on the MACI, is the best known workshop presenter on the topic. He wrote this book to provide, in a single reference source, an in-depth examination of what is now the most frequently used adolescent test on personality and psychopathology in current clinical practice. It is much more than a compilation of how to do this or that. It provides the reader with significant information concerning how the test was developed, how it can be administered, and, most importantly, how to interpret the characteristics and problems that typify troubled youngsters. Dr. McCann's desire was to provide both students and practitioners with a significant body of clinical knowledge so that the instrument could be used in a competent and thoughtful way. The use of objective psychological tests in evaluating adolescents is a major skill that must be acquired by any clinician employed in residential, outpatient, court, prison, or school settings.

There has been a marked increase in our understanding of adolescent difficulties in the past two or three decades; violence and general delinquency have been most noteworthy. Despite the growth of this knowledge, there has been no book that deals with the utility of the MACI as an assessment and diagnostic instrument. Dr. McCann has successfully remedied this problem. His book has been so carefully written as to enable the inventory to be useful to individuals with only a modest background in objective tests and/or adolescent difficulties. Moreover, the book can serve as an introduction to a cognitive and behavioral understanding of adolescents, and may be of considerable value to undergraduates and beginning graduate students who are becoming involved in techniques for assessing adolescents and their problems. Not unimportantly, the book may also be of interest to physicians, social workers, and psychiatrists who work with adolescents in trouble.

It has been especially gratifying that objective inventories are being interpreted increasingly in terms of personality characteristics and traits. Their data are interpreted more and more in the form of configural profiles. No longer are personality functions appraised as if they were a set of independent trait scales; they are now analyzed as holistic integrations that possess clinical significance only when seen as the interrelated and Gestalt composites they are.

The development of the MACI coincided with a time when the field of psychological assessment came under severe restrictions. Owing to the attitudes and behavior of Managed Care providers, the much-maligned projective techniques were cast aside, viewed as quaint and costly tools for clinical assessment. Fortunately, the MACI (and the MCMI) came into play, providing many clinicians with a brief and largely inexpensive tool that could furnish a broad and dynamic interpretation of patients in all mental health settings. Tests such as the MACI have rapidly emerged as major new tools, not only to accommodate the economic and cultural forces seeking simple and quick-fix techniques, but also to provide extensive information for understanding the lives and troubles of adolescents.

Assessment with the MACI will enable the student and the clinician to develop a sophisticated basis for disentangling the many variations among youngsters, to assess both their assets and liabilities, to determine the presence of clinical disorders, and most importantly, to provide a full picture that can serve as the basis for making decisions regarding each adolescent's welfare, that is, to be able to outline a logical course of treatment which may prove optimally efficacious. This is one of the great values of Dr. McCann's book. It will guide the reader to transform the raw MACI test data, coordinate these data with the history of the youngster's experiences, as well as with observational and interview information, facilitating interpretive syntheses and providing thereby a basis to help link assessment to psychotherapy.

Although experienced professionals will likely want to create data syntheses that require a certain amount of clinical imagination on their part, McCann wisely includes Appendix A, which provides a series of subfacets, that is, facets that represent a series of trait subareas composing each scale. For example, he takes each personality/coping scale, and indicates not only the factors of which it is composed, but also the specific item groups contained therein. Thus, for the "Oppositional scale" (Negativistic tendencies), he notes the following major facets: self-punitiveness, angry dominance, resentful discontent, social inconsiderateness, and contrary conduct. In describing the facets of the "Conforming scale" (Obsessive-Compulsive tendencies), he records the following: interpersonal restraint, emotional rigidity, rule adherence, social conformity, and responsible conscientiousness. In this way, he provides significant information that should reduce the clinician's need to depend on speculative hypotheses for reports.

Also of special interest to those who have used the MACI previously is Dr. McCann's recognition that the vast majority of teenagers in trouble represent what I have termed "mixed personality types." In his text, he guides the reader toward an integrated perspective of the person, and demonstrates how each elevated scale is only one relevant part of the overall configural result. Also attractive is that McCann brings the instrument to life by recognizing its complexities and its richness of detail, and does so in a manner that makes it easy for the reader to retain a focus on its essentials. Equally valuable is his objectivity, evident in numerous ways, such as taking into account not only the instrument's strengths, but also a number of its limitations.

This book fills an important gap in the clinical literature, as well as one found in many training programs. Dr. McCann is justly considered a clinician of renown, known for his acumen in personality assessment and for his exceptional teaching talents. For every instructor of a personality assessment course who seeks a way to expose students to the intriguing problems of teenage life, and for every student who worries about translating general theories into everyday clinical practice, this book will provide relevant insights as well as practical assistance. Its clear style, vivid language, and excellent organization will make it a superb text for both advanced undergraduate and graduate assessment courses. This text is insightful and comprehensive, a work of inestimable value to both practicing clinicians and students. Far more detailed than the test's official manual, this book provides readers with a basis for making unusually accurate and clinically useful analyses of adolescent behaviors and vulnerabilities.

THEODORE MILLON

Preface

THIS BOOK is a culmination of several years of using the Millon Adolescent Clinical Inventory (MACI) in clinical and forensic settings as well as a synthesis of information I have presented in workshops on the instrument. I have found the MACI to be an extremely valuable assessment tool when conducting psychological evaluations with adolescents. Any clinician working with this population knows that it can be challenging, and the MACI offers several distinct advantages that facilitate the assessment process. Despite the strengths of the MACI, however, I also have attempted to provide a balanced presentation that recognizes the limitations of the instrument. Although I have found the strengths to far outweigh the limitations of the MACI, sound clinical assessment practices require a fair appraisal of an instrument. Thus, I point out limits in using the MACI in certain situations.

This book is an interpretive guide directed at the novice MACI user as well as the clinician who has extensive experience with the instrument. To my knowledge, this is the first book devoted entirely to the MACI and given the apparent growing use of this test, this book will fill the void in published literature on the instrument.

The dearth of empirical research on the MACI has created some challenges in writing this book. Initially, I was somewhat hesitant in taking on the project because I had hoped that more published research would appear and thus provide a body of literature from which to draw. It seems I have had that sentiment for the past 5 years, beginning at the time the MACI was first published. Although some scattered publications are available, there are also some significant unpublished studies. I have drawn on both published and unpublished data to the extent it facilitates interpretation. I also present some new analyses on existing data in the manual to highlight key issues with interpretation.

It is unclear why the MACI has not received more extensive attention in the empirical literature because the instrument has many advantages in clinical practice. Nevertheless, I have drawn on several sources of information to provide support for the discussions in this book. In particular, I have drawn on data in the MACI manual, published research studies, unpublished research, theoretical literature, workshop materials I have used in the past, and my own experiences with the test.

I hope that this book meets two major goals. The first goal is that clinicians who use the MACI will find it to be a helpful guide for understanding the test, interpreting results in clinical evaluations, and making appropriate recommendations for treatment and case management. A second goal is that the book will draw more attention to the MACI as an adolescent assessment instrument and that this attention will stimulate research into the many issues that have yet to be explored.

JOSEPH T. MCCANN

Acknowledgments

As with any project of this scope, there are several individuals whose assistance and support deserve special recognition because they provided a valuable contribution and made the process of writing more bearable.

I am particularly grateful to those who have shared so many interesting MACI cases with me over the years. The numerous participants in workshops I have presented have helped me to learn more and I appreciate their input and feedback. Also, I thank my colleagues at the Binghamton Psychiatric Center, Pam Vredenburgh, Allan Hochberg, Connie Kinch, and Linda Huntley, for sharing their cases with me. Martha Mason deserves a special note of thanks for the lending of her excellent library skills that have so reliably helped to track down and secure articles for my research.

Other people have been consistent sources of support and professional stimulation: Chuck Ewing, Frank Dyer, and Robert Tringone have willingly discussed cases and professional issues with me.

At NCS Assessments, Virginia Smith, Kristi Everson, Mark Caulfield, Kathy Gailucca, and Ann Stocker have consistently been supportive and responsive over the years. I am extremely grateful for their support. Also, Jeff Kim was able to secure copyright permission to reproduce selected materials that contribute to the overall presentation of the material. MACI™, MCMI-III™, and Millon™ are trademarks of DICANDRIEN, Inc. and permission to refer to them in this book is appreciated.

As always, Ted Millon has provided me with support in my work. He was one of the major motivating forces behind this book, and I very much appreciate his encouragement. In addition to his highly respected and valued work, I am indebted to him for the advice he has offered to me over the years. Also, Roger Davis at the Institute for Advanced Studies in Personology and Psychopathology has been extremely helpful. He answered several critical questions about development of the MACI and also made his research available for inclusion in the book. As such, his contributions are very much appreciated.

Finally, I want to recognize the considerable support of my family. My wife Michele continuously gives her love and guidance and provides me with the inspiration to continue my work. My son Alexander has given me a newfound appreciation for learning and he is a constant source of joy. Whereas this book is the product of my physical and mental efforts, it is the product of their generosity and support.

J.T.M.

Contents

CHAPTER 1

Basic Issues and Theoretical Foundations

THE PAST decade has not been particularly kind to teenagers because many alarming trends have received a great deal of media attention. During the 1997–1998 academic year, five schools became sites of tragedy when a student opened fire with a weapon on a group of teachers or classmates. In Mississippi, a teenager shot and killed two girls, one of whom had broken up with him earlier. In Kentucky, a 14-year-old shot and killed three students and wounded five others for reasons that were never made clear in media coverage. In Arkansas, an 11-year-old and 13-year-old student lured teachers and peers outside a middle school by pulling a fire alarm and then shot at them; in the end, four students and a teacher were killed. Although national statistics have shown a decline in violent crime overall in recent years, the data mask an alarming increase in violent crime perpetrated by teenagers. According to statistics published by the Federal Bureau of Investigation (1993), the arrest rate for violent crime rose 45% among teenagers between 1988 and 1992. Although juvenile homicide apparently dropped 30% between 1994 to 1996, more than 2,000 juvenile homicides were still reported in 1996 (Schiraldi, 1998).

Criminal violence is not the only concern for young people in this country. Over a 30-year period going back to 1957, the overall suicide rate for people age 15 to 24 tripled (Berman & Jobes, 1991). After a peak suicide rate in the late 1970s, suicide among young people appears to have leveled off, but the rate remains high nevertheless, with about 12 suicide deaths per 100,000. These statistics point to an increased demand for assessing and treating the mental health problems of adolescents. Where inpatient and outpatient clinics once focused on adults, and the occasional child or adolescent, there are now specialized outpatient clinics

1

and inpatient hospital units, residential treatment programs, and substance abuse units that focus on adolescents.

The mental health problems of adolescents and their increasing involvement in the criminal justice system have created a pressing need for accurate and useful methods for assessing adolescent personality and psychopathology. This book presents information on clinical use of the Millon Adolescent Clinical Inventory (MACI; Millon, Millon, & Davis, 1993), including an overview of the instrument's development, approaches to interpretation, and use of the test results for developing treatment plans for adolescents receiving mental health services. This chapter provides a brief overview of the MACI, followed by a discussion of general issues that set forth a context in which both novice and experienced MACI users can understand how to utilize the results from this psychological test.

The first portion of this chapter provides a brief summary of the MACI, including its format and foundations. This section is followed by an overview of adolescent development and the assessment of psychopathology in adolescence. A complete analysis of these issues is beyond the scope of this chapter; however, this discussion points out the unique psychological processes that occur in this critical period of development. The chapter then closes with a summary of Theodore Millon's theory of personality and psychopathology. An understanding of this theoretical model is critical to the interpretation of MACI test results because the theory served as a guiding framework for development of the instrument. Moreover, the theory is a major source of information for interpretation of the MACI.

OVERVIEW OF THE MACI

The MACI is a 160-item, 31-scale self-report inventory designed to assess personality styles, significant problems or concerns, and clinical symptoms in adolescents. Using a true-false format, the MACI surveys a wide range of personality characteristics and clinical symptoms that tend to be a focus in psychological evaluations of teenagers who either have or are suspected of having emotional or behavioral difficulties. Responses of adolescents on the MACI items are scored and individual scales are plotted in a profile as illustrated in Figure 1.1. The MACI can be used in several settings to evaluate the psychological status of adolescents: inpatient and outpatient mental health clinics; residential treatment centers; correctional facilities; and educational institutions where professionals suspect psychological difficulties are affecting a teenager's school performance.

Multiscale personality inventories such as the MACI are designed to improve the clinician's understanding of an adolescent's personality and clinical symptoms, but there are other reasons for using such instruments. The MACI can be helpful in formulating diagnostic hypotheses,

MACI™
ID 8681

PERSONALITY CODE: -**74<u>53</u>//-**F*-//-**-*EECC//

VALID REPORT   DATE: 12/17/97

CATEGORY		SCORE		PROFILE OF BR SCORES				DIAGNOSTIC SCALES
		RAW	BR 0	60	75	85	115	
MODIFYING	X	274	37					DISCLOSURE
INDICES	Y	15	78					DESIRABILITY
	Z	1	35					DEBASEMENT
	1	17	38					INTROVERSIVE
	2A	9	28					INHIBITED
	2B	7	31					DOLEFUL
	3	48	68					SUBMISSIVE
	4	49	74					DRAMATIZING
PERSONALITY	5	47	68					EGOTISTIC
PATTERNS	6A	25	45					UNRULY
	6B	6	18					FORCEFUL
	7	62	82					CONFORMING
	8A	14	33					OPPOSITIONAL
	8B	6	16					SELF-DEMEANING
	9	1	4					BORDERLINE TENDENCY
	A	7	31					IDENTITY DIFFUSION
	B	3	15					SELF-DEVALUATION
	C	0	7					BODY DISAPPROVAL
EXPRESSED	D	24	51					SEXUAL DISCOMFORT
CONCERNS	E	9	54					PEER INSECURITY
	F	37	76					SOCIAL INSENSITIVITY
	G	7	40					FAMILY DISCORD
	H	1	9					CHILDHOOD ABUSE
	AA	0	6					EATING DYSFUNCTIONS
	BB	5	11					SUBSTANCE-ABUSE PRONENESS
	CC	31	66					DELINQUENT PREDISPOSITION
CLINICAL	DD	9	27					IMPULSIVE PROPENSITY
SYNDROMES	EE	28	71					ANXIOUS FEELINGS
	FF	1	13					DEPRESSIVE AFFECT
	GG	1	11					SUICIDAL TENDENCY

CONFIDENTIAL INFORMATION FOR PROFESSIONAL USE ONLY

Figure 1.1   The MACI profile. Copyright © 1993 DICANDRIEN, INC. All rights reserved. Published and distributed exclusively by National Computer Systems, Inc. (NCS). Reproduced with permission by NCS.

confirming clinical diagnoses, formulating treatment plans, or making decisions about case management and disposition planning. In addition, the MACI can be used as an outcome measure to evaluate changes in an adolescent's functioning as a result of treatment and intervention. The MACI can also be effective in research studies to investigate a range of issues that pertain to adolescent psychopathology, personality, and treatment response.

In the following chapters, numerous issues will be discussed on development of the MACI, its psychometric properties, interpretation of results, and its use in assessing a wide range of diagnostic and treatment issues. However, some basic principles are relevant to understanding the full range of applications of the test and warrant discussion here. The MACI is based on an approach to test development that departs from the way clinicians approached adolescent assessment a decade ago. Traditionally, adolescents were often viewed as "miniadults": personality assessment instruments developed on adult populations were administered to adolescents with the adoption of specific age-referenced norms. However, some problems, social pressures, and developmental considerations are unique to adolescents, and adult personality measures tend not to capture these issues. The MACI was developed specifically for adolescents and the item content and scales were designed with these unique issues in mind. In addition, the MACI, like its adult counterpart the Millon Clinical Multiaxial Inventory-III (MCMI-III; Millon, Davis, & Millon, 1997), is based on a comprehensive theory of personality and psychopathology (Millon, 1969, 1981, 1990; Millon & Davis, 1994). Many clinical assessment instruments are not necessarily grounded in a comprehensive theoretical model; however, the theory developed by the MACI author, Theodore Millon, offers a logical, coherent, and internally consistent model for developing item content, scale composition, and a general framework for understanding test results. Therefore, the theoretical model can inform test interpretation in the same way that psychometric properties and research results can inform the interpretive process.

In light of these issues, it is important to recognize the unique problems that adolescents encounter and the underlying theory of personality and psychopathology on which the MACI rests. The remainder of this chapter describes these issues and will provide MACI users with a context for understanding the material in the remainder of this book.

ADOLESCENT DEVELOPMENT

In everyday language use, adolescence is a term that generally refers to the teenage years. However, strict chronological age can be problematic in defining when specifically adolescence occurs. Among most people who study this period of development, there is a consensus that adolescence is a stage of considerable transition. As noted by Coleman (1992):

> The transition, it is believed, results from the operation of a number of pressures. Some of these, in particular the physiological and emotional

pressures, are internal; while other pressures, which originate from peers, parents, teachers, and society at large, are external to the young person. Sometimes these external pressures carry the individual towards maturity at a faster rate than he or she would prefer, while on other occasions they act as a brake, holding the adolescent back from the freedom and independence which he or she believes to be a legitimate right. It is the interplay of these forces which, in the final analysis, contributes more than anything to the success or failure of the transition from childhood to maturity. (pp. 10–11)

This observation by Coleman captures the many different pressures and struggles that characterize adolescence. Biological, psychological, and social pressures contribute to the tension between independence and dependence on the family.

There are many ways to define adolescence (Petersen, 1988). Chronological age is one means, but this approach is limited because it does not fully identify this period's developmental aspects. If one assumes the teenage years of 13 to 19 define adolescence, then these age parameters do not encompass other essential features. Puberty is often a biological marker that is used to mark the onset of adolescence; however, some teenagers reach puberty prior to age 13 while others may have a delayed onset. Thus, chronological age is not often an accurate marker. Other gauges have included specific grade levels (e.g., junior and senior high school), cognitive factors such as the onset of formal operations, or the structure of an individual's social environment (e.g., involvement with certain peer groups, leaving the parental home). Some have viewed adolescence broadly as encompassing the second decade of life (Petersen, 1988).

In this book, adolescence is generally conceptualized as the teenage years from 13 to 19. Although this definition has limitations, it also defines the age range for which the MACI can be appropriately utilized. Within the developmental stage of adolescence, several factors are significant. The transitional nature of this period creates a tension between adequate adjustment and turmoil. This conflict is characterized in the quotation from Coleman's (1992) work cited at the beginning of this section. Moreover, it is implicit in this characterization of adolescence as a transitional period that a certain degree of emotional and psychological upheaval is to be expected. Despite these challenges, evidence supports the conclusion that whereas most teenagers can cope with the demands and turmoil of adolescence, some cannot and come to the attention of the mental health or juvenile justice system (Petersen, 1988).

Adolescents can potentially experience problems with adjustment in several areas of functioning. In the biological realm, adolescents experience physical changes related to puberty, and marked changes in hormonal activity bring on increased sexual interest and tension. Therefore, adolescents can experience concerns about their physical development, sexuality, and body image. Some of these concerns may be transient and relatively common, but others may reflect psychological discomfort and maladjustment. In the psychological realm, adolescents face changes in identity, self-concept, and cognitive maturity in response to gradually increasing demands to select a career path and set of life goals. Again, these challenges may be relatively common, but in some cases the adolescent may develop marked discomfort or confusion about his or her identity or self-worth. In the social realm, adolescents face tension between developing greater interests with peers or adopting group norms and the demand to maintain some emotional and financial dependence on parents. This tension again can be the source of normal conflict between the adolescent and the family, but it can also escalate into marked disturbances such as insecurity among peers, oppositional or defiant acting-out, or a lack of empathy toward others.

The unique challenges of adolescence dictate that the assessment of adolescents must include measures that take these issues into account. In many respects, the MACI addresses these issues by including scales that measure concerns that are of most salience in the lives of adolescents.

ASSESSING ADOLESCENT PSYCHOPATHOLOGY

It should come as no surprise that the transition's adolescence and the turmoil that characterizes this stage of development create unique challenges for the clinician who is assessing for psychopathology. The *Diagnostic and Statistical Manual of Mental Disorders-IV* (DSM-IV; American Psychiatric Association, 1994) constitutes the most widely adopted diagnostic framework in clinical practice and is therefore a useful starting point for analyzing the diagnosis of psychopathology, or mental disorders, in adolescents.

The *DSM-IV* defines a mental disorder as "a clinically significant behavioral or psychological syndrome or pattern that occurs in an individual and that is associated with present distress ... or disability ... or with a significantly increased risk of suffering death, pain, disability, or an important loss of freedom" (p. xxi). This definition emphasizes that the behavioral or psychological syndrome must be a source of distress for the person or a cause of some impairment in functioning and not merely a deviation from normality. With respect to diagnosing a mental disorder in adolescents, the *DSM-IV* approach makes two general provisions that offer some guidelines. The first is the identification of specific disorders that are usually diagnosed during infancy, childhood, or adolescence and the second is a special section of "Specific Culture, Age, and Gender Features" for other disorders that may be diagnosed in children, adolescents, or adults (e.g., major depression). Despite these provisions, there are still difficulties associated with the practice of diagnosing psychopathology in adolescents.

Although specific disorders in *DSM-IV* are identified as being first diagnosed in childhood and adolescence (e.g., conduct disorder, oppositional defiant disorder, mental retardation), sometimes these disturbances are not identified until adulthood. For example, attention deficit hyperactivity disorder is included in the "Disorders Usually First Diagnosed in Infancy, Childhood, or Adolescence," but in some cases the symptoms may not be accurately identified as being due to this condition until much later in life, even though the individual might have had some difficulties in childhood or adolescence. Also, the *DSM-IV* notes that the identification of specific disorders as having their onset in childhood or adolescence should not prevent clinicians from exploring other diagnoses that may be present in young people (e.g., major depression, posttraumatic stress disorder, schizophrenia). In those disorders that are found throughout the *DSM-IV*, the clinician must thus attend to the particular age features outlined for a specific disturbance.

The *DSM-IV* makes a number of provisions for diagnosing disorders in adolescence based on factors such as the specific age of the individual, the duration of time that symptoms should be present, and the expected age of onset for a particular form of psychopathology. Moreover, many of these provisions take into account research findings on the manifestation of psychopathology in adolescents. For example, antisocial personality disorder has as one of its criteria that the diagnosis cannot be made unless the person is at least 18 years of age. If a teenager below the age of 18 exhibits symptoms such as antisocial acting-out, chronic impulsivity, violation of the rights of other people, and similar features associated with antisocial personality, then a diagnosis of conduct disorder is appropriate. Moreover, *DSM-IV* notes that conduct disorder is an appropriate diagnosis only when "the behavior in question is symptomatic of an underlying dysfunction within the individual and not simply a reaction to the immediate social context" (American Psychiatric Association, 1994, p. 88). More importantly, research shows that conduct disorder in adolescence does not predict antisocial personality disorder in adulthood because some forms of adolescent antisocial behavior are limited to this phase of development, whereas other forms of such behavior are indicative of a life course of antisocial disturbance (Moffitt, 1993).

Another provision made by *DSM-IV* that is relevant to use of the MACI in clinical assessment is the specific caution made about diagnosing personality disorders in adolescents. Widiger and his colleagues (Widiger, Mangine, Corbitt, Ellis, & Thomas, 1995) urge caution in making personality disorder diagnoses in adolescents because many personality traits do not stabilize until the third decade of life and personality disorder diagnoses show limited stability from adolescence into early adulthood. As such, *DSM-IV* permits the diagnosis of all personality disorders except antisocial in children or adolescents, so long as "the individual's particular maladaptive personality traits appear to be pervasive, persistent, and unlikely to be limited to a particular developmental stage or an episode of an Axis I disorder" (American Psychiatric Association, 1994, p. 631). Moreover, the *DSM-IV* requires that the features of a personality disorder must be present for at least one year before making a diagnosis.

The overall structure of the MACI reflects this level of caution, as well as the controversy surrounding personality disorder diagnosis in adolescents. In particular, the Personality Patterns scales have names that reflect intermediate levels of disturbance. Although each of these scales parallels a specific *DSM* personality disorder, the scale names do not directly reflect these diagnoses as do the names of the personality scales on the adult version of the Millon inventories, the MCMI-III. Thus, Scale 1 on the MACI, while based on the construct of schizoid personality disorder, is called Introversive; Scale 2 on the MACI is named Inhibited instead of Avoidant, and so on. This subtle name alteration reminds MACI users that although the scales are designed to measure disturbed personality traits, judicious use of the scales and a conservative approach to diagnosis of personality disorders in adolescents are warranted.

In light of the challenges that arise when assessing psychopathology in adolescence, it is extremely helpful to have some guiding framework for making a diagnosis. The literature on adolescent psychopathology and specific diagnostic criteria as outlined in *DSM-IV* help to inform the assessment process. Instruments specifically designed for adolescents, such as the MACI, are another useful source of information. A unique aspect of the MACI is that it is based not only on traditional psychometric principles, but also on a comprehensive theory of personality and psychopathology. An understanding of this theoretical framework is necessary for a full appreciation of the MACI's development and for interpreting the test results. The remainder of this chapter describes the theoretical model on which the MACI rests. For readers who want a more detailed review of Theodore Millon's theory, Millon and Davis (1994) provide the most comprehensive and updated presentation.

MILLON'S THEORETICAL MODEL

The human personality can be studied and defined in many ways including descriptive or explanatory perspectives that focus on psychological, social, and biological factors. The theoretical approach to personality and psychopathology developed by Theodore Millon is a comprehensive and integrative approach to personality that is biopsychosocial in nature.

Originally formulated within a social learning model (Millon, 1969, 1981), the theory has expanded into an evolutionary one (Millon, 1990; Millon & Davis, 1994) in which the underlying constructs and principles are rooted in evolutionary theory and reflect many of the principles found in all sciences.

The most basic notion is the principle that individual personality traits lie along a continuum from normal traits and styles, to intermediate levels of disturbance, to abnormality involving disorders of personality. A central framework used to describe this continuum includes the concept of three dimensions, or polarities, each defining a separate aspect of human personality. The first polarity consists of *pain versus pleasure* and refers to the notion that human existence is directed toward maximizing pleasurable or life-enhancing experiences, and minimizing painful or life-threatening experiences. As such, individuals are generally oriented to seek out pleasure and minimize discomfort. A second polarity consists of *active versus passive* and refers to the typical ways of behaving that permit the person to seek out pleasure and minimize pain. The two ways of achieving pleasure include active means, such as manipulating and changing one's environment, and passive means such as accommodating and adapting to one's environment. The third polarity is *self versus other* and represents the source of reinforcing or life-enhancing experiences. This polarity recognizes the social nature of human existence in that some life-enhancing experiences come about through the self, such as getting what one wants or having one's needs met; and some experiences involve others, such as performing altruistic acts or having close interpersonal relationships. At the heart of this theory is the notion that normal functioning involves flexibility and adaptability because the person has a healthy balance between all these polarities. That is, flexibility exists between self and others and the capacity to be active or passive as the situation requires. Moreover, the normal personality is characterized by a clear focus on maximizing pleasurable life experiences and coping effectively with painful situations.

Disturbances in personality arise when the person becomes more rigid in a particular approach to coping, perpetuates vicious cycles in which the same difficulties arise in the person's life, and there is greater susceptibility to psychological distress or decompensation. Moreover, clinical symptoms such as anxiety, depression, or thought disorder are viewed as extensions of personality disturbances. Using the three polarities, Millon outlines five disruptions that can occur in the person's functioning that give rise to personality disturbances and psychopathology. The first disruption can arise in the person's instrumental style of coping in that he or she becomes fixated on either an *active* or a *passive* mode of coping. The second disruption in functioning can arise in the source of the person's life-enhancing experience when there is an excessive reliance on either the self *(independent)* or others *(dependent)*. The three other disruptions all arise in the pain versus pleasure polarity. The person can be *detached*, with an unwillingness or inability to experience pleasure in life. Another disruption can occur when the individual reverses the polarities of pain and pleasure, deriving pleasure from experiences that are normally painful and pain in situations that are normally pleasurable; this disruption is called a *discordant* personality pattern. The other disruption occurring in the pain versus pleasure realm is the *ambivalent* pattern whereby the person is conflicted between seeking out self-oriented versus other-oriented experiences.

These disturbances in polarities can be used to form a 2 (active-passive) × 5 (independent-dependent-discordant-ambivalent-detached) table that represents 11 basic personality styles. Table 1.1 outlines each of these styles with the labels reflecting intermediate levels of disturbance and the corresponding *DSM* personality disorder in parentheses. The active-independent personality is characterized by manipulation and self-centered acting-out that is represented in the unruly personality, corresponding to the antisocial personality disorder. The passive-independent style is characterized by a lack of empathy for others, feelings of entitlement, and grandiosity that define the egotistic personality, or the narcissistic personality disorder. Active-dependent personality is defined by gregariousness, attention-seeking, and emotionality that is meant to draw attention to one's self and to make others want to be around the person; this dramatizing style corresponds to the histrionic personality disorder. The passive-dependent personality is characterized by submissiveness, passivity, and inadequacy and reflects a submissive style that parallels the dependent personality disorder. The active-discordant style is characterized by hostile acting-out, the intentional infliction of pain, either verbally or physically, and excessive efforts to exert power over others; this forceful style corresponds to the sadistic personality disorder. Passive-discordant

Table 1.1
Personality Disorders in Millon's Theoretical Framework

Instrumental Style	Polarity Disruption				
	Independent	Dependent	Discordant	Ambivalent	Detached
Active	Unruly (Antisocial)	Dramatizing (Histrionic)	Forceful (Sadistic)	Oppositional (Negativistic)	Inhibited (Avoidant)
Passive	Egotistic (Narcissistic)	Submissive (Dependent)	Self-Demeaning (Self-Defeating)	Conforming (Compulsive)	Introversive (Schizoid) Doleful (Depressive)
Severe Patterns	Paranoid	Borderline	Borderline/ Paranoid	Borderline/ Paranoid	Schizotypal

types are self-loathing and pessimistic, and they feel deserving of their suffering and unhappiness; this self-demeaning type corresponds to the self-defeating personality disorder. The active-ambivalent personality experiences excessive irritability and moodiness, skepticism, and oppositional behavior; this style corresponds to the negativistic personality disorder. Passive-ambivalent types are conflicted and overcompensate by adopting a rigid adherence to rules and order, tight controls over emotions, and inflexibility; this conforming style corresponds to the compulsive personality disorder. In the detached personality type, there is an active variant that is characterized by withdrawal from others, heightened social anxiety, and the expectation of rejection and ridicule by others; this inhibited type corresponds to the avoidant personality disorder. Finally, there are two variants of the passive-detached style. The introversive style, corresponding to the schizoid personality disorder, is characterized by bland emotions, a lack of interest in relationships, and a lethargic and unemotional demeanor. The doleful style, corresponding to the depressive personality disorder, is characterized by pessimism, hopelessness, and chronic unhappiness. The major distinguishing feature between these two passive-detached types is that the introversive style is generally devoid of any emotional experience whereas the doleful style passively accepts a painful and dysphoric existence.

Millon also conceptualizes three personality disorders, the schizotypal, borderline, and paranoid, as severe variants of the more basic personality disorders. These three disorders are considered more severe because of the manifestation of transient psychotic episodes, severe disruption in identity, and more extreme levels of emotional dysregulation. Only the borderline personality is represented on the MACI because of the wide clinical interest in borderline disturbances in adolescents. The other two severe personality disorders are not represented on the MACI due to the low prevalence of these disturbances in the clinical sample that made up the instrument's normative sample.

The theoretical framework outlined here and schematically displayed in Table 1.1 has direct application to the clinical interpretation of the MACI. The individual scales on the MACI profile are arranged in accordance with this theoretical framework. In Figure 1.1, Scales 1, 2A, and 2B are arranged side by side and correspond to the inhibited, introversive, and doleful personalities; all three of these scales thus reflect the detached personality types in Millon's theory. Scales 3 and 4 in Figure 1.1 represent the submissive and dramatizing personality styles and also correspond to the dependent types. Scales 5 and 6A represent the egotistic and unruly personalities, which have the independent polarity disruption as the unifying theme. Scales 7 and 8A represent the conforming and oppositional personalities and have the ambivalent polarity disruption as their unifying theme. Only the two discordant types, forceful and self-demeaning, are placed next to scales that have similar behavioral and clinical presentations, but do not comprise a discordant dimension in side-by-side scales.

This arrangement of the MACI scales has some practical implications for interpretation because some MACI profiles with multiple scale elevations can be understood using the theoretical framework. If Scales 1, 2A, and 2B are all elevated, a general social detachment and lack of pleasure in life is represented in the profile. If Scales 2A and 2B are elevated, but Scale 1 is not, then social detachment associated with painful emotional experiences is being tapped. Likewise, if Scales 5 and 6A are elevated, the MACI profile is reflecting a general self-centeredness that may be manifest in both entitlement and expectation of special treatment as well as manipulative and antisocial acting-out. Because the discordant and ambivalent types experience conflict either in the nature or source of reinforcement, Scales 6B, 7, 8A, and 8B reflect a cluster of scales that reveal how the adolescent deals with internal conflict and tension. This issue is discussed in Chapter 5.

Another important concept in Millon's theory of personality is the prototypal model of individual personality types. A prototype represents a common set of features or characteristics describing members of a category that constitutes an ideal standard to evaluate individuals in the real world (Everly, 1995). What makes the prototypal model useful is that it provides different domains of personality to allow for the heterogeneity among people in actual practice. For example, clinicians rarely encounter a "pure" narcissistic or antisocial personality disorder; rather, people represent mixes and blends of personality styles, or two individuals with a specific personality disorder (e.g., narcissistic) may manifest different clusters of traits of the disorder.

The concept of domain of personality is important because it provides the basis for understanding the different personality styles discussed earlier. Millon defines two general features of personality: structural and functional. Structural attributes of personality "represent a deeply embedded and relatively enduring template of imprinted memories, attitudes, needs, fears, conflicts, and so on that guide experience and transform the nature of ongoing life events" (Millon & Davis, 1994, p. 144). Functional attributes of personality "represent dynamic processes that transpire within the intrapsychic world and between the individual's self and psychosocial environment" (p. 141). These structural and functional domains of personality are then organized at four levels: behavioral, phenomenological, intrapsychic, and biophysical.

The behavioral level of personality domains represents those aspects that deal with what a person does and what can be directly observed. The two domains of personality at this level are *expressive acts* and *interpersonal conduct*. Expressive acts are "readily observable by others" and "enable the clinician to define, through inference, valuable qualities of the patient's overall characterological presentation" (Everly, 1995, p. 29). Interpersonal conduct is "the way one relates to others" and "allows the clinician to declare qualities of personal competence, self-esteem," and needs for affiliation (p. 29). Both expressive acts and interpersonal conduct are functional attributes of personality.

At the phenomenological level, there are three domains of personality. These have the common theme of deciding how the person experiences him- or herself in the world. The three domains at this level are *cognitive style, object representations,* and *self-image.* Cognitive style represents how people "perceive events, focus their attention, process information, organize their thoughts, and communicate their reactions and ideas to others" (Everly, 1995, p. 30). Object representations constitute "an inner imprint, a structural residue composed of memories, attitudes, and affects" that are products of significant experiences with others and which guide perceptions and reactions to current life events (p. 30). Self-image refers to the perception that people have of themselves and their consistent image of who they are. Of these three domains of personality, cognitive style is a functional attribute and object representations and self-image are both structural attributes.

The intrapsychic level of functioning encompasses two domains of personality representing unconscious processes that reflect how the person deals with internal conflict. The two domains at the intrapsychic level are *regulatory mechanisms* and *morphologic organization.* Regulatory mechanisms are internal psychological processes that provide self-protection, self-defense, need gratification, and conflict resolution when the person experiences internal or external psychological threats; they are generally inferred and unobserved features of the personality. Morphologic organization refers to the general configuration of the internal psychic structure, including the degree of cohesiveness, balance, and tension that exists among the internal personality structures. The regulatory mechanisms constitute a functional attribute of personality, whereas morphologic organization is a structural component of personality.

The fourth level of data on personality functioning is the biophysical level, which encompasses one domain, namely mood or temperament. This is a structural attribute and represents the persistent moods and emotional features that occur in a wide range of experiences and across various relationships.

In all, eight domains of personality are organized around the two general themes of the dynamic nature of the domain (i.e., structural and functional) and the level of data they represent (i.e., behavioral, phenomenological, intrapsychic, and biophysical). This domain model permits a description of each personality style in Millon's prototypal approach to be defined at each of these levels. In Appendix A, each of the personality styles measured by the MACI Personality Patterns scales is presented along with the individual domains for each personality style. These descriptions represent Millon's theoretical prototypic descriptions of each personality style at each level and domain of personality. More importantly, these tables in Appendix A can serve as reference materials when interpreting the MACI Personality Patterns scales. When an elevation occurs on a particular scale, the table for that scale can be consulted to generate diagnostic and clinical hypotheses.

SUMMARY

Many challenges occur in the assessment of adolescents. Because this transitional period of development sometimes requires unique provisions when assessing psychopathology in young people, clinicians must have specialized techniques and instruments to assess the most significant concerns and difficulties of adolescence. The Millon Adolescent Clinical Inventory (MACI) was designed specifically for adolescents and is a theory-based instrument with a wide range of applications. This chapter provides a general overview of the issues relevant to adolescent development and the assessment of psychopathology in teenagers. In addition, it summarizes Millon's theory of personality and psychopathology, which served as the guiding framework for developing the MACI. The text stresses the relevance of adolescent development and assessment and the principles in Millon's theory to clinical use of the MACI. This introductory chapter thus gives a context for the material presented in the remaining chapters.

CHAPTER 2

Development of the MACI

SEVERAL UNIQUE characteristics distinguish the MACI from other instruments that are used to evaluate psychopathology in adolescents. For one, the MACI was constructed to provide information on the issues and concerns that are unique to adolescent clinical populations. Unlike psychometric instruments originally designed for adults and later modified for or renormed on adolescent populations, the MACI reflects experiences and concerns that are typical of adolescents. Another distinguishing feature of the MACI is that it was constructed using an underlying theory of personality and psychopathology that guided selection of items, scales, and certain psychometric properties.

The underlying comprehensive theory used in constructing the test is extremely important for two reasons. First, the theory helps to explain why various features were purposely designed into the test, such as item overlap or profile adjustments. Second, the underlying theory assists with interpretation because the selection of items and the scale composition follow directly from the theoretically based formulation of personality styles and clinical syndromes as outlined by Millon (1969, 1981, 1990; Millon & Davis, 1994). When clinicians understand the psychometric properties and the underlying theory of the MACI, they can interpret the test without the need for a comprehensive "cookbook." Although an actuarially derived database for codetype interpretation is desirable, the theory has much clinical utility and facilitates interpretation of the instrument. Psychometric properties, which are discussed in Chapter 3, provide the empirical basis that also informs interpretive strategies discussed in later chapters.

This chapter provides users of the MACI with an outline of the procedures that were utilized in constructing the test and standardizing the administration and scoring. It includes an overview of the way in which items were selected and individual scales were constructed. Also presented is a discussion of the standardized administration and scoring procedures and a description of the normative sample on which the MACI was developed. The various scales and item content of each are then presented. The chapter closes with an overview of the strengths and weaknesses of the MACI. Although there is no diagnostically perfect psychometric instrument, clinicians can enhance effective and proper use of any instrument when they recognize its strengths and limitations and supplement the assessment with methods that complement the other techniques utilized.

A few distinguishing features of the MACI are an item-weighting system, base rate scores to transform raw scores into interpretable scores, and profile adjustments that compensate for factors that can impact on the scores for particular scales. In many ways, these features are part of the development and standardization process for the MACI and could conceivably be presented in this chapter. However, they are intimately tied to the psychometric properties of reliability and validity and are also critical to interpretive strategies discussed in later chapters. Therefore, these features are discussed in Chapter 3, on psychometric properties of the instrument.

MACI VERSUS MAPI

An appropriate starting point for exploring the development of the MACI is to consider its predecessor, the Millon Adolescent Personality Inventory (MAPI; Millon, Green, & Meagher, 1982). The MAPI received favorable reviews when it was originally published. In particular, the MAPI was seen as "an excellent addition to the instrumentation available for use with adolescents" in which the psychometric and construction procedures were viewed as modern approaches to test development (Brown, 1985, p. 979). Likewise, the MAPI was seen as unique in its approach to assessing concerns and issues that were specific to adolescents (Dyer, 1985). It was noted, however, that additional empirical support was needed to document the validity of the interpretive conclusions provided by the MAPI (Widiger, 1985).

The MAPI was originally divided into two forms: a clinical version for use in aiding mental health professionals in evaluating adolescents in clinical settings and a guidance form for use in school settings to help counselors identify teenagers who might benefit from more extensive psychological evaluation (Millon et al., 1993). Because norms for the MAPI were based on a mixed sample of clinical and nonclinical adolescents, a more purely clinical normative sample was sought so that scales could be added to evaluate a broader range of clinical concerns. Therefore, Millon and his colleagues undertook to develop a clinical instrument that ultimately resulted in the MACI. Many specific changes occurred during this development. As outlined in Millon et al. (1993), four new personality scales were added (Doleful, Forceful, Self-Demeaning, and Borderline Tendency); the Expressed Concerns scales were renamed to reflect a more clinical focus; Modifier Indices were added to evaluate response styles; new Clinical Syndrome scales were added; an item-weighting system (to be fully discussed in Chapter 3) was added; and interpretive texts to reflect these changes were written for inclusion in the computerized interpretive reports.

To fully appreciate the significance of the changes between the MAPI and MACI, it is important to recognize that only 49 (31%, or about one-third) of the items from the MAPI were retained on the MACI. Of the 160 items on the MACI, 111 (69%, or over two-thirds) are new and did not appear on the MAPI. Also, Table 2.1 provides a side-by-side comparison of the scales that appear on each version of these two instruments. The MACI has 14 scales that do not appear on the MAPI, and 5 scales on the MAPI are not found on the MACI. Based on the dramatic change in item content, scale composition, and the different normative samples, it can be stated fairly that the MAPI and MACI represent two different psychometric instruments.

A common question that arises from time to time is whether the MAPI continues to have any application. A fair response is that the MAPI appears to have some utility in school settings where the focus is on specific academic concerns. The MAPI scales having to do with such issues as Academic Confidence (Scale H), Scholastic Achievement (Scale UU), and Attendance Consistency (Scale WW) are of particular interest to counselors and mental health professionals working in school settings where the focus may be on a teenager's adjustment to school or perception of his or her academic or scholastic skills. Also, the normative sample for the MAPI is particularly appealing for those in school settings because of the inclusion of nonclinical subjects in the sample. Therefore, the MAPI continues to have some targeted applications in school settings.

Despite these uses of the MAPI, the MACI represents a significant revision that has a clinical focus. For those clinicians working with teenagers who exhibit emotional or behavioral disturbances, the MACI is the instrument of choice. Even in school settings where the focus is primarily clinical, such as the potential impact of depression, substance abuse, or personality disturbances on learning, the MACI remains a useful instrument and is appropriate for such applications. There are no definitive rules for when to use the MAPI instead of the MACI: such

Table 2.1
Scales of the MACI and MAPI

Scale	MACI	MAPI
Modifier Indices		
RR	—	Reliability Index
VV	Reliability Index	—
X	Disclosure	—
Y	Desirability	—
Z	Debasement	—
Personality Patterns		
1	Introversive	Introversive
2A	Inhibited	Inhibited
2B	Doleful	—
3	Submissive	Cooperative
4	Dramatizing	Sociable
5	Egocentric	Confident
6A	Unruly	Forceful
6B	Forceful	—
7	Conforming	Respectful
8A	Oppositional	Sensitive
8B	Self-Demeaning	—
9	Borderline Tendency	—
Expressed Concerns		
A	Identity Diffusion	Self-Concept
B	Self-Devaluation	Personal Esteem
C	Body Disapproval	Body Comfort
D	Sexual Discomfort	Sexual Acceptance
E	Peer Insecurity	Peer Security
F	Social Insensitivity	Social Tolerance
G	Family Discord	Family Rapport
H	Childhood Abuse	Academic Confidence
Clinical Syndromes		
AA	Eating Dysfunctions	—
BB	Substance-Abuse Proneness	—
CC	Delinquent Predisposition	—
DD	Impulsive Propensity	—
EE	Anxious Feelings	—
FF	Depressive Affect	—
GG	Suicidal Tendency	—
Behavioral Correlates		
SS	—	Impulse Control
TT	—	Societal Conformity
UU	—	Scholastic Achievement
WW	—	Attendance Consistency

decisions will be dictated by the specific needs of the case. However, the MACI is the preferred instrument for clinical assessment of adolescents in a variety of settings.

NORMATIVE SAMPLE

The specific procedures that were followed to develop the MACI into its final form are outlined in detail in the manual (Millon et al., 1993). Nevertheless, it is worth reviewing critical aspects of the MACI's development that pertain to frequent questions about the appropriate application and use of the instrument.

The first step in development of the MACI was the creation of a research form of the instrument, consisting of a 331-item form that included the 150 items from the MAPI and 181 new items. The new items reflected changes to be implemented with the MACI, including items for the new Personality Patterns, Expressed Concerns, and Clinical Syndrome scales, the greater clinical focus of the instrument, and changes in diagnostic criteria for constructs from the *DSM-IV* that are assessed with the MACI.

For the normative sample, 1,017 adolescents were administered the research form of the MACI and this sample was divided into a development group (579 adolescents) and two cross-validation samples (Sample B with 139 adolescents and Sample C with 194 adolescents). The development group was used to select test items based on the frequency of item endorsement and the correlation of item responses with overall scales scores; the development sample was also used to develop the base rate conversions for raw scores into interpretable base rate scores (to be discussed in Chapter 3).

The MACI normative sample consists of male and female adolescents aged 13 to 19, inclusive, selected from mental health treatment settings. More specifically, the normative sample was drawn from outpatient mental health clinics, private practice settings, inpatient psychiatric and general medical units, and residential treatment settings. Therefore, the MACI normative sample consists of adolescents engaged in an active course of mental health treatment or who were in the beginning phases of assessment for emotional and behavioral problems. With respect to racial and ethnic diversity, the MACI development and cross-validation samples were primarily white (79%), with representations of African American (8%), Hispanic (6%), Native American (3%), and Asian (<1%) subjects; data are not reported on the racial makeup of the remainder of the sample. Because the MACI normative sample was drawn from clinical settings, the demographic characteristics are not census-matched, as with other psychometric instruments that are based on an approach which assumes a normal distribution of constructs being measured.

Representations of various racial and ethnic groups in the MACI normative sample reflect the diversity in the clinical settings from which the sample was drawn.

Another important feature of the MACI normative sample is that it is divided into four different normative groups for the purpose of converting raw scores into base rate scores. Separate norms exist for males aged 13 to 15, males aged 16 to 19, females aged 13 to 15, and females aged 16 to 19. This demarcation of separate norms for younger and older adolescents is particularly useful because it recognizes that not all adolescents are the same. Those youths entering the teenage years are likely to have different types and prevalence rates of concerns and clinical issues than teenagers who are close to entering young adulthood. The MACI norms are designed to take such developmental considerations into account.

Based on the foregoing discussion, the MACI is appropriate for use with male and female adolescents aged 13 to 19 who are undergoing a psychological examination for emotional and behavioral problems. Concerns are sometimes raised about the MACI's development on adolescents undergoing mental health treatment; it is therefore claimed that it is suitable only for clinical populations. Objections may be raised over its use in so-called gray areas of application where the clinical nature of the setting is less clear. Child custody evaluations or examinations of learning-disabled teenagers are often viewed as nonclinical or school-based and thus not appropriate for the MACI. However, this conclusion does not have strong support if one is familiar with the MACI's psychometric principles. Mental health professionals have been successful over the years in demonstrating to courts, for example, that clinical issues are important to consider in child custody arrangements. In particular, if child custody situations were truly nonclinical, then the question follows: Why are clinical mental health professionals such as psychologists and psychiatrists asked to conduct examinations at all? The answer is that these settings are highly contentious and conflicted and thus likely to result in some form of stress or emotional distress in teenagers caught in the middle of a parental divorce. Likewise, evaluations of learning-disabled children often involve careful attention to emotional difficulties that may result from or contribute to learning problems in the classroom. Therefore, the MACI is useful in most settings where clinicians practice and assessment or screening is needed for clinical syndromes, personality difficulties, or other forms of psychopathology in adolescents.

Applications that are not well suited for use of the MACI include settings where psychological testing results have little or no relevance to emotional or behavioral difficulties. Examples include school counseling situations where the focus is on career planning or curriculum scheduling for a student with minimal evidence of psychopathology, or cases where the psychological testing is used for self-exploration or out of curiosity. In these situations, the MACI is not likely to yield useful information.

SCALE COMPOSITION

A distinguishing feature of the MACI is the unique fashion in which the items were selected and scales were constructed. Rather than being limited to one method for constructing a psychometric instrument, the MACI was designed using a three-stage validation procedure that included the following steps: (1) theoretical-substantive; (2) internal-structural; and (3) external-criterion. The specific items generated during the development of the MACI had to pass each of these stages, not any one particular approach to test construction. Items were first generated to reflect the content of the specific scales that represent the various personality patterns, expressed concerns, and clinical symptoms assessed by the MACI; this initial stage assured that the items had some face-valid connection to the theoretical and substantive content of the scales. Items were then examined in terms of their internal-structural properties such as item endorsement frequencies and correlations between item responses and scores on individual scales. Finally, the items and scales had to correlate with external-criterion measures of the constructs being measured; these external measures were clinicians' judgments based on familiarity with particular cases. As the manual describes, items went through iterative processes whereby there was a reduction in the number of items down to the 160 items that were finally included on the MACI.

The individual scales and indices contained on the MACI profile were chosen using several criteria (Millon et al., 1993). One of the major factors was developing scales that would adequately assess the basic personality patterns that are a central component of Millon's theory of personality and psychopathology (Millon & Davis, 1994). There has also been increased interest in borderline personality disturbances in adolescents, thus prompting development of a scale measuring this particular personality pattern.

For the MACI to be of greatest use to practicing clinicians, the developers of the instrument introduced scales that would assess clinical syndromes and concerns that are of significance to clinicians working with adolescents in a variety of settings. These scales were designed to measure eating disturbances, delinquency predisposition, impulsivity, substance abuse, anxiety, depression, and suicidal tendencies. Because adolescence brings unique conflicts and pressures, several scales were also included to assess problems related to adolescent identity concerns, self-image, body image, sexual concerns, social insensitivity, insecurity in peer relationships, childhood abuse, and family problems. Again, these scales were selected based on their relevance to the major issues encountered when evaluating and treating adolescents in clinical settings.

A final concern when constructing the MACI was to include scales and indices that evaluate the impact of various response sets and self-reporting strategies. In particular, there is a distinct need to have ways of determining whether a particular adolescent is responding to a self-report instrument in a manner that will have an adverse impact on the validity of the test results. Whether or not an adolescent is responding inconsistently, defensively, or in a manner that exaggerates symptoms and concerns are all important interpretive considerations. Therefore, response style indices were developed for the MACI profile.

These considerations resulted in the formulation of 31 scales and indices that appear on the MACI profile. Table 2.2 outlines the names of each MACI scale, along with the number of items contained on it and a sample item that reflects the content.

ADMINISTRATION AND SCORING

Two formats are available for administering and scoring the MACI, one for hand scoring and another for computer scoring (Millon et al., 1993). Because the scoring algorithms and profile adjustments are complex, computer scoring of the MACI is generally the preferred method. Through NCS Assessments, the publisher of the MACI, computer scoring services are available, including mail-in and on-site scoring. Hand scoring is useful when MACI results require rapid turnaround and on-site computer scoring is unavailable. Also, hand scoring is desirable when only the profile of results is needed and a computer interpretive report is not needed, such as in academic and training settings where students are learning to interpret the MACI. McCann (1997) has also made the point that hand scoring of the MACI is a useful learning tool for gaining a more detailed and in-depth understanding of MACI scoring, including item weighting, conversion of raw scores to base rate scores, and profile adjustments. Thus, hand scoring is useful for beginning users of the MACI who would like a better understanding of the test.

As noted, the MACI may be administered to any adolescent between the ages of 13 and 19 who is undergoing psychological assessment for emotional and behavioral difficulties. It is also important to recognize that a *sixth-grade reading level* is required of any teenager who completes the MACI. In some instances, the clinician will be faced with wanting to use the MACI on an adolescent who has limited reading skills. In these cases, some alternate administration procedures are possible. Oral administration of MACI items is possible either by using an audiotape format that is available from NCS Assessments or by having the examiner

Table 2.2
MACI Scales and Sample Items

Scale	Number of Items	Sample Item
Modifier Indices		
VV. Reliability Index	2	I flew across the Atlantic thirty times last year.
X. Disclosure	N/A[a]	N/A
Y. Desirability	17	I always try to do what is proper.
Z. Debasement	16	So little of what I have done has been appreciated by others.
Personality Patterns		
1. Introversive	44	I don't need to have close friendships like other kids do.
2A. Inhibited	37	I often feel that others do not want to be friendly to me.
2B. Doleful	24	It's not unusual to feel lonely and unwanted.
3. Submissive	48	I worry a great deal about being left alone.
4. Dramatizing	41	I seem to fit in right away with any group of new kids I meet.
5. Egotistic	39	Some people think of me as a bit conceited.
6A. Unruly	39	Punishment never stopped me from doing whatever I wanted.
6B. Forceful	22	I sometimes scare other kids to get them to do what I want.
7. Conforming	39	I always try to do what is proper.
8A. Oppositional	43	I often resent doing things others expect of me.
8B. Self-Demeaning	44	I guess I'm a complainer who expects the worst to happen.
9. Borderline Tendency	21	I seem to make a mess of the good things that come my way.
Expressed Concerns		
A. Identity Diffusion	32	I often feel as if I'm floating around, sort of lost in life.
B. Self-Devaluation	38	I see myself as falling far short of what I'd like to be.
C. Body Disapproval	17	Most people are better looking than I am.
D. Sexual Discomfort	37	Thinking about sex confuses me much of the time.

(continued)

Table 2.2 (Continued)

Scale	Number of Items	Sample Item
E. Peer Insecurity	19	Most other teenagers don't seem to like me.
F. Social Insensitivity	39	Becoming involved in other people's problems is a waste of time.
G. Family Discord	28	I would rather be anyplace but home.
H. Childhood Abuse	24	I hate to think about some of the ways I was abused as a child.
Clinical Syndromes		
AA. Eating Dysfunctions	20	Although people tell me I'm thin, I still feel overweight.
BB. Substance Abuse Proneness	35	I used to get so stoned that I did not know what I was doing.
CC. Delinquent Predisposition	34	I'm no different from lots of kids who steal things now and then.
DD. Impulsive Propensity	24	As soon as I get the impulse to do something, I act on it.
EE. Anxious Feelings	42	I often fear I'm going to panic or faint when I'm in a crowd.
FF. Depressive Affect	33	Things in my life just go from bad to worse.
GG. Suicidal Tendency	25	More and more often I have thought of ending my life.

[a] Disclosure is calculated based on the sum of differentially weighted raw scores from Scales 1 through 8B.
Note. Sample items are from the Millon Adolescent Clinical Inventory. Copyright © 1993 DICANDRIEN, INC. All rights reserved. Published and distributed exclusively by National Computer Systems, Inc. (NCS). Reproduced with permission by NCS.

read the items to the test subject who then places his or her responses on the MACI answer sheet.

No research is available on the relative impact of these alternate methods of administration on the test results. However, specific procedures can be followed to minimize any adverse effects of presenting the items orally to the respondent. Audiotape administration permits the adolescent taking the MACI to be outside the presence of the examiner or any other person who may have an impact on the adolescent's responding. Also, if the MACI is read to the subject, it is preferable for the adolescent to mark his or her responses on the answer sheet, rather than answer the examiner verbally for each item. This minimizes the impact of interpersonal variables on

MACI test responses. Because there are only 160 items on the MACI, it can be administered orally in a relatively brief amount of time to those teenagers whose reading level falls below the sixth-grade level. The examiner must be sure, however, that the adolescent does not have other cognitive deficits or auditory processing or comprehension deficits that may interfere with oral administration.

Another important consideration for practicing clinicians is what test to administer to older adolescents, aged 18 or 19. As noted, the normative age range for the MACI extends up to age 19 and yet the adult version of the Millon inventories, the Millon Clinical Multiaxial Inventory-III (MCMI-III; Millon, 1994), has norms that begin at age 18. Therefore, with older adolescents, clinicians must decide which instrument should be used. There are no clear decision rules that can be followed when making the choice between the MACI and MCMI-III for an 18- or 19-year-old subject (McCann, 1998). The decision will be guided more by the specific issues being evaluated, as well as by developmental considerations related to the adolescent's life circumstances.

If the older adolescent is attending high school, living at home with his or her parents, and in other ways functioning as an adolescent, then the MACI is probably preferable because it is likely to reveal issues of direct relevance to the adolescent's functioning. If, instead, the teenager is attending college or working full-time, lives independently, or in other ways functions as an autonomous adult, then the MCMI-III is probably the preferred instrument because such issues as family discord (MACI Scale G) or peer insecurity (MACI Scale E) may be of minimal relevance to the clinical issues being assessed. On the other hand, the MACI does not directly measure severe forms of psychopathology such as thought disorder, paranoia, bipolar mood disturbances, or severe schizotypal and paranoid personality disorders. If these clinical issues are relevant to the assessment of older adolescents, then the MCMI-III would be the appropriate assessment instrument. No clear decision rules govern selection of one instrument over the other when evaluating older adolescents. Selection of either the MACI or MCMI-III in the older adolescent is guided by the judgment of the clinician, which must take into account the issues being assessed and the teenager's developmental status.

STRENGTHS AND LIMITATIONS OF THE MACI

When clinicians recognize the strengths and limitations of the methods they use, they can approach the assessment process more competently. Knowledge of the advantages and limitations of psychological assessment techniques permits tests to be selected for measurement of constructs for which they are well suited; and other sources of information, such as case history, clinical interviews, projective techniques, structured interviews, and collateral interviews, can supplement the assessment, creating a genuine multimethod approach to assessment. Therefore, an analysis of the strengths and weaknesses of the MACI will help the clinician make effective use of the instrument and supplement MACI results with other techniques when appropriate.

With respect to the strengths of the MACI, it is best to begin with the length of the test. According to Dyer (1985), test length is a critical consideration in adolescent psychodiagnostic testing. Clinicians who regularly work with adolescents know they are generally reluctant or unwilling participants in the assessment process. Therefore, getting teenagers to cooperate in completing psychological testing can be a challenge. The MACI is much shorter, relative to other multiscale personality measures such as the Minnesota Multiphasic Personality Inventory—Adolescent (MMPI-A; Butcher et al., 1992). Most clinicians will find that the adolescent is much more willing to complete the 160-item MACI, as opposed to the 478-item MMPI-A. Thus, brevity of the MACI is a particularly important advantage in assessing adolescents.

A second strength of the MACI is its multiscale format that assesses a wide array of concerns and psychological difficulties. The Personality Patterns, Expressed Concerns, and Clinical Syndrome Scales represent a broad-based approach to assessing adolescent psychopathology that recognizes the importance of many different facets of the adolescent's psychological functioning. In light of its brevity, the MACI is suitable not only as a broad-based psychodiagnostic measure, but also as a screening instrument for psychological difficulties. Related to the broad spectrum of constructs being measured by the MACI is that the instrument is anchored in a comprehensive theoretical approach to understanding personality and psychopathology as outlined in Chapter 1. The fact that theory is a major cornerstone of the MACI makes for a logical and rational connection between item content, psychometric properties, and scale composition. As a result, interpretation of the MACI is facilitated by the presence of a theoretical model as the guiding framework for test construction.

From a practical standpoint, there are other advantages and strengths of the MACI. The normative age range is broader than most other adolescent self-report instruments. For example, the MMPI-A has a lower age limit of 14 and an upper limit of 18, while the MACI has a lower age limit of 13 and an upper limit of 19, thus permitting a broader range of applications. Also, the normative sample of the MACI is stratified into two age groups, 13- to 15-year-olds and 16- to 19-year-olds, to differentiate between early and late adolescence. Additionally, the sixth-grade reading level of the MACI is lower than the required seventh-grade reading level for the MMPI-A.

Other strengths of the MACI related to psychometric principles are discussed in the next chapter. Briefly, the MACI has superior internal-consistency reliability, an indicator of precision of measurement, and was developed with a modern approach to test construction that uses theoretical-substantive, internal-structural, and external-criterion forms of validity (see Chapter 3). The item-weighting system also facilitates test interpretation, as outlined in subsequent chapters. The MACI's numerous advantages as a psychometric instrument render it both practical and extremely useful for assessing personality and psychopathology in adolescents.

Regardless of the advantages with a particular psychological assessment technique, there is no diagnostically perfect test. Recognition of a test's limitations does not mean that it should not be used, unless the limitations far outweigh any benefits. Rather, recognizing a test's limitations represents an effort to encourage competent and ethical use of the test results and to avoid over- or underinterpreting the data.

A major limitation of the MACI is that it does not have any scales measuring many of the more severe forms of psychopathology. There is no scale for assessing formal thought disorder, paranoid thinking, or bipolar mood disturbances, although some MACI scales may be used as indirect measures of some of these constructs (e.g., Peer Insecurity as a measure of interpersonal hypersensitivity). Also, there are no scales designed to measure severe character disturbances such as schizotypal and paranoid personality disorder. Therefore, clinicians who have concerns about the more severe forms of psychopathology will need to supplement MACI results with other methods and instruments such as structured interviews, clinical interviews, and projective techniques.

Another limitation of the MACI is that although validity data are available in the manual, and external validity concerns were addressed in the developmental stages of the MACI, there is still limited independent research that can assist in outlining how the test performs across a variety of settings. To the extent such research exists, these findings will be presented in this text. However, more independent research is needed.

A particularly interesting concern about the MACI that has been raised is the excessive item overlap; that is, with 160 items used to construct 31 scales and indices, multiple items are keyed with assignments to several different scales. This limitation is addressed in some detail in Chapter 3. This concern, however, has been addressed with differential weighting of items, which in turn provides clinicians with a useful interpretive tool to enhance their interpretation of the MACI: the examination of individual item responses to particular items. This approach is discussed elsewhere in this book. For now, it should be noted that item overlap is expected on theoretical grounds and is not a limitation per se of the MACI.

SUMMARY

The development of a psychometric instrument is generally laid out in a technical manual, and the specific procedures followed in constructing the instrument, although necessary components that a test user must study, are often not seen as critical to test interpretation. With the MACI, development of the instrument, including the rationale for selecting the normative sample, item content, and scale composition, and specific scoring algorithms, is useful for developing specific interpretive strategies. Because of the manner in which the MACI was developed and the theoretical underpinnings of the test, the process of test development and psychometric properties are intricately connected. This chapter has provided a brief overview of the differences between the MACI and its predecessor, the MAPI, as well as a review of the normative sample, scale composition, and administration and scoring issues. Also, the strengths and limitations of the MACI were addressed with the goal of providing users of the instrument with a balanced appraisal of how the MACI can be useful and where additional procedures must supplement the assessment. Many innovative aspects of the MACI's properties are also part of the development process but are more appropriately considered under psychometric characteristics because they pertain to issues of validity.

CHAPTER 3

Profile Features and Psychometric Characteristics

ONE OF the innovative features of the Millon inventories is a multistep validation process that departs from the traditional methods for developing self-report instruments. In an empirical approach to test construction, developers select items for inclusion based on their capacity to discriminate between groups of individuals with and without the construct being measured. Still other instruments are based on the construct validity method: items are selected because of their capacity to adequately sample the entire content of features defining the construct. Although each approach has its advantages, each also has limitations. For example, the empirical method produces scales that may have adequate discriminant validity, but are composed of items with highly different content that result in low internal consistency or precision of measurement.

Instead of relying on any one particular approach to test construction, the selection of items and development of scales on the MACI utilized three stages of validation: (1) theoretical-substantive, (2) internal-structural, and, (3) external-criterion. The reason for this multistage approach to validation was to adhere to principles outlined in modern test construction theory (Loevinger, 1957). The three-stage approach supports a commitment to using diverse validation methods to maximize the validity of the instrument after it is completed (Hase & Goldberg, 1967). Therefore, the MACI departs from other personality measures typically used with adolescents in that the three main issues related to test development (substantive content validity, internal-structural stability, and external criterion validity) were part of the development process, rather than issues to be explored after completion of test construction. Although some comparisons between the MACI and other instruments such as the MMPI-A are useful to illustrate similarities and differences, the MACI has psychometric properties and basic structural aspects that are different from many other adolescent self-report measures.

Even though the MACI was developed according to the three-stage process, it is more appropriate to discuss these procedures under psychometric considerations because they were part of the framework for constructing the test. In the first validation step (*theoretical-substantive* considerations), items were written to reflect the content covered by the constructs measured by each scale. Millon's formulation of personality types as outlined in Chapter 1, as well as the expressed concerns and clinical syndromes, served as the taxonomy for drafting items. The MACI manual outlines these substantive areas for each scale (Millon et al., 1993). During the second stage (*internal-structural* validation procedure), the items were tested to verify that they would produce scales that are homogeneous, have adequate stability, and measure constructs in a congruent and theoretically meaningful fashion. Items also need to show adequate endorsement frequencies, good internal consistency, and temporal stability. Furthermore, items must correlate with the construct they measure in a theoretically expected fashion. Finally, the third stage of development (*external-criterion* validation) subjected MACI scales to comparison against external variables once items and scales had met theoretical-substantive and internal-structural requirements. The purpose of this final stage was to assure that the MACI would have adequate validity against external variables to produce measures with convergent and discriminant validity.

A detailed discussion of the intricacies of this process is provided in the MCMI-III manual (Millon et al., 1997) and will not be repeated here. It is important to note, however, that the three validation steps, while sequential, are not independent of one another. Rather, the process is iterative in that once items were drafted and subjected to internal-structural analyses (e.g., endorsement frequencies or item-to-scale correlations), theoretical-substantive revisions were undertaken to eliminate, revise, or reassign items to scales to account for the internal-structural properties. This avoided several problems. If an item correlated moderately with a scale but had no theoretically clear connection to the construct, the item was rewritten or dropped from the scale. Likewise, external criterion results were utilized to modify the substantive and structural properties of scales, again through modification of item wording or adjustment of scale length, to maximize external validation properties.

As a result of the validation process, the MACI became a multiscale inventory with homogeneous scales possessing a high degree of precision in measurement. Likewise, the scales have good stability and relate meaningfully to external variables and criteria such as clinician judgment and other self-report measures. From an interpretive standpoint, the MACI items and scales have many properties that are not found on other psychometric instruments and that add to the techniques available to interpret the profile.

The review of profile features and psychometric properties in this chapter provides MACI users with the fundamental principles of these innovative properties and will facilitate interpretation as discussed in subsequent chapters. The major topics covered here include an overview of the use of differential weighting of items when computing total scale raw scores. Although at first glance item weighting appears to be a basic scoring matter, it has an impact on the MACI user's understanding of the theoretical composition of each scale and the meaning of scale elevations as they affect interpretation. A second major topic is the use of base rate (BR) scores when transforming scale raw scores into meaningful and interpretable scores. The third issue is the use of profile adjustments on the MACI to correct for various factors that can affect the nature of the subject's self-reports. Finally, the more traditional psychometric properties of reliability and validity will be discussed as they pertain to the MACI. Because the intent of this chapter is not to repeat material that can be accessed in the manual, technical details are provided only to the extent needed to illustrate profile features and psychometric properties that inform and guide the interpretation process.

ITEM WEIGHTING

Most multiscale psychological tests assign individual items to one or more scales in such a way that when the item is endorsed in the required direction, one raw score point is added to the total scale score. In actual practice, most tests are scored in this fashion: a template is placed over the answer sheet and the answers appearing in the template windows are counted to yield the scale raw score. Such scoring represents a one-to-one item weight in which each item weighs equally on the scale.

On the MACI, a differential item weighting scheme was implemented such that items on each scale are given a weight of 1, 2, or 3 raw score points. Items weighted 3 raw score points are called *prototypic* items and represent those items that most strongly represent the construct being measured. Items with weights of 2 raw score points are called *secondary* items and assess features and aspects of the construct that are significantly related to the construct. Those items with raw score weights of 1 are called *tertiary* items and reflect aspects of the construct that are associated somewhat with the construct being measured by the scale. Because of the weights given to items, any scale on the MACI will have a maximum possible raw score total that exceeds the total number of items on the scale. For example, Scale AA (Eating Dysfunctions) has 20 items, but the maximum possible raw score total is 44 because there are 10 prototypic items ($3 \times 10 = 30$), 4 secondary items ($2 \times 4 = 8$), and 6 tertiary items ($1 \times 6 = 6$).

Another important consideration is that each item on the MACI, with the exception of the two items on Scale VV, serves as a prototypic item for one and only one scale; an item may be included on other scales but only as a secondary or tertiary item. For example, Item 2 on the MACI reads: "I'm pretty sure I know who I am and what I want in life." This item is a prototypic item (3 raw score points) on Scale A (Identity Diffusion) when answered "False," and it does not appear as a prototypic item on any other scale. However, Item 2 serves as a secondary item (2 raw score points) on Scales 1 (Introversive), 8B (Self-Demeaning), and 9 (Borderline Tendency) when answered "False," and as a tertiary item (1 raw score point) on Scales 5 (Egotistic) and D (Sexual Discomfort) when answered "True." Each MACI item is treated in a similar fashion.

Selection of the item weight given to each item was guided by the three-step validation process outlined at the beginning of the chapter. For prototypic items, weights were assigned based on a consideration of theoretical-substantive and internal-structural considerations. More specifically, for an item to be assigned as a prototypic item to a scale there had to be a clear substantive connection between the item content and the construct it purports to measure. In other words, an item must have clear face validity. Second, responses from an item had to correlate higher with the total score of the scale to which it was assigned than with the total scores from other scales on the MACI profile. Secondary and tertiary item weights were assigned based on a process of making initial item assignments, calculating internal-structural and external criterion statistics for item responses and then dropping, adding, or reweighting items and recalculating the statistics (Roger Davis, personal communication, February 16, 1998). Consequently, the weights assigned to individual MACI items are the result of empirical analyses.

The major reason behind implementing the differential item weights was to reduce the effects of item overlap. Because the MACI has 160 items used to score 31 scales, containing anywhere from 16 to 44 items per scale, there is a considerable degree of item overlap that could potentially result in weak discriminant validity and multiple scale elevations due to shared items rather than the specific symptoms or traits being measured. Although no research has been done on the impact of this weighting scheme on the MACI, some have criticized the same weighting scheme that was used on the MCMI-II as being unnecessary and cumbersome because it does little to reduce the intercorrelations between scales (Retzlaff, Sheehan, & Lorr, 1990). However, others have documented that the impact of item overlap on convergent and discriminant validity is not as significant as originally argued by others (McCann, 1990, 1991).

Despite the arguments against differential weighting, the recognition of items having varying degrees of face validity and statistical relationship to the construct being measured is a useful feature of the MACI that facilitates interpretation. In essence, prototypic items for each scale represent subsets of items that can be utilized to examine what specific elevations, or the lack of elevations, might mean. Therefore, I strongly advocate the item-weighting system as a tool for facilitating MACI interpretation as outlined in the following section.

THE EFFECT OF ITEM WEIGHTS ON SCALE ELEVATIONS

An interesting question that can be asked about the MACI is, "What effect does the relative composition of each MACI scale have on the conversion of raw scores to base rate scores?" Base rate scores are discussed more fully later in this chapter, but the heart of this question focuses on the impact of item weights on MACI interpretation. More specifically, is it possible to obtain a clinically significant elevation on a MACI scale without a subject endorsing the most diagnostically significant items (prototypic items)? This issue is similar to the use of subtle versus obvious items for interpreting psychometric scales on psychological tests.

These issues are clinically important because all the MACI scales are made up of face-valid prototypic items as well as more subtle secondary and tertiary items that measure related but less direct aspects of the construct. The clinical and practical significance of this issue is illustrated with an example. Suppose an adolescent endorses all the prototypic items on Scale GG (Suicidal Tendency); the important interpretive question becomes whether this pattern of item endorsement is sufficient to yield a clinically significant elevation on Scale GG if none of the secondary or tertiary items, measuring such things as sullen affect or poor self-image, are endorsed. If prototypic items alone are not sufficient to produce a clinically significant elevation when raw scores are converted to BR scores, then the clinician using the MACI may commit a false negative error by incorrectly assuming that the lack of a Scale GG elevation means that the adolescent is not experiencing suicidal symptomatology. Similarly, if secondary and tertiary items alone are sufficient to raise Scale GG, but no prototypic items are endorsed and a clinical elevation occurs, the clinician may make a false positive error by concluding incorrectly that the adolescent is actively suicidal when the item content reveals that this is not true.

To answer such critical questions as this, clinicians can examine the relative raw score contributions of prototypic, secondary, and tertiary items for each MACI scale and compute the BR score that is possible for each item set (these computations and the results are presented in detail in Appendix B). Based on this analysis, it will be evident which scales can yield clinically significant elevations (BR ≥ 75) even if the subject fails to endorse the most diagnostically significant items (prototypic items). Also, it is possible to determine which MACI scales can be clinically elevated based on endorsement of prototypic items alone or whether some MACI elevations are based on endorsement of subtle items (secondary and tertiary) as opposed to prototypic items.

The results from the analysis reported in Appendix B show that no MACI scale can produce a clinically significant elevation by endorsement of prototypic items alone. A few scales come close, particularly Scales 2B (Doleful), 6B (Forceful), and AA (Eating Dysfunctions) in that a BR score in the 72 to 73 range is possible based on endorsement of all prototypic items on these scales. A more significant finding from the data in Appendix B is that most MACI scales can be elevated in the clinically significant range based on endorsement of secondary and tertiary items but no prototypic items. I have categorized each of the MACI scales into one of three groups that I call *low, moderate,* and *high threshold* scales. Low threshold scales are those MACI scales that can be elevated at or above a BR score of 85 (prominent clinical elevation; see next section) based solely on secondary and tertiary items. These scales can thus be influenced by other factors related to, but somewhat different from what is actually being measured. Moderate threshold scales can be elevated in the BR = 75 to 84 range based only on secondary and tertiary items; for these scales to exceed a BR score of 84, at least some prototypic items must be endorsed. High threshold scales cannot be elevated in a clinically significant range unless some prototypic items are endorsed. Table 3.1 outlines the specific classification for each scale on the MACI into either low, moderate, or high threshold.

This table illustrates how most MACI scales can be elevated when factors associated with the construct being measured are present. For example, Scale 1 (Introversive) represents personality features associated with the schizoid personality, such as social alienation or withdrawal, lack of pleasure, lethargy, and emotional blunting. These characteristics are found in schizoid and introversive adolescents, but other forms of psychopathology can produce elevations on the scale because they have similar symptoms, including depressive disorders, social phobia, or other introverted personality types.

Throughout the remainder of this book, we will return to the concept of the face validity of certain items on the MACI when interpreting scales or analyzing puzzling or challenging diagnostic issues.

BASE RATE SCORES

One of the major distinctions between the MACI and other adolescent self-report instruments is that the MACI utilizes base rate (BR) scores to

Table 3.1
Sensitivity of MACI Scales to Elevation Based on Subtle Item Content[a,b,c]

Low Threshold Scales (BR ≥ 85)	
1. Introversive	B. Self-Devaluation
2A. Inhibited	E. Peer Insecurity
2B. Doleful	F. Social Insensitivity
6A. Unruly	G. Family Discord
8A. Oppositional	CC. Delinquent Predisposition
8B. Self-Demeaning	EE. Anxious Feelings
A. Identity Diffusion	FF. Depressive Affect
Moderate Threshold Scales (BR = 75–84)	
3. Submissive	H. Childhood Abuse
6B. Forceful	GG. Suicidal Tendency
D. Sexual Discomfort	
High Threshold Scales (BR < 75)	
4. Dramatizing	AA. Eating Dysfunctions
5. Egotistic	BB. Substance-Abuse Proneness
7. Conforming	DD. Impulsive Propensity
C. Body Disapproval	

[a] Base rate score ranges are based on raw scores calculated with secondary and tertiary items only.
[b] Scale 9 (Borderline Tendency) does not have any prototypic items and therefore could not be considered in this analysis.
[c] These classifications do not consider the fact that profile adjustments may contribute to individual scale elevations.

convert raw scores into an interpretively meaningful scale. The concept of a BR score is quite different from standard norm-referenced scores such as T-scores, which are used on many psychological tests. What distinguishes BR scores from other scores such as T-scores is that BR scores are established on the premise that personality disturbances and clinical symptoms are not normally distributed in the general population. For example, a scale designed to measure suicidal tendencies is addressing a problem that is not normally distributed; there is no average suicidal risk that each person has in the population at large. Instead, suicidal tendency is a clinical issue that is typically evaluated in terms of its presence or absence and its relative level of severity.

It is useful to first look at how BR scores differ from T-scores. On the MMPI-A, for example, raw scores on each scale are converted to T-scores in which the mean raw score corresponds to a T-score of 50 and a standard deviation of 10. Moreover, the T-score distribution is normally shaped. Additionally, the MMPI-A utilizes uniform T-scores in which the percentile values for a particular score are equivalent across the different scales. Therefore, a T-score on one scale represents a percentile rank that is the same as the percentile rank for the equivalent T-score on another scale.

The MACI uses a completely different approach to the conversion of raw scores to BR scores such that the same BR score reflects a different percentile value on each scale. The underlying rationale is that disturbed personality traits, expressed concerns, and clinical syndromes are not normally distributed in the general population. Clinical assessment seeks to identify the presence and relative degree of severity of various forms of psychopathology and the prevalence of disorders and syndromes across different categories. The BR score of the MACI represents a standardized scale that reflects these varying percentages or prevalence rates of disorders in the population against which an individual's scores can be compared.

When the MACI was being developed, the standardization procedures called for each adolescent included in the normative sample to be rated by a clinician on each of the personality styles, expressed concerns, and clinical syndromes that are on the MACI profile. These ratings consisted of a rating on a Likert scale in which each adolescent was rated on the 11 Personality Patterns, 9 Expressed Concerns, and 9 Clinical Syndromes. To standardize these ratings and impose some uniformity, the rating forms contained brief definitions of each category. These descriptions are provided in the MACI manual (Millon et al., 1993). Another part of the rating process required that each clinician choose one Personality Pattern, one Expressed Concern, and one Clinical Syndrome that most closely approximated the clinician's impression of the adolescent. A second Personality Pattern, Expressed Concern, and Clinical Syndrome was then obtained that was a close fit, but which did not apply as well as the first rating. As a result of these ratings, three pieces of data were available for each scale on the MACI that served as one external criterion for assessing validity of the test: (1) the dimensional rating; (2) the percentage of cases in the normative sample that had the one personality pattern, expressed concern, and clinical syndrome rated as prominent or the best fit; and (3) the percentage of the normative sample that was rated as having a personality pattern, expressed concern, and clinical syndrome present as a secondary component.

The conversion of raw scores to BR scores on the MACI was then instituted in the following manner. Four anchor points were selected on the BR scale to correspond to specific raw score values; these anchor points were 0, 75, 85, and 115. The BR score values of 0 and 115 were assigned to the minimum (i.e., 0) and maximum possible raw score for each scale respectively. The BR score of 75 was assigned to the raw score value that corresponded to the percentile value that also represented the percentage of the normative sample that had the construct being measured rated as present. A BR score of 85 was assigned to the raw score value that corresponded to the percentile value that also represented the percentage of adolescents in the normative sample that had the construct being measured rated as prominent. For example, suppose that 9% of the normative sample had dramatizing personality rated as the most representative of the adolescent's personality style and another 12% had this personality style rated as a second most likely fit (these percentages are only examples and may not reflect actual percentages in the normative sample). A BR score of 85 would be assigned on Scale 4 (Dramatizing) to the raw score representing the 91st percentile $(100 - 9 = 91)$ so that 9% of the sample would obtain a score above a BR score of 85, corresponding to the 9% prevalence rate of the dramatizing personality pattern in the normative sample. A BR score of 75 would be assigned to the raw score representing the 79th percentile $(100 - [9 + 12] = 79)$ reflecting the prevalence of adolescents having dramatizing personality traits as present; it is important to remember that those rated as having a construct rated as prominent would also have the characteristic rated as being present.

The conversion of raw scores to BR scores followed a similar procedure for each of the MACI scales, with the exception of the three Modifying Indices (Scales X, Y, and Z) which had different BR score conversions that are outlined in the next chapter. The specific BR score values between the anchor points were then obtained through algebraic interpolation. Because of these procedures, specific features define the nature of BR scores on the MACI. First, since each personality pattern, expressed concern, and clinical syndrome had different prevalence rates, the percentile values associated with a BR score on each MACI scale are different from those of other scales. The percentile values correspond to the prevalence rates of the characteristics being measured. Second, the distribution of BR scores is not normal; thus the distance between a BR score 65 to 75 is different from the distance between 75 and 85. As such, BR scores represent a nominal scale of measurement that can also be characterized as an ordinal measure if one assumes that the direction of scores goes from less pathological (BR = 0) to moderate levels of disturbance, to more extreme levels of psychopathology at higher levels on the scale.

The MACI manual also notes some slight modifications that were made in the BR conversions for Scales 1 (Introversive) through 8B (Self-Demeaning) such that "the proportion of times a specific scale score was observed to be the *highest* score for an individual matched the target prevalence rate for *most prominent* characteristic" and "the portion of times a specific scale score was observed to be second highest score for an individual matched the target prevalence rate for the *presence* of the characteristic" (Millon et al., 1993, p. 29). These modifications were made whether or not the BR scores rose above the 75 level. As such, when all the Personality Pattern scales fall below a BR score of 75, the MACI computerized interpretive reports are based on an analysis of the first- and second-highest scales, relative to the others.

The practice of interpreting MACI scales that fall below a BR score of 75 as being clinically significant is not recommended for several reasons. For one thing, when the Personality Patterns scales all fall below 75, there is the strong possibility of a low disclosure level that reflects a response set that can cloud the overall results. In addition, the lack of elevation on any Personality Patterns scale may also represent a lack of clinical disturbance. Also, some sophisticated adolescents who nevertheless have some level of psychopathology may be able to minimize major areas of disturbance. Therefore, the following general guide is offered for interpreting BR scores.

When BR scores fall below 60, this should generally be taken to mean that the adolescent is not reporting any significant difficulties in that particular area. Whether this is an accurate portrayal of the self, however, must be determined by considering various pieces of data including case history, collateral information, and other assessment data. For BR scores in the 60 to 74 range, the scale may reflect either no substantial evidence of the characteristic being measured, particularly if the score is close to 60, or the possibility of some traits or aspects of the construct being measured being present at subclinical levels if scores approach 75. The general rule for clinical interpretation of BR scores is outlined in Table 3.2. When BR scores are at or above 75, this reflects the *presence* of traits or features of the construct being measured at a level that is likely to be clinically significant. When BR scores are at or above 85, the *prominence* of traits or features of the construct being measured is at a highly clinically significant level. There are a few instances where the presence or absence of a scale elevation is due to some alternative factors and in later chapters these possibilities are explored.

UNDERSTANDING PROFILE ADJUSTMENTS

Once raw scores have been converted to BR scores, four possible adjustments can be made to the BR scores prior to the MACI profile being

Table 3.2
Interpretation of BR Scores on the MACI

BR Score	Description
≥ 75	Characteristic being measured is present and significant.
≥ 85	Characteristic being measured is prominent and highly significant.

plotted. These four adjustments are based on complex mathematical algorithms that will not be repeated here. The reader is referred to the MACI manual for a more detailed outline of these calculations (Millon et al., 1993). However, it is important to briefly review these adjustments and the rationale for their use when scoring the MACI so that the clinician has some understanding of their impact on the profile.

The four profile adjustments on the MACI were implemented to control for the impact of various self-report styles on the accuracy of the adolescent's responses to the items. Each of these adjustments raises or lowers specific scale scores to correct for any potential distortions that might occur as a result of biased self-reports. Each adjustment attempts to control for distortions that may occur from different types of response bias.

The first adjustment that might be made is referred to as the *disclosure* adjustment. It is based on the raw score value of Scale X (Disclosure) and is defined as follows. When the raw score of Scale X is between 275 and 400 inclusive, no disclosure adjustment is made. If the raw score of Scale X is low (< 275) then the BR scores on Scales 1 (Introversive) through 9 (Borderline Tendency) are increased in proportion to how low the raw score on Scale X actually is. If the raw score of Scale X is high (> 400), then the BR scores of Scales 1 through 9 are all reduced in proportion to how high the raw score of Scale X is. This adjustment is based on the logical assumption that how open and self-revealing the adolescent is (i.e., disclosing) will affect the MACI results. Adolescents who are very nondisclosing will have relatively low BR scores while those adolescents who are very over-disclosing will have extremely high BR scores. This adjustment seeks to correct scores on the Personality Patterns scales for the relative level of openness that an adolescent has.

The second profile adjustment is called the *anxiety/depression* adjustment and is based on the fact that adolescents who are in an acute state of emotional turmoil may distort some of their self-reports. Therefore, no adjustment is made if both Scales EE (Anxious Feelings) and FF (Depressive Affect) are below a BR score of 85. If either or both of these scales are above 85, then an adjustment is made by reducing Scales 2A (Inhibited), 2B (Doleful), 8B (Self-Demeaning), and 9 (Borderline Tendency) in proportion to the relative combined elevations on Scales EE and FF. Again, this adjustment reflects that adolescents in an acute state of anxiety and/or depression are likely to overreport inhibited, depressive, self-demeaning, and borderline personality traits.

The third profile adjustment—*desirability/debasement*—compensates for the distinct tendency of some respondents to either minimize or exaggerate personal difficulties and concerns on self-reports. This adjustment is based on the relative elevation of Scales Y (Desirability) and Z (Debasement). When the difference between BR scores on these two scales is less than 4, no adjustment is made. When the difference is equal to or greater than 4, adjustments are made to all of the Expressed Concerns scales (A through H) and four Clinical Syndrome scales (AA, EE, FF, and GG). The BR scores on these scales are increased when Scale Y exceeds Scale Z by 4 or more points, and they are reduced when Scale Z exceeds Y by 4 or more points. This adjustment is based on a similar principle to the F-minus-K index that is often cited in the MMPI literature as a useful measure of biased responding.

The fourth modification on the MACI profile is the *denial/complaint* adjustment. This factor is based on the notion that certain personality traits or styles are associated with either defensiveness and denial or a propensity to exaggerate and complain. Adjustments are made to Scales A (Identity Diffusion), B (Self-Devaluation), G (Family Discord), EE (Anxious Feelings), FF (Depressive Affect), and GG (Suicidal Tendency). The personality patterns associated with denial are dramatizing, egotistic, and conforming; thus when Scale 4, 5, or 7 is the highest among all Personality Patterns BR scores, the scores are increased on the six scales listed previously. Those personality patterns associated with a tendency to exaggerate or complain are inhibited, doleful, and self-demeaning; thus when Scale 2A, 2B, or 8B is the highest among all Personality Patterns BR scores, the scores on these six scales are decreased.

A few comments should be made about these profile adjustments to assist the user of the MACI. One major point is that the adjustments are carried out sequentially in the order they were presented. Therefore, the disclosure adjustment is made, followed by anxiety/depression, desirability/debasement, and denial/complaint. As such, subsequent adjustments are based on the BR score values that result from previous adjustments. For example, the relative elevations of Scales EE and FF used to determine whether the anxiety/depression adjustment is necessary are those that exist after the disclosure adjustment, if any, has been made. Also, some scales can theoretically have several adjustments that increase, decrease, or both raise and lower the BR score.

Another major issue is the rationale for implementing these adjustments. Some researchers have criticized similar adjustments used on the adult version of the Millon inventories, the MCMI-II. More specifically, it has been noted that these adjustments are cumbersome and do not appreciably increase the diagnostic accuracy of the inventory. For example, the raw score of Scale X (Disclosure) is used to raise or lower the Personality Patterns scales; however, these scales are used to calculate the final raw score for Scale X. At first glance, there would appear to be a confusing circularity present in the adjustments. Although these issues are important to recognize, there is a more significant reason for these adjustments that overrides any other concerns. *The purpose of the MACI profile adjustments is to maintain the prevalence rate based percentiles that define elevations at the BR*

≥ *75 and BR* ≥ *85 levels.* Thus, when disclosure is too low or too high, the Personality Patterns will tend not to be elevated at the BR score levels of 75 and 85 at a rate that corresponds to the prevalence of the personality style when it is present or prominent. Likewise, when one or both of Scales EE and FF are elevated over a BR of 85, the prevalence rate based percentiles on Scales 2A, 2B, 8B, and 9 become distorted and thus an adjustment becomes necessary. The adjustments are implemented to make sure that all the MACI scales are greater than or equal to a BR of 75 at a rate that corresponds to the percentage of adolescents in the normative sample rated as having the trait or characteristic present. Likewise, the adjustments help ensure that the MACI scales are greater than or equal to a BR of 85 at a rate that corresponds to the percentage of adolescents in the normative sample rated as having the trait or characteristic as most prominent. Although these adjustments do not typically enter into the interpretation process, it is important to at least be aware of their presence, the impact they have on scale elevations, and the general rationale for their use.

RELIABILITY

INTERNAL CONSISTENCY

The internal consistency of MACI scales was computed using the alpha coefficient on two samples, the development and cross-validation samples in the standardization sample. Overall, these coefficients are quite respectable and support the MACI scales as uniform and precise measures of the constructs being measured. The MACI manual reports the alpha coefficients for each scale, and thus these data will not be repeated here (Millon et al., 1993). In the development sample, the coefficients range from 0.73 on Scales D and Y to a high of 0.91 on Scale B. Of the 29 MACI scales for which internal consistency coefficients can be calculated, 1 has a coefficient above 0.90, 17 others are above 0.80, and the remainder are above 0.70. As such, these data reflect very good internal consistency across the MACI scales. More significant is that this high level of internal consistency was obtained on the cross-validation sample, lending support to MACI precision of measurement.

TEST-RETEST STABILITY

The MACI manual also reports test-retest reliability statistics on a sample of 47 adolescents drawn from the development and cross-validation samples. Test-retest reliability is a measure of the stability of measurement; constructs that vary over time, such as situational anxiety, would be expected to have lower test-retest reliability because of the nature of what is being measured. On the other hand, more stable constructs, such as personality traits, are expected to have higher test-retest reliability coefficients.

The MACI scales have had their stability measured over a test-retest interval of 3 to 7 days with excellent results. Stability coefficients range from a low of 0.63 on Scale 1 to a high of 0.92 for Scale 9. The average stability coefficient for the 12 Personality Patterns scales is a very respectable 0.81, while the average stability coefficients for the 8 Expressed Concerns scales at 0.79 and the 7 Clinical Syndromes scales at 0.83 are also very high. On the three Modifier Indices, Scales X, Y, and Z, the stability coefficients are 0.86, 0.71, and 0.84 respectively.

Overall, the stability of the MACI over a relatively short period has been established. However, there appears to be no appreciable difference between the more stable constructs of personality style and the more transient constructs such as clinical symptomatology. The long-term stability of the MACI over months or even years is an area in need of further study.

VALIDITY

The validity of the MACI was evaluated using external criteria. Data were utilized from measures such as clinicians' ratings and judgments for each of the constructs being measured by the MACI scales as well as five collateral test instruments that measure similar or nearly identical constructs. These five measures were the Beck Depression Inventory (Beck & Steer, 1987), Beck Hopelessness Scale (Beck & Steer, 1988), Beck Anxiety Inventory (Beck & Steer, 1990), Eating Disorder Inventory-2 (Garner, 1991), and the Problem Oriented Screening Inventory for Teenagers (POSIT; National Institute on Drug Abuse, 1991). This section presents some general comments rather than the findings from the validity studies of the MACI provided in the manual. Specific validity coefficients are reported in Chapters 5, 6, and 7.

The correlations calculated between BR scores on the MACI and clinicians' judgments in the cross-validation sample were significant for 20 out of 24 scales when clinicians were permitted to make a broader range of diagnostic judgments about the adolescents they were evaluating. The highest correlations were obtained for Scale CC (Delinquent Predisposition), EE (Social Insensitivity), and BB (Substance Abuse Proneness) at 0.34, 0.39, and 0.52 respectively. Still, the correlations between clinician judgments and MACI BR scores were not significant for Scales 1, 3, 8A, and C; and those that were significant were uniformly low. The best correspondence between clinicians' judgments and MACI BR scores was obtained for the Clinical Syndrome scales. These findings are consistent with a body of research in personality disorder research that has found moderate correspondence between self-report measures and clinicians' ratings (cf. Rogers, 1995). The low correlations tend to reflect method variance in which different types of information, such as self-report instruments versus the judgments and observations of others, project different representations of the person's functioning. What a person reports on psychological testing may or may not be the way others view the person. Therefore, both forms of data are a useful and important part of the psychological assessment process.

In general, the pattern of correlation between MACI BR scores and the collateral self-report measures utilized in the standardization sample supports the criterion-related validity of the scales. However, although the data in the MACI manual support the scales as measures of the constructs they have been designed to measure, independent research is needed and criterion validity is an area ripe for further study. A broader range of external criterion measures can be used to examine the relationship between MACI scores and such things as formal *DSM-IV* diagnoses, prognosis in treatment, and other relevant variables. Prediction studies and longitudinal investigations will assist in the treatment and disposition planning for adolescents who undergo psychological evaluation. More research is needed on the MACI in a variety of settings.

SUMMARY

This chapter reviews the major features of the MACI profile that can affect the interpretation process. These features include differential weighting of items when scoring the test, conversion of raw scores into BR scores, and the use of profile adjustments to control for distortion in test results. Also reviewed are general psychometric properties such as reliability and validity. Although there is a need for independent research on the MACI in a variety of settings, the instrument has excellent reliability properties and adequate validity to support its use in clinical contexts. In subsequent chapters, specific reliability and validity coefficients are reported as each individual scale is reviewed, and interpretive strategies are provided. In Chapters 5, 6, and 7, the Personality Patterns, Expressed Concerns, and Clinical Syndromes scales are discussed to assist the MACI user in formulating clinically useful and accurate interpretive conclusions. Before considering interpretation of the MACI profile, the evaluation of profile validity must be first reviewed.

CHAPTER 4

Assessing Profile Validity

A MAJOR concern when using self-report instruments is that the individual may distort his or her responses to such an extent that the reliability and validity of the information obtained may be called into question. Furthermore, self-reports can vary in terms of both the type and relative degree of distortion that occurs (Rogers, 1997). Individual response sets can consist of defensive responding in which subjects attempt to consciously deny or minimize personal concerns or symptoms to present themselves in a favorable light. There is also malingering or negative impression management in which an adolescent consciously fabricates or exaggerates symptoms to achieve some external goal. Another form of distortion includes irrelevant responding in which questions are answered without regard to item content. All these distorted response styles can cast doubt on the accuracy and consistency of psychological test results. A fourth possibility is that the subject is responding honestly to test items.

Complicating the issue are other potential sources of bias in self-reporting on psychological test instruments. There is the possibility of what Rogers (1997) refers to as hybrid responding, where the subject responds with a combination of any of the major response styles. For example, a respondent might begin answering questions honestly and then become fatigued or disinterested and complete the latter portion of the test with a random or irrelevant response style. Another major factor that complicates self-report validity is the degree to which the response bias is something of which the respondent is unaware. In some instances the subject may engage in self-deception and has little or no awareness of the bias in his or her self-reports. Examples of such responding are when an adolescent has strong needs for approval and acceptance and endorses socially desirable responses as part of a pervasive personality style, or the adolescent who overreports symptoms and concerns unintentionally due to severe breakdown of psychological defenses.

Several factors may predispose a particular adolescent taking the MACI to distort results. In some cases, the stigma of seeking mental health treatment or a general lack of trust in adults may cause an adolescent to intentionally deny or minimize symptoms or problems, thus making treatment difficult. In other cases, severely decompensated adolescents or those attempting to feign psychiatric disturbance may overreport clinical symptoms. Regardless of the particular motivation underlying a distorted response style, any self-report instrument that measures clinical symptoms and personality characteristics should have some means of assessing the consistency and accuracy of self-reports.

This chapter provides information on the indices and scales of the MACI that evaluate response style. These measures fall under the general name of Modifier Indices and are designed to indicate the degree to which an adolescent is responding in a random, socially desirable, malingered, exaggerated, or honest manner.

MODIFIER INDICES

The four scales or indices on the MACI measuring response style and test-taking attitude are the Reliability Index (Scale VV), and the Disclosure (X), Desirability (Y), and Debasement (Z) scales. Together they can be used to discern adolescents who respond to test questions honestly, distort their results with a tendency toward denial and underreporting, magnify problems, and are careless or in other ways inaccurate in their self-reports. The interpretation of Scales X, Y, and Z is based on an analysis of BR scores for each scale; however, it is important to recognize that the BR score anchoring points for the Modifier Indices were established differently than were anchoring points for other MACI scales. Rather than being based on prevalence rates of response styles, the BR scores for Scales X, Y, and Z are based on the raw score frequency distributions for each scale. In this way, a BR ≥ 85 represents the highest 10% of the normative sample, BR scores of 75 to 84 represent the next 15%, scores from 35 to 74 represent approximately the next 60%, and BR < 35 reflects the lowest 15% of the normative sample. Specific BR scores falling between the anchor points of 35, 75, and 85 were derived through algebraic interpolation. Table 4.1 contains the actual frequency distribution obtained for the MACI normative sample.

Therefore, a BR score of 75 or greater on Scales X, Y, and Z places a given adolescent's score in the upper quartile, or highest 25% of the normative sample. Scores of 85 or above place the adolescent's score in the

Table 4.1
Distribution of BR Scores for Scales X, Y, and Z in the
MACI Normative Sample

	Scale		
BR Score Range	X (%)	Y (%)	Z (%)
00–34	13.0	12.1	6.4
35–74	62.7	66.1	72.5
75–84	14.0	13.1	11.9
85–115	10.4	8.6	9.2

highest 10% of the normative sample, whereas scores below 35 reflect the bottom 15% of the distribution.

SCALE VV—RELIABILITY INDEX

Basic Characteristics

The Reliability Index does not appear as an actual measure on the MACI profile, since it consists of two items (114 and 126) that are bizarre in content and are rarely, if ever, endorsed by even the most disturbed adolescents. Therefore, scores can range from 0 to 2, depending on the number of items endorsed; both are keyed in the True direction. Additionally, the items making up this index are also contained on a similar measure for the adult version of the test, the MCMI-III. Selection of items for the Reliability Index was therefore based on the extremely low endorsement frequency of each item (i.e., less than 0.01%). Research has also shown that this index will accurately identify over 95% of all random response sets when a cutoff of one item is utilized (Bagby, Gillis, & Rogers, 1991).

Significant Elevations

The formal rule governing Scale VV interpretation in the manual is that a score of 0 indicates the MACI results are "Valid"; however, this does not preclude the possibility that the test results may be invalid due to other factors such as over- or underreporting of symptoms. Therefore, a score of 0 is necessary, but not sufficient for a valid MACI profile. Scores of 1 on the Reliability Index are considered, according to the rules outlined in the manual, to reflect a profile of "Questionable Validity" and a score of 2 represents "Invalid" results. When the MACI is computer scored, either "Valid Report," "Questionable Validity," or "Invalid Report" will appear at the top of the profile printout, depending on whether the Reliability Index score is 0, 1, or 2 respectively.

When either item on the Reliability Index is answered in the affirmative, there are several possible interpretations. In general, the index evaluates how well the adolescent paid attention to the items while completing the MACI. One possible reason for the positive score may be random responding in which the adolescent indiscriminately responded to the MACI items without regard to item content. Some adolescents who are extremely oppositional to the evaluation process and who resent having to take the MACI may provide a random response set. Other factors may also lead to positive scores; these include concentration difficulties while taking the test, poor reading skills, or extreme confusion that adversely affects the adolescent's ability to accurately report his or her symptoms. Other assessment data, such as measures of attention and concentration or tests of reading level can be useful in helping to determine the source of difficulty. In the case of random responding or confused states, other measures of response consistency, such as VRIN and TRIN on the MMPI-A, can be useful corroborative data to help identify indiscriminate responding.

Another possible interpretation of a positive score on the Reliability Index is malingering. The work of Rogers and his colleagues (Rogers, 1997; Rogers, Bagby, & Dickens, 1992) has shown that a typical response characteristic of individuals who are malingering is that they endorse bizarre, rare, or absurd symptoms in an attempt to portray themselves as severely disturbed. Since the items on the Reliability Index involve highly unusual and bizarre phenomena, such as not seeing a car in the last ten years and flying across the Atlantic Ocean thirty times in a year, the endorsement of one item may raise suspicions about possible malingering if other response styles have been ruled out.

SCALE X—DISCLOSURE

Basic Characteristics

Originally conceptualized and designed as a measure of an adolescent's willingness to be open and self-revealing, Scale X is in theory supposed to be a neutral measure of openness. It is intended to be neutral with respect to negative versus positive impression management, and it is the only scale on the MACI that is regularly interpreted in both directions. Whereas most scales on the MACI are interpreted in terms of whether or not there is a significant elevation, both low and high scores on Scale X are interpreted because the BR scores are based on the frequency distribution of scores in the normative sample instead of diagnostic prevalence rates. Another unique feature of Scale X is that it is not a true scale in terms of having a set of items that are scored. Instead, Scale X is comprised of the differentially weighted raw score totals from the 11 Personality Patterns scales (Scales 1 through 8B). The raw scores for each scale are multiplied by a correction factor to increase or decrease the relative contribution of each scale to the overall raw score, since some scales are considered to be closely associated with openness and others are associated more with guardedness or denial. The resultant sum is then used as the Scale X raw score for conversion into a BR score.

According to guidelines in the manual, Scale X raw scores less than 201 or greater than 589 are considered to be extremes that render the MACI profile invalid. These cutoffs were derived because the diagnostic-based prevalence rates for individual scales cannot be maintained when Scale X scores fall in these extreme ends of the distribution.

Although Scale X is conceptualized as a neutral measure of openness, the scale correlates highly in the positive direction with Scale Z (0.78) and moderately in the negative direction with Scale Y (−0.44). The scale also correlates highly with MACI scales that reflect negative emotions and poor self-appraisal, as evidenced by strong positive correlations with Scales 2B (0.75), 8A (0.80), 8B (0.73), 9 (0.73), A (0.75), B (0.79), FF (0.68), and GG (0.70). Low scores on Scale X are associated with socially desirable response sets and approval needs as evidenced by strong negative correlations with Scales 3 (−0.53), 4 (−0.59), 5 (−0.66), 7 (−0.83), and Y (−0.44). Therefore, the scale is associated with specific response sets and the degree of emotional distress an adolescent is experiencing.

Significant Elevations

Low scores that fall in a BR score range of 0 to 34 represent a response style in adolescents who are defensive and unwilling to bring forth personal attributes and concerns. The lack of openness in teenagers who score in this range on the MACI may be due to any one of several factors, including general concerns about how the clinician will use information, strong needs to appear well adjusted and emotionally stable, and general suspicions or lack of trust in adults. When the raw score of Scale X is less than 201, the MACI profile is considered invalid due to the adolescent providing an insufficient amount of information, responding false to most items, or extreme denial and minimization.

Scores in the BR range of 35 to 74 are considered moderately disclosing. The adolescent has provided enough information about himself or herself to be useful. In treatment settings, adolescents scoring in this range are likely to provide some information in interviews and therapy sessions; however, some defensiveness may also be noted.

High scores on Scale X that fall in a BR score range of 75 to 84 reflect an adolescent who is being quite direct and open about personal concerns and difficulties. Numerous scales may be elevated across the entire MACI profile and the adolescent is likely to engage in some meaningful discussion about concerns. Elevations in this range do not necessarily suggest that the adolescent will have insight into the causes of problems or symptoms and psychological defenses such as projection, acting-out, and displacement are possible.

Where Scale X is highly elevated in the BR score range of 85 to 115, there is the strong likelihood of negative impression management, the overreporting of symptoms, or a "cry for help." The adolescent may be searching for attention, support from others, or some secondary gain. Problems and concerns may be numerous and it can often be difficult to tease out genuinely severe problems from those that are exaggerated. When the raw score of Scale X is greater than 589, the MACI profile is considered invalid because the adolescent has endorsed too many symptoms and concerns to provide a clear diagnostic assessment.

SCALE Y—DESIRABILITY

Basic Characteristics

The major purpose of Scale Y is to evaluate whether a particular adolescent is using some form of positive impression management to create an unrealistically favorable presentation. Rather than include unique items designed specifically for a socially desirable response set, the MACI was designed so that all items on Scale Y are drawn from other scales on the instrument and keyed in the True direction. Of the 17 items comprising Scale Y, 12 are prototypic items from Scales 4 (2 items), 5 (3 items), and 7 (7 items). The five remaining items are prototypic items keyed in the opposite direction on Scales A (2 items), C (2 items), and F (1 item). Consequently, item overlap contributes to rather high positive correlations between Scale Y and Scales 4 (0.51), 5 (0.64), and 7 (0.64) and high negative correlations between Scale Y and Scales 1 (−0.51) and A (−0.54). Therefore, it is not uncommon to see elevations on one or more of these other scales when Scale Y is elevated. In particular, Scales 4, 5, and 7 may be elevated when there is a socially desirable response set.

Significant Elevations

High scores on Scale Y indicate that the adolescent has a need for others to see him or her as well adjusted. Personal faults are minimized and there is an attempt to be seen in an unrealistically favorable light. Moderate elevations in the BR score range of 75 to 84 reflect guardedness and defensiveness and the subject may express morally virtuous ideals or attempt to present as emotionally composed. In treatment settings, Scale Y elevations generally reflect adolescents who approach problems superficially and lack clear insight into why they are in treatment. Where the history reveals evidence of serious psychopathology such as a recent suicide attempt or conduct that violates the rights of others, a Scale Y elevation suggests that the adolescent will be resistant to treatment and this can be a negative prognostic sign.

By itself, an extreme elevation on Scale Y is not sufficient to invalidate the MACI computer interpretive printout. When the BR score exceeds 90, however, serious consideration should be given to the possibility that a socially desirable response set is adversely impacting validity. The reason for this interpretive hypothesis is that BR scores over 90 indicate that the adolescent has endorsed all, or nearly all, of the items on the scale, thus resulting in scores at the highest extreme of the Scale Y distribution. Extreme elevations in this range thus point to the possibility of blatant denial, resistance to self-disclosure, conscious efforts to be viewed as well adjusted and free of psychopathology, or strong personality-based needs for approval from others. An exception to the BR of 90 cutoff would be a MACI profile where despite the Scale Y elevation, the profile reveals psychopathology that is inconsistent with a socially desirable response set, such as elevations on scales reflecting depressive symptoms (e.g., Scales 2B, FF, GG) and negative self-appraisal (e.g., Scales A and B).

An interesting characteristic of Scale Y is that most of the items on the scale are taken from Personality Patterns scales (i.e., Scales 4, 5, and 7). Consequently, many of the items reflect content that is representative of a characterological propensity to seek approval and to be viewed positively by others. Elevations may therefore reflect a socially desirable response set that is situational; the subject may be responding to the obvious content of the items. On the other hand, an elevation on Scale Y may sometimes represent a need for approval that is less situational and more a part of the adolescent's personality style.

SCALE Z—DEBASEMENT

Basic Characteristics

Some adolescents are motivated for one reason or another to present their problems or concerns in a way that emphasizes negative self-attributes or exaggerates minor symptoms. Scale Z is designed to measure such response styles. Like Scale Y, Scale Z does not have any items that are unique to assessing negative impression management, since all 16 items from the scale are found as prototypic items on other MACI scales. Moreover, all items are keyed in the True direction. Fourteen items from Scale Z are found as prototypic items on Scales 2A, 2B, 8B, A, B, FF, and EE, with each of these scales contributing two items to Scale Z. The other two items from Scale Z are provided by Scales 8A and C. There are rather high positive correlations between Scale Z and Scales 1 (0.56), 2A (0.53), 2B (0.77), 8A (0.58), 8B (0.75), 9 (0.71), A (0.66), B (0.85), FF (0.79), and GG (0.71). As expected, there are high negative correlations between Scale Z and those MACI scales associated with socially desirable response sets, including Scales Y (−0.42), 4 (−0.65), 5 (−0.74), and 7 (−0.61). Because of these intercorrelations, elevations are common on several of these other scales when Scale Z is high; in the same way, when depression and negative self-appraisal are part of the adolescent's personality style, Scale Z will also typically be high.

Significant Elevations

High scores on Scale Z reflect an inclination on the part of the adolescent to devalue himself or herself or to present concerns and difficulties as more troublesome than is likely to be the case on objective examination. Typically there is some motivation to exaggerate, overreport, or in some other way distort problems in the negative direction. However, moderate elevations in the BR score range of 75 to 84 do not necessarily reflect an intentional negative response set. It is not unusual to find moderate elevations among adolescents who are emotionally distraught, depressed, or who have a very poor self-image as part of their personality. When the teenager has very few rewarding experiences or has several negative things going on in life, it is understandable that there will be elevations on Scale Z. Therefore, moderate elevations are common in adolescents who are socially detached, depressed, or anxious, and who have feelings of inadequacy and low self-esteem.

As with Scale Y, an extremely high elevation on Scale Z will not, by itself, invalidate the computerized report for the MACI. However, as scores on Scale Z exceed a BR of 90, the subject's score is in the highest extreme of the frequency distribution for Scale Z, because he or she has endorsed almost all of the items on the scale. Therefore, the MACI profile's overall validity should be questioned. Among the possible reasons for an extremely high Scale Z score may be strong feelings of helplessness that render the adolescent unable to communicate distress in effective ways; this response pattern is similar to the psychological "cry for help" commonly seen in adolescents who lack the resources to communicate their inner feelings of distress in a coherent fashion. Other reasons for extreme elevations on Scale Z include malingering or dissimulation in which the adolescent is attempting to exaggerate symptoms to achieve some secondary gain. Integrating other test results, historical information, and clinical observations is necessary to clarify the reasons for extreme elevations on this scale.

MODIFIER INDICES CONFIGURATIONS

HONEST RESPONDING

Generally, an honest MACI response pattern is characterized by Scales Y and Z falling below a BR of 75 and Scale X between a BR score of 35 and 85 (inclusive). The relative configuration between Scales X, Y, and Z is not particularly important when the scales are in these specified ranges. Figure 4.1 presents three different Modifying Indices configurations that all represent honest response patterns. In Figure 4.1(a), Scale Y exceeds Scales X and Z, but all three are well below 75. Figure 4.1(b) reveals Scale Z to be higher than either Scales X or Y; this configuration is also indicative of honest responding. It is also possible that Scale X may exceed a BR score of 75, while Scales Y and Z remain below that level as the configuration in Figure 4.1(c) illustrates. In this example, the response style is honest and reflects a high level of openness and frankness in the adolescent's self-reporting. Because Scales X and Z are

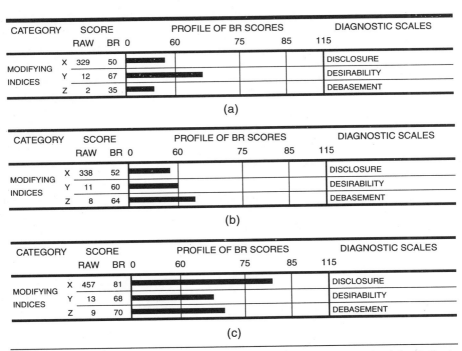

Figure 4.1 Honest response styles on the MACI characterized by (a) relatively higher Scale Y; (b) relatively higher Scale Z; and (c) Scale X elevation. Copyright © 1993 DICANDRIEN, INC. All rights reserved. Published and distributed exclusively by National Computer Systems, Inc. (NCS). Reproduced with permission by NCS.

highly correlated, it would be unusual for Scale X to exceed a BR score of 85, while Scale Z remained below 75.

INCONSISTENT RESPONDING

Because the Reliability Index is quite effective in identifying random responding on the MACI, it is not necessary to be concerned with whether or not there is a typical random response profile. In rare instances, however, Scale VV may be 0 and both Scales Y and Z will be elevated above a BR score of 75, and the MACI profile will be technically valid as defined by formal validity rules in the MACI manual. This profile configuration reflects conflicting and antithetical self-reports in adolescents who are endorsing a number of symptoms and characteristics that often do not go together (e.g., feeling unworthy while also feeling like one fits in at social gatherings).

Two alternative meanings can be attached to this unusual response pattern. In some cases, high scores on Scales Y and Z reflect atypical or rare symptom combinations that often characterize individuals who are dissimulating (Rogers, 1997). These adolescents are attempting to present themselves as disturbed, but are unclear as to what specific items they should endorse; therefore, they sometimes adopt a response style of indiscriminately reporting symptoms. A second possible interpretation for this configuration of Scales Y and Z is based on clinical experiences that have identified the pattern in gregarious, self-centered, or narcissistic adolescents who are experiencing an acute agitated depression. Differentiating between these two interpretive hypotheses often requires careful consideration of the setting in which the test results are obtained (e.g., clinical vs. forensic) and the case history. Concurrent elevations on Scales Y and Z at or above a BR score of 75 where one of the scales exceeds a BR score of 85 are likely to reflect inconsistent responding, whereas when both Scales Y and Z are above 75 but below 85, the results are more likely to reflect an agitated depression. However, these decision rules are not definitive and careful consideration must be given to both the assessment context and case history.

POSITIVE IMPRESSION MANAGEMENT

The two primary indicators of a socially desirable response set on the MACI are Scales X and Y. In particular, when Scale X is below a BR score of 35, the adolescent is responding in a guarded fashion in which there is denial or minimization of problem areas. The other measure is Scale Y, which reflects an attempt to present one's self in a virtuous, socially desirable, or unrealistically positive light.

A typical socially desirable response set is illustrated in Figure 4.2. Scale Y is quite high at a BR of 85 and the rest of the profile is near the mean BR of 60. There is some indication of submissive personality characteristics, passivity, and anxiety. However, the positive impression management contributes to a profile that is lowered overall.

In contrast, Figure 4.3 illustrates a socially desirable response set (Scale Y = 85) that also reveals a low level of disclosure (Scale X = 15). Many of the scales fall below the median BR of 60 and there are a few prominent elevations on Scales 4, 5, and 7. This profile illustrates the high degree of item overlap and significant correlations between Scales Y and Scales 4, 5, and 7, as socially desirable response sets often result in elevations on one or more of these Personality Patterns scales. This profile is from an adolescent with a history of severe conduct problems who was facing placement in a restrictive setting. The MACI profile reflects positive impression management that makes the diagnostic information highly suspect. The delinquency indicator on Scale CC and peer insecurity on Scale E are consistent with the history, but these and other problems are masked by the prominent socially desirable response set.

However, not all single scale or combination of elevations on Scales 4, 5, and 7 represent socially desirable responding. Typically, the relative elevation on Scale Y and the clinical data and case history are helpful in determining whether the profile reflects genuine personality propensities or a socially desirable response pattern. Also, an elevation on Scale Y with extreme elevations on Scale 4, 5, or 7, but not all three together, may also represent a personality disturbance that is ego-syntonic to the adolescent.

NEGATIVE IMPRESSION MANAGEMENT

Scales X and Z are used to evaluate response sets in which there is an attempt to focus on, overreport, or exaggerate problems. A negative response set is typically defined by elevations on Scale Z that equal or exceed a BR score of 75 or a BR score on Scale X at or above 85. Figure 4.4(a) illustrates a configuration that is often accompanied by depressive symptoms, poor self-image, and other symptoms of genuine pathology. Therefore, moderate elevations on Scale Z as shown in this example are not particularly significant. Additionally, there is a high correlation between Scales X and Z, so as one elevates the other follows; this trend is seen by comparing Figures 4.4(a) and 4.4(b). Both of these profiles are technically valid, and they reflect high levels of distress, dysphoric emotions, and negative self-appraisal.

There are also high correlations between Scale Z and several scales that measure such clinical issues as depression, negative self-concept,

MACI   Clinical Interpretive Report

PERSONALITY CODE: -**38A2B6A//-**-*FBE//-**EE*FFDDCC//
VALID REPORT   DATE: 10/29/93

CATEGORY		SCORE RAW	BR	PROFILE OF BR SCORES 0 60 75 85 115	DIAGNOSTIC SCALES
MODIFYING INDICES	X	356	58		DISCLOSURE
	Y	16	85		DESIRABILITY
	Z	4	55		DEBASEMENT
PERSONALITY PATTERNS	1	23	57		INTROVERSIVE
	2A	21	52		INHIBITED
	2B	16	65		DOLEFUL
	3	60	75		SUBMISSIVE
	4	44	57		DRAMATIZING
	5	38	52		EGOTISTIC
	6A	34	64		UNRULY
	6B	13	47		FORCEFUL
	7	50	54		CONFORMING
	8A	25	67		OPPOSITIONAL
	8B	14	24		SELF-DEMEANING
	9	11	40		BORDERLINE TENDENCY
EXPRESSED CONCERNS	A	15	52		IDENTITY DIFFUSION
	B	28	66		SELF-DEVALUATION
	C	8	35		BODY DISAPPROVAL
	D	29	57		SEXUAL DISCOMFORT
	E	12	65		PEER INSECURITY
	F	34	69		SOCIAL INSENSITIVITY
	G	11	53		FAMILY DISCORD
	H	14	59		CHILDHOOD ABUSE
CLINICAL SYNDROMES	AA	5	16		EATING DYSFUNCTIONS
	BB	14	30		SUBSTANCE-ABUSE PRONENESS
	CC	27	61		DELINQUENT PREDISPOSITION
	DD	18	62		IMPULSIVE PROPENSITY
	EE	34	75		ANXIOUS FEELINGS
	FF	15	71		DEPRESSIVE AFFECT
	GG	8	28		SUICIDAL TENDENCY

CONFIDENTIAL INFORMATION FOR PROFESSIONAL USE ONLY

Figure 4.2 Socially desirable response set. Copyright © 1993 DICANDRIEN, INC. All rights reserved. Published and distributed exclusively by National Computer Systems, Inc. (NCS). Reproduced with permission by NCS.

MACI   Profile Report

PERSONALITY CODE: 5**47*36A//-**-*EFG//-**-*CCEE//
VALID REPORT   DATE: 10/23/93

CATEGORY		SCORE		PROFILE OF BR SCORES				DIAGNOSTIC SCALES
		RAW	BR 0	60	75	85	115	
MODIFYING	X	234	15					DISCLOSURE
INDICES	Y	15	85					DESIRABILITY
	Z	0	15					DEBASEMENT
	1	11	32					INTROVERSIVE
	2A	11	40					INHIBITED
	2B	3	23					DOLEFUL
	3	49	74					SUBMISSIVE
	4	44	80					DRAMATIZING
PERSONALITY	5	41	86					EGOTISTIC
PATTERNS	6A	26	60					UNRULY
	6B	5	29					FORCEFUL
	7	56	78					CONFORMING
	8A	5	26					OPPOSITIONAL
	8B	4	22					SELF-DEMEANING
	9	4	27					BORDERLINE TENDENCY
	A	5	25					IDENTITY DIFFUSION
	B	6	22					SELF-DEVALUATION
	C	0	10					BODY DISAPPROVAL
EXPRESSED	D	28	56					SEXUAL DISCOMFORT
CONCERNS	E	12	73					PEER INSECURITY
	F	26	64					SOCIAL INSENSITIVITY
	G	13	60					FAMILY DISCORD
	H	2	14					CHILDHOOD ABUSE
	AA	0	9					EATING DYSFUNCTIONS
	BB	9	21					SUBSTANCE-ABUSE PRONENESS
	CC	31	72					DELINQUENT PREDISPOSITION
CLINICAL	DD	14	42					IMPULSIVE PROPENSITY
SYNDROMES	EE	27	65					ANXIOUS FEELINGS
	FF	4	29					DEPRESSIVE AFFECT
	GG	0	14					SUICIDAL TENDENCY

CONFIDENTIAL INFORMATION FOR PROFESSIONAL USE ONLY

Figure 4.3 Socially desirable response set with concurrent elevations that reflect item overlap. Copyright © 1993 DICANDRIEN, INC. All rights reserved. Published and distributed exclusively by National Computer Systems, Inc. (NCS). Reproduced with permission by NCS.

CATEGORY	SCORE		PROFILE OF BR SCORES				DIAGNOSTIC SCALES
	RAW	BR	0　　　60	75	85	115	
MODIFYING INDICES	X 405	70					DISCLOSURE
	Y 5	15					DESIRABILITY
	Z 13	77					DEBASEMENT

(a)

CATEGORY	SCORE		PROFILE OF BR SCORES				DIAGNOSTIC SCALES
	RAW	BR	0　　　60	75	85	115	
MODIFYING INDICES	X 433	77					DISCLOSURE
	Y 10	54					DESIRABILITY
	Z 14	85					DEBASEMENT

(b)

Figure 4.4 Negative impression management on the MACI characterized by (a) moderate Scale Z elevation; and (b) Scale X and Z elevations. Copyright © 1993 DICANDRIEN, INC. All rights reserved. Published and distributed exclusively by National Computer Systems, Inc. (NCS). Reproduced with permission by NCS.

emotional dyscontrol, and insecurity. Therefore, MACI profiles that are defined by numerous indicators of psychological maladjustment will frequently have a negative response set, as Figure 4.5 shows. Generally, as long as Scales X and Z do not extend well beyond a BR of 90, the profile typically reflects genuine psychopathology and not an invalid profile. In some adolescents with severe psychopathology, such as dissociative symptoms, severe personality disorders, and extreme depression, marked elevations are common on Scales X and Z; these profiles often suggest a psychological "cry for help."

PROFILE VALIDITY RULES

Several considerations enter into the evaluation of the MACI's overall validity. An important first step is to recognize the profile invalidity rules outlined in the manual that define the algorithms for assessing validity of computer-scored tests (Millon et al., 1993). Sometimes a clinician may be unsure why a MACI profile will be computer scored as invalid. There are six computer-defined validity rules, as outlined in Table 4.2; violation of any one of the formal rules is sufficient to invalidate the profile. Also included in Table 4.2 are some additional validity considerations discussed in previous sections.

The *first* general rule is that the MACI cannot be scored if the gender of a particular subject is unknown; the likelihood of an adolescent's gender being unknown in clinical practice is extremely low. This requirement

MACI   Profile Report

PERSONALITY CODE: 92B2A**18B*8A3//B**CGA*E//FF**GGBB*AA//
VALID REPORT   DATE: 10/21 /93

CATEGORY		SCORE		PROFILE OF BR SCORES				DIAGNOSTIC SCALES
		RAW	BR	0	60	75	85	115
MODIFYING	X	405	70					DISCLOSURE
INDICES	Y	5	15					DESIRABILITY
	Z	13	77					DEBASEMENT
	1	40	82					INTROVERSIVE
	2A	46	89					INHIBITED
	2B	38	95					DOLEFUL
	3	59	72					SUBMISSIVE
	4	14	23					DRAMATIZING
PERSONALITY	5	3	3					EGOTISTIC
PATTERNS	6A	19	29					UNRULY
	6B	6	17					FORCEFUL
	7	33	40					CONFORMING
	8A	34	74					OPPOSITIONAL
	8B	52	78					SELF-DEMEANING
	9	32	95					BORDERLINE TENDENCY
	A	32	80					IDENTITY DIFFUSION
	B	59	96					SELF-DEVALUATION
	C	27	82					BODY DISAPPROVAL
EXPRESSED	D	27	41					SEXUAL DISCOMFORT
CONCERNS	E	17	72					PEER INSECURITY
	F	6	7					SOCIAL INSENSITIVITY
	G	27	82					FAMILY DISCORD
	H	13	39					CHILDHOOD ABUSE
	AA	32	62					EATING DYSFUNCTIONS
	BB	34	77					SUBSTANCE-ABUSE PRONENESS
CLINICAL	CC	9	21					DELINQUENT PREDISPOSITION
SYNDROMES	DD	19	57					IMPULSIVE PROPENSITY
	EE	34	58					ANXIOUS FEELINGS
	FF	48	105					DEPRESSIVE AFFECT
	GG	32	83					SUICIDAL TENDENCY

CONFIDENTIAL INFORMATION FOR PROFESSIONAL USE ONLY

Figure 4.5 Negative response set associated with concurrent elevations that reflect psychological maladjustment and item overlap. Copyright © 1993 DICANDRIEN, INC. All rights reserved. Published and distributed exclusively by National Computer Systems, Inc. (NCS). Reproduced with permission by NCS.

Table 4.2
MACI Invalidity Rules

A. Formal rules (based on computer scoring):
1. Gender unknown or not indicated.
2. Age less than 13, greater than 19, or unknown.
3. 10 or more items missing or double marked.
4. Scale VV = 2.
5. Raw score of Scale X < 201 or > 589.
6. All of Scales 1 through 8B at BR = 59 or below.

B. Additional considerations:
1. Try to have no item responses missing or double marked.
2. Scale VV should be 0.
3. If both Scales Y and Z ≥ 75, consider inconsistent responding or dissimulation.
4. Scale Y > 90 indicates strong positive impression management.
5. Scale Z > 90 indicates strong negative impression management.
6. If Scales 4, 5, and 7 are all elevated, consider socially desirable response set.

typically refers to instances where gender is accidentally omitted from the computer answer sheet; this variable must be known to choose the correct base rate transformation tables. A *second* general rule is that the MACI is considered invalid if the adolescent's age is less than 13, greater than 19, or unknown. Again, this variable is required to select the appropriate base rate transformation table. A *third* formal rule governing MACI validity is that if 10 or more items are missing or double marked, the results are considered invalid. This rule is based on the fact that 10 or more omissions may compromise the scoring of each scale in that there may not be a sufficient number of items completed for each scale. It is recommended, however, that clinicians make every effort to have no omissions on the MACI. With 160 items used to score 31 scales and indices, item responses are valuable and given the relative brevity of the test, a clinician can easily scan the items and have the adolescent complete or mark any omitted or double-marked responses. A *fourth* formal rule of MACI validity is that the test is considered invalid if both items on Scale VV (Reliability Index) are endorsed. However, given the sensitivity of these items to random responding and malingering, a recommendation is outlined in Table 4.2 that Scale VV should be zero. This cutoff is more conservative and is more likely to eliminate test results that are unreliable or of questionable accuracy. The *fifth* formal validity rule is that the MACI is considered invalid due to underreporting of symptoms if the raw score of Scale X is less than 201 and invalid due to overreporting if the raw score of Scale X is greater than 589. Other considerations have been discussed in this chapter pertaining to the accuracy of MACI results and these are mentioned in Table 4.2. Finally, a *sixth* validity rule states that if all of the BR scores on Scales 1 through 8B are below 60, then the MACI is considered invalid. Under these conditions, the adolescent's scores on the Personality Patterns scales have all fallen below the median for the normative sample and no clear personality style emerges from the test data.

If any one of the six formal validity rules in Table 4.2 is violated, the MACI results are considered invalid. When all six rules are satisfied, the computer will score the test results and yield a profile. Nevertheless, satisfaction of each rule as defined by the computer does not necessarily guarantee the validity of the MACI, as some of the examples in this chapter have shown. In later chapters, various approaches will be discussed for deriving useful information from technically valid profiles that do not appear to fit the case history or clinical presentation.

SUMMARY

The reliability and validity of results from self-report psychological tests are extremely important considerations that must be addressed prior to undertaking profile interpretation. Four major indices or scales on the MACI are used to evaluate the response style utilized by the adolescent when taking the MACI: the Reliability Index (Scale VV) and Scales X (Disclosure), Y (Desirability), and Z (Debasement). This chapter outlines the meaning of elevations on these measures and various Modifying Indices configurations are presented to assist in identifying specific response sets. Formal rules for determining whether MACI results are invalid are presented, including the computer-defined rules outlined in the MACI manual as well as some additional rules that will help the MACI user reduce the likelihood of errors when judging the validity of the MACI profile.

CHAPTER 5

Personality Patterns Scales

TWELVE SCALES make up the section of the MACI profile known as the Personality Patterns scales. Each of these scales was designed to measure one of the basic personality prototypes formulated by Millon (1969, 1981, 1990; Millon & Davis, 1994). As noted, there is some controversy surrounding the practice of diagnosing personality disorders in adolescents. However, the MACI Personality Patterns scales, while corresponding to individual personality disorders in *DSM-IV* (American Psychiatric Association, 1994), are more appropriately labeled to reflect individual personality styles that in exaggerated or rigid form can represent disturbances in personality. When personality traits become fixed or inflexible and perpetuate the same types of maladaptive coping and ineffective problem-solving, then those traits may be viewed as forms of psychopathology.

The Personality Patterns scales measure individual personality types along a continuum from normal variants of personality to extreme levels of disturbance and psychopathology. From an interpretive standpoint, this continuum is represented in the BR scores that are used to plot individual MACI scales. Therefore, when interpreting these scales, only scores that exceed a BR of 75 are considered clinically significant. Scores exceeding a BR of 85 are considered more prominent, and as scores rise above this level, the higher BR values are associated with more extreme levels of disturbance. When BR scores fall between 60 and 74, the MACI Personality Patterns scales can be viewed as possibly reflecting personality traits that may be helpful in describing the adolescent's functioning, but the inference of a disturbance in personality should be avoided with scores in this range. This is not to say that personality disturbances are not present when MACI BR scores fall below a BR of 75 because the low scores may be due to other factors such as socially desirable responding, defensiveness, or other forms of denial. In these cases, the clinician must rely on other pieces of data to arrive at an appropriate assessment of the adolescent's personality.

In this chapter, we explore the interpretive significance of elevations on the MACI Personality Patterns scales. The first section examines each scale individually in terms of general psychometric properties and characteristics of the scale's composition as it bears on interpretation. Thus, interpretation of each scale is outlined by describing meanings that can be attributed to significant elevations (BR ≥ 75 or BR ≥ 85). The material for these discussions is drawn from the MACI manual (Millon et al., 1993), previously published material on MACI interpretation (McCann, 1997), and clinical experience with using the instrument in a variety of settings. With respect to research on the MACI personality scales, one study has investigated the dimensions underlying each of these scales by developing content scales through a process of factor analysis and refinement of the scales through rational analysis (Davis, 1994). Content scales for the MACI developed by Davis for the Personality Patterns scales represent empirically based dimensions that reflect the construct validity of these scales and they can aid interpretation. In this chapter, these dimensions are discussed in general terms. For those interested in obtaining a more detailed outline of the items comprising these content scales and their psychometric properties, Appendix C provides this information.

The second major section of this chapter outlines configurations that are often found when using the MACI. These configurations can be classified based on common behavioral constellations and theoretical constructs that may be represented in multiple scale elevations. Traditionally, the interpretation of multiscale inventories has been most effective when clinicians recognize that a single scale can take on added significance or slightly different meaning if it is elevated in combination with one scale versus another. Personality Patterns scale configurations can be classified according to theoretical dimensions such as interpersonal detachment and emotional instability or according to constellations of behavior such as externalization versus internalization.

INDIVIDUAL SCALES

SCALE 1: INTROVERSIVE

Scale Characteristics

The major purpose of Scale 1 is to measure introversive personality traits that include a deficiency in the adolescent's capacity to experience pleasurable or painful responses to life events. Moreover, it is designed as a measure of personality traits associated with the schizoid personality as outlined in *DSM-IV* and the passive detached style in Millon's theoretical model.

Scale 1 is made up of 44 items; it shares a significant number of items (20 items) with Scale 2A and a moderate number of items with Scales 2B (6 items), 8B (9 items), and 9 (6 items). The internal consistency of Scale 1 is very good with an alpha coefficient of 0.83 in the development sample. Stability is the lowest among all Personality Patterns scales at 0.63, suggesting that some change in Scale 1 scores may be due to state aspects of personality (to be commented on more fully later). The concurrent validity of Scale 1 reveals high correlations with the Ineffectiveness (0.54) and Social Insecurity (0.49) subscales of the Eating Disorder Inventory-2 (EDI-2). Scale 1 also correlates significantly with the Beck Depression Inventory (0.46) and the Beck Hopelessness Scale (0.42). As such, some of the transient features measured by Scale 1 appear to be associated with depressive symptomatology. Of all MACI scales, Scale 1 was one of a few that did not correlate significantly with clinician judgments of introversive personality traits, again suggesting that this scale may represent a more heterogeneous set of characteristics.

Davis (1994) identified four major content dimensions measured by Scale 1. The first is *existential aimlessness* reflecting a general lack of clarity with the meaning of one's life and a lack of clear identity. A second content domain is *anhedonic affect* reflecting a lack of any pleasurable feelings in one's life and a lack of interest in activities that add pleasure to life. The third content domain is *social isolation* representing difficulty fitting in with peers and a lack of close relationships. The fourth content domain represents *sexual indifference* and reflects a lack of interest in sexual matters or in forming romantic attachments. These empirically established dimensions support the construct validity of Scale 1.

Significant Elevations

High scores on Scale 1 reflect a diminished capacity for experiencing either psychic pleasure or pain in one's life. The range of emotions typically displayed by the adolescent is likely to be very narrow, particularly if this scale is much higher than any other personality scale or if there are no other scales reflecting emotionality (e.g., Scales 9, EE, or FF) that are elevated. On the surface, the adolescent may appear apathetic, remote, and lacking in vitality. In relationships with others, they are likely to be detached and they will have very few, if any, close interpersonal relationships, including with family members. Overall, the adolescent with a high score on Scale 1 tends to prefer solitary activities and he or she will avoid those activities that are likely to force contact or interactions with others. If demands are placed on them, these adolescents are likely to respond with bland indifference; if they experience anxiety or tension, they are likely to mask it with the appearance of indifference or little apparent discomfort.

The problem-solving strategies of adolescents with primary Scale 1 elevations tend to be underdeveloped and limited. They do not focus on complex aspects of the environment and have difficulty reaching out to others for help. When discussing problems, they have difficulty voicing their concerns. Overall, they appear aimless, lacking in direction, and unaffected by the difficulties they may encounter. These adolescents also experience feelings of hopelessness, yet they may express little desire to take any steps to change the quality of their lives.

Because of the lower stability and the significant correlations with measures of depression, Scale 1 elevations may also reflect depressive symptomatology. The apathy, lethargy, anhedonia, and social withdrawal measured by this scale may reflect a chronic depression such as dysthymia. Also, the lack of capacity for experiencing psychological pleasure or pain may in some cases reflect a psychological numbing that is common in victims of severe trauma. Therefore, in adolescents whose clinical histories reflect physical or sexual abuse or loss of a significant attachment figure, Scale 1 elevations may represent a reaction to these psychosocial stressors.

SCALE 2A: INHIBITED

Scale Characteristics

Scale 2A provides a measure of inhibited personality traits that are represented not only in the adolescent's difficulty in experiencing pleasure in life, but also in the teenager's hypersensitivity to and expectation of psychological pain. In addition, this scale is designed to correspond to personality traits that are associated with the avoidant personality in *DSM-IV* and the active detached style in Millon's theoretical model.

Scale 2A is made up of 37 items and several of them are shared with other scales, including Scales 1 (20 items), 2B (7 items), and 8B (15 items). Concurrent elevations on these other scales may therefore occur when Scale 2A is highly elevated. The internal consistency of Scale 2A is very good, with an alpha coefficient of 0.86 in the development sample. Test-retest reliability is acceptable with a coefficient of 0.70, although again some state qualities of personality may be represented in elevations. The concurrent and discriminant validity of Scale 2A has some support as seen by significant correlations with the Ineffectiveness subscale (0.41) of the EDI-2 and low correlations with measures of affective disturbance with the Beck Depression Inventory (0.21), Beck Hopelessness Scale (0.19), and Beck Anxiety Inventory (0.08). Among the Personality Patterns scales, Scale 2A had one of the stronger correlations with clinicians' judgments of personality, with a 0.27 correlation coefficient between BR scores and clinicians' ratings of inhibited personality traits.

Six content dimensions were identified for Scale 2A by Davis (1994) that are supportive of the construct validity of the scale. The first dimension is *existential sadness* representing general feelings of unhappiness about one's self and the quality of one's life. A second dimension is *preferred detachment*, which reflects a desire to avoid interpersonal contact and to do things alone. The third dimension is *self-conscious restraint* representing a hesitance in taking action or in doing things impulsively or spontaneously. *Sexual aversion*, the fourth dimension, reflects a lack of interest, with active avoidance of sexuality. The fifth dimension of Scale 2A is *rejection feelings* and reflects a sense of being left out or being uncomfortable in social situations due to a fear of rejection or ridicule. The sixth dimension on Scale 2A, *unattractive self-image*, represents discomfort with one's physical appearance and self-consciousness about how others see the adolescent. These six dimensions represent many of the features associated with the inhibited personality.

Significant Elevations

Elevations on Scale 2A represent an extreme sensitivity to rejection and humiliation that causes significant difficulties in the adolescent's ability to enjoy life and to experience pleasure. Frequently, the behavior of adolescents with high scores is inhibited and they lack initiative because they fear that others will be critical and rejecting. On the surface, these teenagers appear shy, uncomfortable in social settings, and awkward when they interact with others. As such, they are often lonely and detached. When pressure is placed on them to become more sociable or outgoing, they become anxious and actively avoid activities that bring them into contact with others.

A major feature of adolescents who score high on Scale 2A is that they have a very poor self-image and lack confidence in their ability to do things well. Because they often fear that they will do things poorly or that everything they touch becomes "spoiled," these adolescents do not plan their activities. They are ineffective problem-solvers because they are often paralyzed by their own fears.

In relationships with others, they may be seen as needy and clingy because they require constant reassurance that they are doing things adequately or that they are accepted and tolerated despite their self-perceived shortcomings. Although inhibited teenagers may avoid relationships out of fear of rejection, they will actively hang on to those relationships they have developed once they have been given reassurance of being accepted. They remain sensitive to criticism and rejection.

Based on the general nature of the items on this scale, there is a general psychological maladjustment component that is represented in very high elevations. Generalized feelings of unhappiness, lack of close relationships, and self-deprecation may also be present and are likely to be associated with concurrent elevations on Scales 2B, 8B, 9, B, and E. A primary difference between Scales 2A and 1 is that the inhibited adolescent wants relationships but is isolated and detached because of fears of rejection and humiliation. The introversive adolescent is indifferent to relationships and has little interest in forming connections to others.

Scale 2B: Doleful

Scale Characteristics

The major personality features measured by Scale 2B are a sense of significant loss of important attachment figures, feelings of wanting to give up, and hopelessness that happiness can ever be attained. This scale is a measure of the characteristics associated with the depressive personality outlined in the appendix of *DSM-IV* and a variant if the passive-detached personality style outlined by Millon.

Scale 2B has 24 items; there is extensive overlap with Scale 8B (13 items), and moderate overlap with Scales 8A (9 items), 9 (8 items), 1 (6 items), and 2A (5 items). As such, Scale 2B correlates highly with each of these scales. The reliability of Scale 2B is very good, with an internal consistency coefficient of 0.86 in the development sample and a test-retest reliability coefficient of 0.83. Therefore, the stability of this scale is high and suggests that it measures fairly long-standing and chronic forms of depression. The correlation between Scale 2B BR scores and clinicians' ratings of doleful personality traits is significant, but a modest 0.22. Concurrent validity of Scale 2B is supported by significant correlations between the Mental Health concerns subscale (0.47) of the POSIT, Body Dissatisfaction (0.58) and Ineffectiveness (0.52) subscales of the EDI-2, the Beck Depression Inventory (0.58), and the Beck Hopefulness Scale (0.54). Overall, Scale 2B appears to be a stable measure of chronic or long-standing depression and hopelessness.

The content dimensions of Scale 2B were established through factor analysis of the items by Davis (1994). He found four subscales that support the construct validity of the scale. The first dimension—*brooding melancholia*—represents excessive rumination, hopelessness, and preoccupation with the negative aspects of one's life. A second dimension is *social joylessness* and represents a prominent lack of pleasure in being with people and general anhedonia. *Self-destructive ideation*, the third content dimension of Scale 2B reflects suicidal ideation and thoughts of hurting one's self. The fourth content dimension is made up of several prototypic items and was labeled *abandonment fears*; it reflects prominent feelings of being unwanted, unloved, and alone. This last factor reflects the attachment loss that is a major theoretical construct distinguishing the doleful personality from the introversive and inhibited personality measured by Scales 1 and 2A respectively.

Significant Elevations

A major feature associated with high scores on Scale 2A is long-standing feelings of depression and unhappiness. Adolescents with high scores on this scale have much difficulty experiencing joy and pleasure because they have chronic feelings of hopelessness. Their apathy is based largely on lack of hope that anything will change the unhappy nature of their life. If others do something nice for them or take steps to improve unpleasant circumstances, these teenagers are likely to respond with pessimism or feelings of unworthiness.

Pessimism also carries over into other areas of the adolescent's functioning, such as self-image and interpersonal relationships. Adolescents with high scores on Scale 2B have very low self-esteem, feelings of worthlessness, and inadequacy. Therefore, they do not see themselves as effective or competent problem-solvers. These feelings of inadequacy usually stem from feelings of abandonment and loss of important attachment figures. Such adolescents generally feel that they must be less than adequate mostly because others have left or rejected them. In social situations, therefore, these teenagers are likely to be seen as withdrawn, isolated, and disinterested in friendships because of the expectation that others will leave or abandon them. The expectation is that nothing positive will result from forming close relationships.

On a behavioral level, the adolescent with high scores on Scale 2B is prone to worry and ruminate about the negative quality of his or her life. There may be feelings of wanting to die and suicidal ideation and/or intent may also be present. In this regard, Scale GG elevations should be considered and face-valid items representing suicidal preoccupation should be reviewed (see Chapter 10). A range of mood disturbances can be found with Scale 2B elevations, including dysthymia and chronic depression. Whether the diagnostic picture is a victim of childhood trauma or abuse or a conduct disorder in an acting-out adolescent, the Scale 2B elevation generally represents the adolescent's feelings of having lost a significant attachment figure (e.g., an absent father or mother) or chronic hopelessness and dysphoria. There may also be feelings of guilt over past misbehavior or transgressions that may be either real or exaggerated.

SCALE 3: SUBMISSIVE

Scale Characteristics

The major purpose of Scale 3 on the MACI is to measure personality characteristics associated with passive dependency in which the adolescent finds happiness and security in relationships with others, with a marked tendency to ignore one's own needs or wishes. As such, this scale is designed as a measure of the dependent personality as outlined in the DSM-IV and the passive-dependent personality style outlined in Millon's theoretical model.

The 48 items on Scale 3 overlap with other scales, including Scales 7 (16 items), 2A (7 items), and 8B (5 items). Despite the item overlap, Scale 3 correlates highly only with Scale 7 (0.73). The internal consistency of Scale 3 is adequate, with an alpha coefficient of 0.74 obtained in the developmental sample. Test-retest reliability is very good, with a coefficient of 0.88. Although Scale 3 was one of only a few Personality Patterns scales to not correlate significantly with clinicians' judgments of submissive personality traits, other correlations with collateral measures support the concurrent validity of the scale. Significant correlations were obtained between the Maturity Fears subscale (0.52) of the EDI-2 and a negative relationship with the Family Relations subscale (-0.44) of the POSIT, reflecting a need for harmonious family relationships.

The construct validity of Scale 3 was supported by factor analytic studies conducted by Davis (1994) in which he identified six content dimensions that reflect the personality traits associated with the submissive personality. The first content dimension is *deficient assertiveness*, which represents a resistance toward acting impulsively or against the wishes of others. *Authority respect*, the second content subscale, represents a propensity to defer to those in authority and to conform to the wishes of parents and other authority figures. The third dimension of Scale 3 is *pacific disposition*, which represents a tendency to be easygoing, passive, and unassertive. A fourth dimension, *attachment anxiety*, measures heightened concerns about being left alone and fears of having to function autonomously. The fifth dimension is *social correctness*, representing a preoccupation with doing what is proper and expected by others. *Guidance seeking*, which is the sixth dimension of Scale 3, reflects a need to have others assume direction and take responsibility for one's life. Overall, these six factors support the construct validity of Scale 3 as a measure of submissiveness, passivity, and other traits associated with dependence.

Significant Elevations

A major attribute of adolescents who score high on Scale 3 is passivity and submissiveness in interpersonal relationships. These teenagers avoid taking any leadership roles in social settings, and in relationships with peers they tend to be concerned that others will not be there for them. They tend to be clingy and avoid situations where they will have to assume more mature roles. Family relationships may be enmeshed and the teenager may allow parents to assume responsibility for things that the adolescent should be doing on his or her own, such as homework, the planning of social activities, and getting extra help for school work.

There are underlying fears that others will not be there for the adolescent or that important people may abandon him or her. To foster more dependent relationships, the adolescent with a high Scale 3 score will tend to view him- or herself as ineffective or inept and personal abilities and achievements are downplayed. It is expected that others will assume a more active role and will take charge in times of crisis or stress. High scores also reflect a lack of self-confidence in many areas, and reassurance from others is needed to maintain feelings of adequacy and security. Strong interpersonal ties may be developed with those adults or peers who are viewed by the submissive teenager as capable of assuming a more assertive and active role. Moreover, close relationships are often viewed in sentimental ways, even if those relationships are problematic.

Because some attributes measured by this scale have positive connotations in some settings (e.g., unassertiveness and passivity in a residential or correctional setting; respect for authority), elevations may reflect the adolescent's wish to portray these attitudes. Therefore, the context in which Scale 3 elevations arise should be considered.

SCALE 4: DRAMATIZING

Scale Characteristics

This scale measures the active-dependent personality style formulated by Millon; it also corresponds to the histrionic personality outlined in the *DSM-IV*. A major feature of this personality style is a dramatic, manipulative, gregarious, or attention-seeking series of behaviors that seek to increase protection and nurturance from others.

This scale is made up of 41 items and there is moderate item overlap between Scale 4 and other MACI scales, including Scales 5 (18 items) and 6A (11 items). However, there is a high correlation between Scales 4 and 5 only (0.83). As expected from a theoretical perspective, there is a high negative correlation between Scale 4, which reflects high levels of sociability, and the MACI scales measuring detached styles, including Scales 1 (−0.82), 2A (−0.74), and 2B (−0.58). Internal consistency of Scale 4 is quite high with an alpha coefficient of 0.82 in the development sample. The stability of Scale 4 is acceptable at 0.70. The relationship between Scale 4 BR scores and clinicians' judgments of dramatizing personality traits, while statistically significant, is low at 0.15. Concurrent validity is supported by correlations that are significant and in the expected direction between the Ineffectiveness (−0.54), Interpersonal Distrust (−0.41), and Social Insecurity (−0.47) subscales of the EDI-2.

Five content dimensions were identified through factor analysis that support the construct validity of Scale 4 (Davis, 1994). The first of these dimensions is *convivial sociability,* which measures an adaptive set of social skills that allow the teenager to fit in with a group of peers. The second dimension—*attention-seeking*—is a group of mostly prototypic items that reflect dramatic and attention-getting perceptions of the self. The third dimension for Scale 4 is *attractive self-image,* in which the adolescent has a positive body image and a perception of being well liked by others. *Optimistic outlook,* the fourth dimension, measures denial of pessimistic attitudes and a lack of hopelessness. The fifth dimension of Scale 4 that Davis identified is *behavioral disinhibition* reflecting a proclivity for sensation-seeking behavior and a need for excitement. These five factors represent major features of the dramatizing personality.

Significant Elevations

Teenagers who score high on Scale 4 are sociable and need a lot of stimulation in their lives. It is important to them to have numerous friendships and to have many people available to add stimulation and excitement. A major feature associated with high scores is a dramatic display of emotions; oftentimes the emotions of dramatizing adolescents are seen by others as highly changeable and at times shallow. Because of their variable emotions, as well as their changeable attitudes, the behavior of these teenagers is often poorly planned and impulsive. They often make decisions without much forethought—on the spur-of-the-moment or for fickle reasons.

In social settings, the behavior of adolescents with high Scale 4 scores can be characterized by excessive talkativeness and gregariousness. There is also a strong need to draw attention to oneself, frequent risk-taking, or sensation-seeking behavior. These characteristics are often directed at drawing attention and creating an appearance that will make others think that the teenager is likable and interesting. Most relationships for dramatizing adolescents are either superficial or short-term. They do not tolerate long-term relationships very well because they become bored and need to move on to have life stay interesting. Others may find the teenager fun at first, but the dramatizing teenager's superficial approach to relationships causes friends and acquaintances to lose interest. The view that others have of the adolescent often conflicts with dramatizing adolescent's self-image of being a fun-loving, interesting, and friendly individual.

Because many of the items on this scale pertain to personal attributes with a positive tone, such as sociability and a positive outlook on life,

Scale 4 is sometimes elevated when an adolescent adopts a socially desirable response set. When Scale 4 is moderately elevated (i.e., BR 75–84) and Scale 7 is also a primary or secondary elevation, then a socially desirable response set is possible. If Scale 4 is significantly elevated (e.g., BR ≥ 85), Scale 7 is not elevated, and other personality scales are elevated (e.g., Scales 3, 5, 6A, or 6B), then dramatizing personality traits are present and are contributing to the difficulties the adolescent may be experiencing. Although the dramatizing personality may exhibit changeable, fickle, or scattered decision making, this cognitive style is not strongly represented in the items on the scale. Therefore, the relationship between Scale 4 elevations and behavioral disorders such as attention-deficit/hyperactivity disorder cannot be directly inferred from this scale and other assessment measures should be included to assist in making such a diagnosis.

SCALE 5: EGOTISTIC

Scale Characteristics

The major purpose of Scale 5 is to measure personality traits associated with narcissism and self-aggrandizement that render the adolescent feeling entitled and lacking in empathy for others. This scale also assesses features of the narcissistic personality in *DSM-IV* and the passive independent style formulated by Millon.

There are 39 items on Scale 5 and a moderate overlap with Scales 4 (18 items) and 6A (8 items). Scale 5 correlates highly in the positive direction with Scale 4 (0.83) and in the negative direction with Scales 1 (–0.74), 2A (–0.69), 2B (–0.65), 8B (–0.64), and 9 (–0.59). In the developmental sample, internal consistency of Scale 5 was good with an alpha coefficient of 0.80. Stability of the scale was also very good with a test-retest reliability coefficient of 0.82. The correlation between Scale 5 BR scores and clinicians' ratings of egotistic personality traits was a significant, but modest 0.20. Concurrent validity of Scale 5 was supported by significant correlations in the expected direction with the Body Dissatisfaction (–0.78), Ineffectiveness (–0.74), and Social Insecurity (–0.54) subscales of the EDI-2.

As with the other MACI personality scales, Davis (1994) conducted a factor analysis of the items of Scale 5; he found six factors that support the construct validity of the scale. The first content dimension is *admirable self-image*, encompassing items that measure a favorable body image and satisfaction with one's appearance. A second factor is *social conceit*, which reflects feelings of being the center of attention. The third content dimension is *confident purposefulness*, which represents a feeling of having direction in life and a clear identity. *Self-assured independence* is the fourth dimension identified for Scale 5 and represents items measuring a denial of clinging behavior or neediness. The fifth content factor, *empathic indifference,* represents a lack of empathy for others. Finally, Davis identified *superiority feelings* as a sixth factor for Scale 5, representing grandiosity and self-aggrandizement. Overall, these six factors represent many of the characteristics associated with the narcissistic or egotistic personality.

Significant Elevations

The adolescent who scores high on Scale 5 can be adequately described as overly self-confident and self-assured. As a result, others tend to view the teenager as self-centered, arrogant, and conceited. In general, the self-image of superiority tends to be either unsubstantiated or is an exaggerated self-perception of the teenager's talents and abilities. This grandiosity causes difficulties in interpersonal relationships.

Around others, the adolescent with a Scale 5 elevation requires a very high level of admiration and respect. When these accolades do not come forth, the teenager is likely to respond with anger, rage, or the appearance of cool indifference. Because the teenager expects others to recognize his or her talents and abilities in the same aggrandized manner, there is likely to be an angry or terse response when others fail to award adequate recognition or credit. A sense of entitlement and of being owed benefits leads to the egotistic teenager exploiting others to get the desired recognition. An equally significant interpersonal attitude displayed by egotistic adolescents is a lack of empathy or concern for others. As a result, they show very little respect to others and may appear pleasant only if it will result in some benefit to themselves.

The thinking of adolescents with high Scale 5 scores tends to be focused on thoughts of unlimited success, power, or rewards. At times, these thoughts may preoccupy the teenager's thoughts to the point that he or she appears quiet and aloof. Chronic feelings of being unappreciated or taken for granted are common.

When Scale 5 elevations occur in combination with other personality scales, there tends to be a strong resistance to seeing one's self as having problems. Thus, the adolescent has an ego-syntonic view of any maladaptive characteristics or traits. This can create strong resistance in treatment. In other cases, extremely high Scale 5 scores represent prominent grandiosity that can be found in paranoid and hypersensitive adolescents.

SCALE 6A: UNRULY

Scale Characteristics

The major purpose of Scale 6A is to assess personality traits characterized by the shunning of socially acceptable behavior and the adopting of deceitful, illegal, or exploitive behaviors to benefit oneself or to retaliate against others. This scale thus serves as a measure of traits associated with the antisocial personality in *DSM-IV* and the active-independent personality outlined by Millon.

There are 39 items on Scale 6A, and moderate item overlap exists between this scale and Scales 4 (11 items), 5 (8 items), 6B (12 items), and 8A (13 items). Rather high positive correlations exist between Scale 6A and Scales 6B (0.75) and 8A (0.48). The internal consistency of Scale 6A is very good, with an alpha coefficient of 0.84 obtained in the development sample. Test-retest reliability is also good with a coefficient of 0.79. The correlation between Scale 6A BR scores and clinicians' ratings of unruly personality traits was one of the highest among the Personality Patterns scales at a modest 0.27. Concurrent validity of the scale is supported by significant positive correlations between the Substance Use or Abuse (0.41), and Family Relations (0.46) subscales of the POSIT and a negative correlation with the Maturity Fears (−0.48) subscale of the EDI-2.

Six content dimensions were identified by Davis (1994) that support the construct validity of Scale 6A. The first factor, *impulsive disobedience,* measures a propensity to act out in an impulsive manner without much planning or thought as to consequences. A second factor on Scale 6A is *socialized substance abuse,* which represents a positive endorsement of the use of drugs and alcohol, particularly in social situations. *Authority rejection,* the third content scale, measures a refusal to follow direction from authority. The fourth content dimension is *unlawful activity,* representing a tendency to engage in criminal activities or to commit illegal actions. The fifth content scale—*callous manipulation*—measures an unempathic attitude toward the using of others to get what one wants. The sixth content dimension of Scale 6A is *sexual absorption,* which represents comfort with sexual matters. These six dimensions represent the major features measured by the scale and are supportive of the construct validity.

Significant Elevations

A major feature of teenagers scoring high on Scale 6A is the presence of many conduct problems that are the result of the teenager's rejection of socially acceptable standards and norms for behavior. Because their rebelliousness involves a rejection of any limits being placed on their actions, unruly teenagers are oppositional, combative, and uncooperative. They will have difficulty observing a curfew, following rules, or doing things that are expected of them. At times, the adolescent with a Scale 6A elevation will appear cooperative and compliant, but this generally represents either a manipulative facade or a cooperative stance toward others who share similar antisocial attitudes. Cooperative group-oriented behavior is generally directed at achieving goals that are rebellious or illegal.

Adolescents who score highly on Scale 6A have a strong need for autonomy and independence. When limits are placed on their behavior, they become defiant. At times when they are being manipulative, their behavior can be more controlled, and at other times their behavior is impulsive and irresponsible. There is a high degree of illegal activities associated with high scores, including stealing, truancy, fighting, and general rejection of social norms.

The relationships of unruly teenagers are often characterized by a lack of compassion or empathy for others. Moreover, they are also characterized by the adolescent's negative views of human nature. These teenagers tend to see others as untrustworthy and lacking in sincerity. Unruly teenagers are quick to seek revenge for some perceived injustice such as when they feel others are taking advantage of them. Over time, experience proves to be a very limited teacher because unruly adolescents do not learn from the mistakes or problems they have encountered. If they act out and suffer adverse consequences, they either superficially adopt a cooperative and compliant set of values with no clear plan for carrying through or they casually promise to change their behavior with no intent of carrying through on the promise. Thus, they strive to find other manipulative or antisocial ways to avoid future problems. Nevertheless, there tends to be a maladaptive cycle of behavior involving acting-out, limits or correction being given, followed by rebellious and angry acting-out, with instances of revenge-seeking behavior as well.

A diagnosis of conduct disorder should be considered with Scale 6A elevations, although other disruptive behavior disorders may also be a viable diagnosis, including oppositional-defiant disorder. In adolescents with no history of conduct problems, high Scale 6A scores tend to reflect attitudes involving a negative and highly misanthropic view of others. There may also be a strong identification with a peer or intimate partner who has antisocial tendencies.

SCALE 6B: FORCEFUL

Scale Characteristics

The major purpose of Scale 6B is to measure personality traits associated with aggressive control, domination, and intimidation of others. Moreover, the forceful personality views the infliction of pain and discomfort as a preferred mode of relating to others. As such, the scale is intended as a measure of the sadistic personality outlined in the appendix of *DSM-III-R* and the active discordant type formulated by Millon.

The scale is made up of 22 items, making it one of the shortest Personality Patterns scales. Of the other personality scales, those sharing a significant number of items with Scale 6B are Scales 6A (12 items) and 8A (11 items). Despite being one of the shortest scales, Scales 6B had very good internal consistency in the development sample with an alpha coefficient of 0.83. Test-retest reliability was also very good with a coefficient of 0.85. Among the Personality Patterns scales, Scale 6B had the highest correlation between scale BR scores and clinicians' judgments of forceful personality traits at 0.28, although this correlation is somewhat low. The concurrent validity of Scale 6B was supported by significant correlations in the expected direction with the Substance Abuse (0.45) and Aggressive Behavior/Delinquency (0.29) subscales of the POSIT and the Maturity Fears (0.32) subscale of the EDI-2.

In a factor analytic study of the MACI personality scales, Davis (1994) found three major content dimensions that define the major characteristics of Scale 6B. The first of these dimensions is *intimidating abrasiveness*, representing a disposition toward hurting or acting cruelly against others. The second content dimension is *precipitous anger*, which reflects impulsive anger and lack of thought about the effects of one's actions. The third dimension of Scale 6B is *empathic deficiency*, which pertains to the lack of empathy that sadistic and forceful individuals exhibit. These three content scales reflect major components of the forceful personality construct.

Significant Elevations

High scores on Scale 6B reflect a prominent need for self-determination and control of others. These adolescents appear hostile, combative, and indifferent to the destructive or unpleasant consequences of their actions on other people. As a result, their behavior brings them into constant conflict with adults in positions of authority. Such teenagers are intolerant of being controlled or of having limits placed on their behavior. They view limit setting and other restrictions as a challenge to be met with blunt and hostile retaliation.

Another major characteristic of adolescents who score highly on Scale 6B is the perception they have of themselves as tough and intimidating toward others. Because they lack empathy and have no sensitivity to the feelings of others, their social behavior often appears caustic, insulting, or abrasive. Moreover, they tend to derive satisfaction from humiliating, verbally attacking, or in other ways impinging on other people's sense of well-being. Efforts to confront these contentious social behaviors are frequently met with hostility and a combative demeanor.

Conduct disorders and antisocial behavior are common with Scale 6B elevations; however, the relative absence of this diagnosis and symptomatology in teenagers who score high on the scale is also a strong possibility. If the adolescent demonstrates conduct disturbances, the scale 6B elevation generally denotes that the teenager derives pleasure and satisfaction from the harm and turmoil that the acting-out creates for others. When the history or clinical picture does not reveal a significant pattern of conduct disturbance or antisocial acting-out, several alternative hypotheses can be considered. In some cases, the teenager may be quite sophisticated and has eluded getting caught in many situations; perhaps other, less assertive peers have been coerced or manipulated into doing the "dirty work" for the forceful adolescent. Another possibility is that the adolescent has strong negative and hostile views of others and sees authoritarian and dominant forms of behavior as a desirable means for protecting one's self; the guiding life philosophy might be characterized by the phrase, "the best defense is a good offense." In these instances, the forceful attitudes may be a reaction to psychosocial pressures (e.g., peer pressure, reactions to being severely victimized) or a strong identification with an aggressive/sadistic peer or peer group (e.g., gang identification, strong identification with a forceful boyfriend or girlfriend).

SCALE 7: CONFORMING

Scale Characteristics

One of the main purposes of Scale 7 on the MACI is to provide a measure of behavioral restraint, rigidity, and excessive conformity to external rules and expectations of others. The major constructs that served to guide development of this scale were the obsessive-compulsive personality in *DSM-IV* and the passive-ambivalent personality style outlined by Millon.

Scale 7 consists of 39 items which are shared at a moderate level with Scale 3 (16 items); Scale 7 correlates highly with Scale 3 (0.74) and moderately with Scales 4 (0.46) and 5 (0.55). The internal-consistency of Scale 7 was 0.86 in the development sample, which is very high and represents good precision of measurement. Test-retest reliability was also excellent, with a coefficient of 0.91 that was highest among all MACI scales. The correlation between Scale 7 BR scores and clinicians' judgments of conforming personality traits was a modest, but significant 0.25. Data on the concurrent validity of Scale 7 reflects a general denial of psychological concerns and high levels of efficiency. Significant positive correlations were obtained between Scale 7 and the Interoceptive Awareness (0.45) subscale of the EDI-2 and negative correlations were obtained between Scale 7 and the Ineffectiveness (−0.47) and Impulse Regulation (−0.41) subscale of the EDI-2. In addition, there were high negative correlations between Scale 7 and the Beck Depression Inventory (−0.62) and Beck Hopelessness Scale (−.063), which reflects an inverse relationship between Scale 7 scores and depressive symptomatology.

In a factor analytic study of the content dimensions of Scale 7, Davis (1994) identified five subscales that reflect major attributes associated with the conforming personality type. The first content dimension identified by Davis is *interpersonal restraint*, which represents a tendency to think before acting and a reduced tendency to act impulsively. A second content subscale is *emotional rigidity*, which reflects a lack of pessimistic thinking and other symptoms of depression as well as the presence of a secure sense of self. *Rule adherence* is the third content dimension identified for Scale 7 and represents a preference for routine and a set way of carrying out activities. The fourth dimension of Scale 7 is *social conformity* and reflects the adoption of law-abiding behavior and a denial of antisocial attitudes. Davis labeled the fifth content subscale *responsible conscientiousness* representing a strong tendency to do things properly and according to the expectations of those in authority. Together, these five content subscales represent the major features of the conforming personality type.

Significant Elevations

More than any other Personality Patterns scale on the MACI, Scale 7 is one that is heavily influenced by factors other than the personality traits it was designed to measure. This does not mean that elevations cannot reflect conforming personality traits; rather, the scale must be interpreted within the context of other MACI scale elevations as well as the case history.

Because many characteristics of the conforming personality are desirable (e.g., following rules, conscientiousness, conforming behaviors), it is common to observe Scale 7 elevations in those teenagers who are exhibiting a socially desirable response set and not necessarily a compulsive personality style. Thus, some impulsive, acting-out, emotionally unstable adolescents may yield a Scale 7 elevation because they want to create a positive impression by appearing to be hard-working, compliant, emotionally restrained, and conforming. Typically, Scale 7 elevations that represent a socially desirable response set are those where either no other Personality Patterns scales are elevated or Scales 4 and/or 5 are moderately elevated. If Scale 7 is elevated in combination with any other Personality Patterns scales (e.g., 2A, 3, or 8B), the scale usually reflects aspects of the compulsive personality, such as rigidity or behavioral restraint that are part of the adolescent's personality style. Another hypothesis to consider is that the rigid defenses of the adolescent are brittle and overcontrol his or her emotions. Also, when Scale 7 is the primary or single elevation and the BR score is very high (e.g., BR > 85), then conforming personality traits are more prominent.

A Scale 7 elevation that represents the presence of conforming personality traits reflects an adolescent who is emotionally constricted and very serious-minded. There is usually a history of subjection to intense discipline and restraint rendering the teenager hesitant to assert his or her own needs and wishes. These teens hold rigid ideas and beliefs about what is morally right and wrong and there is strict compliance with rules and the expectations of those in authority. The denial of one's own needs and impulses serves to avoid punishment or intimidation from others.

In relationships, the conforming teenager keeps a tight seal over feelings, yet anxiety and anger arise when peers go against the conforming adolescent's fixed beliefs and ideas. When other teenagers favor a spontaneous and unpredictable way of doing things, the conforming adolescent has difficulty accepting this way of acting because it conflicts with a self-image of being industrious, hard-working, and dependable. Therefore, the conforming teenager may be viewed by peers as intolerant, judgmental, and rigid.

Beneath the surface of restraint and rigidity, the conforming adolescent also may have intense anxiety and ambivalence over the wish to assert his or her own needs and wishes versus the need to conform and show self-restraint. Thus, there may be periods of oppositional and angry responses followed by guilt and constraint of emotions.

SCALE 8A: OPPOSITIONAL

Scale Characteristics

Despite its label, Scale 8A is not designed as a direct measure of oppositional-defiant disorder as outlined in *DSM-IV*. Rather, it reflects the characteristics of the passive-aggressive/negativistic personality as well as the conflicted active ambivalent personality style outlined by Millon. The major feature of this personality type is an intense ambivalence characterized by vacillating self-image, irritability, negative attitudes about others, and passive-aggressive or resistant behavior.

Forty-three items make up Scale 8A, with moderate item overlap between this scale and Scales 2B (9 items), 6A (13 items), 6B (11 items), and 8B (14 items). As such, Scale 8A elevations may occur in combination with one or more of these other scales. The internal consistency of Scale 8A was very respectable, with an alpha of 0.85 obtained in the development sample. Stability of Scale 8A, as measured by a test-retest reliability coefficient, was acceptable at 0.76. No relationship was observed between Scale 8A BR scores and clinicians' ratings of oppositional personality traits (0.02), suggesting that there may have been some confusion between the clinicians' understanding of the construct being measured and the theoretical construct guiding scale development. That is, the clinical diagnosis of oppositional-defiant disorder may have informed the clinicians' ratings, which would reflect ratings that do not necessarily represent the theoretical and clinical construct of passive-aggressive/negativistic personality. The concurrent validity of Scale 8A is supported by noting significant correlations with the Mental Health (0.50) and Family Relationship (0.48) subscales of the POSIT, reflecting general psychological disturbance and family difficulties associated with Scale 8A elevations. In addition, significant correlations were noted between Scale 8A and the Body Dissatisfaction (0.67), Ineffectiveness (0.64), and Impulse Regulation (0.63) subscales of the EDI-2.

A factor analysis of the items from Scale 8A uncovered five content dimensions that support the construct validity of Scale 8A (Davis, 1994). The first of these dimensions, *self-punitiveness*, reflects a preoccupation with suicidal thoughts and a feeling that the world would be better off if the adolescent was dead. The second content subscale is *angry dominance*, which measures a tendency to bully others and to use intimidation to get what one wants. *Resentful discontent* represents a third dimension and is made up of many prototypic items; it reflects general negative attitudes about one's self and relationships with others. The fourth content dimension is *social inconsiderateness* and represents a lack of sensitivity to the feelings of others. The fifth content subscale, *contrary conduct*, represents defiant and acting-out behavior. Overall, major components of the negativistic personality were represented in Davis' factor analytic study.

Significant Elevations

High scores on Scale 8A indicate strong feelings of resentment over having limits placed on one's behavior. Teenagers with elevations on this scale are very resistant in their behavior, and when people ask them to do something, they often respond with resentment and irritability. They are prone to procrastinate or engage in other passive-aggressive behavior because they have difficulty asserting themselves appropriately.

A major characteristic of the adolescent with high scores on Scale 8A is an irritable and moody temperament that often creates the appearance of chronic discontent. Negativistic teenagers do not necessarily show more chronic irritation; instead, they are more quick to arouse into anger or irritability at the slightest provocation. As a result of this irritability, others tend to react with frustration or irritability of their own. Consequently, negativistic teenagers may feel that no one understands or appreciates them and their mood can quickly shift to sullenness and dysphoria.

Overall, significant ambivalence and inconsistency is noted in the disposition of adolescents with Scale 8A elevations. They tend to be confused about themselves and their future, and have difficulty controlling their moods. They manifest their resentment and oppositionality by spoiling the pleasures or enjoyment others feel through passive-aggressive and indirect hostile comments. Peers who are the object of these barbs will shun the teenager, contributing further to feelings of being misunderstood and unappreciated. In addition to poor peer relationships, problems with teachers, parents, and other authority figures are also present. Thus, elevations on this scale denote possible active resistance to treatment.

Elevations on Scale 8A may reflect symptoms of oppositional-defiant disorder; however, this scale was not designed as a direct measure of this diagnostic construct. Therefore, adolescents with oppositional-defiant disorder may or may not have an elevation on this scale.

In addition, Scale 8A (along with Scale 8B) is a useful measure of how the adolescent deals with internal conflict and tension. When Scale 8A is elevated, it represents a tendency to externalize emotional conflict through acting-out with defiance, hostility, or antisocial behavior. When Scale 8A is not elevated, there is either no emotional conflict or the adolescent tends to internalize conflict, in which case Scale 8B would be elevated. If both Scales 8A and 8B are elevated, there is likely to be significant conflict and emotional turmoil that is dealt with in a highly variable and chaotic manner, including both internalizing and externalizing behavior.

Scale 8B: Self-Demeaning

Scale Characteristics

The major purpose of Scale 8B is to measure the self-effacing and self-punitive attitudes that characterize adolescents who focus on their own worst features. Although self-defeating personality was dropped from *DSM-IV*, this personality type served as a major guiding construct for development of Scale 8B, as did the passive discordant type outlined by Millon. Aside from the controversy surrounding the self-defeating personality, Scale 8B is a useful scale for measuring the internalization of emotional conflict and self-effacing attitudes that are part of several forms of psychological disturbance.

Of the 44 items in Scale 8B, there is considerable item overlap with Scales 2A (15 items), 2B (13 items), 8A (14 items), 9 (12 items), and 1 (9 items). The highest correlations are between Scale 8B and Scales 2B (0.74), 9 (0.67), and 5 (−0.64). Overall, the reliability of Scale 8B is excellent, with internal consistency high at an alpha of 0.90 in the development sample and a test-retest reliability coefficient of 0.88. The correlation between Scale 8B BR scores and clinicians' judgments of self-demeaning personality traits is a significant but modest 0.20. Concurrent validity data reveal some support for the validity of Scale 8B, with significant correlations between Scale 8B and the Mental Health (0.44) and Social Skills (0.44) problem subscales of the POSIT and the Body Dissatisfaction (0.74), Ineffectiveness (0.69), Interoceptive Awareness (0.58), and Impulse Regulation (0.62) subscales of the EDI-2. There are also moderate correlations between Scale 8B and the Beck Depression Inventory (0.42) and Beck Hopelessness Scale (0.43). These results indicate that Scale 8B is measuring problems associated with dissatisfaction with the self, disruptive negative or depressive emotions, and poor adjustment.

In a study of the content dimensions of Scale 8B, Davis (1994) identified four subscales through factor analysis that support the construct validity of Scale 8B. The first of these content subscales is *self-ruination,* which reflects a negative outlook on one's life and future that creates a feeling of aimlessness. A second content subscale is *low self-valuation,* which represents a negative self-image and poor self-esteem. *Undeserving self-image,* the third content subscale, measures feelings of unworthiness and a perception that one's negative experiences in life are deserved. *Hopeless outlook* is the fourth content subscale and measures a general pessimism and negative outlook toward the future. Davis' factor analysis is consistent with the criterion validity reported in the MACI manual and supports the construct validity of Scale 8B.

Significant Elevations

Adolescents who score high on Scale 8B generally focus on their worst personal attributes and are self-effacing and self-loathing. They have poor self-esteem and tend to undermine or sabotage opportunities for personal growth and fulfillment. A major force that holds them back is the feeling that they do not deserve success or rewards in life. Thus feelings can stem either from a chronic depression or from a personality trait that has its roots in a childhood where the adolescent was made to feel unworthy due to physical and/or psychological abuse or neglect. As a result, these adolescents tend to put other people's needs ahead of their own.

The interpersonal relationships of adolescents who score high on Scale 8B are characterized by the hindering of attempts by others to offer help or support. Because self-demeaning adolescents feel unworthy of help, they tend to undermine the helpful actions of others. Moreover, they will often provoke aggravation in others by voicing beliefs that nothing can be done to change their life. As such, others are likely to view the adolescent with high Scale 8B scores as a complainer and as difficult to please.

Another major feature of high scores is the handling of emotional conflict by the use of internalizing defenses. When under stress, the teenager will tend to blame him- or herself for problems and expect the worst to happen. Thus, Scale 8B elevations reflect pessimism and hopelessness. Moreover, suicidal rumination and ideation may be present. Diagnostically, depression is a common issue with Scale 8B elevations, including dysthymia, and major depression. There may also be a history of having been abused or neglected at an early age with long-standing issues that have not been adequately worked through. In treatment, adolescents with Scale 8B elevations may be difficult because of their feeling that they do not deserve help.

SCALE 9: BORDERLINE TENDENCY

Scale Characteristics

Scale 9 measures more severe personality disturbances that are characterized by marked ambivalence in the adolescent's perceptions of self, relationship to others, and the regulation of affect. The adolescent has identity diffusion, intense mood fluctuations, and chaotic interpersonal relationships. The borderline personality in *DSM-IV* and the severe ambivalent personality outlined by Millon both served as constructs that guided development of the scale.

Scale 9 has 21 items and is unique in that other than the Modifier Indices, Scale 9 is the only MACI scale that does not have any prototypic items; all the items from this scale were taken from other MACI scales. There is significant item overlap with Scales 8B (12 items), 8A (9 items), 2B (8 items), 1 (6 items), 6A (5 items), and 6B (5 items). The highest correlations exist between Scale 9 and Scales 8A (0.67), 8B (0.67), and 2B (0.67); there is also a strong negative correlation between Scales 9 and 7 (−0.71). The reliability of Scale 9 is excellent with a high alpha coefficient of 0.86 found in the development sample and a test-retest reliability coefficient of 0.92 reported in the manual. Correlations between Scale 9 BR scores and clinicians' ratings of borderline personality traits are not reported in the manual. Criterion validity is supported as indicated by high correlations between Scale 9 and the Social Skills (0.63) subscale of the POSIT and the Body Dissatisfaction (0.67), Ineffectiveness (0.60), Interoceptive Awareness (0.55), and Impulse Regulation (0.62) subscales of the EDI-2. Moderate elevations between Scale 9 and the Beck Depression Inventory (0.47), Beck Hopelessness Scale (0.50), and Beck Anxiety Inventory (0.33) support Scale 9 as a measure of emotional turmoil.

In a factor analytic study of the content dimensions of Scale 9, Davis (1994) identified four content subscales that reflect major features of the borderline personality. The first content scale is *empty loneliness,* which represents feeling alone and empty. A second content subscale is *capricious reactivity,* which measures impulsivity that is characteristic of the behavior in borderline personality. *Uncertain self-image,* the third content dimension, reflects identity diffusion and uncertainty about one's self and direction in life. The fourth major content subscale is *suicidal impulsivity* representing thoughts of suicide and intense emotions that could precipitate a suicide attempt. These four dimensions are consistent with the guiding theoretical construct of borderline personality and support the validity of the scale.

Significant Elevations

Adolescents who score high on Scale 9 will typically have elevations on several other Personality Patterns scales, such as Scales 2B, 8A, and 8B, due to the sharing of items. Nevertheless, high scores represent adolescents who experience significant emotional turmoil and instability. Their emotions tend to fluctuate from periods of anxiety, to anger, depression, happiness, or irritability. Others are likely to characterize the adolescent as moody. Moreover, the teenager tends to be impulsive and to have poor behavioral controls. Their emotions can easily precipitate acting-out in the form of temper tantrums, suicidal gestures, hostile lashing out, sexual promiscuity, or self-punishing behaviors.

In addition to emotional turmoil, there tends to be a considerable amount of instability in other areas of the teenager's life. Interpersonal relationships are often intense and chaotic, as the adolescent has changing feelings and attitudes toward important people in their life that go from idealization to devaluation and rejection. As such, others who are close to the adolescent may often feel confused, bewildered, and frustrated over the teenager's rapidly changing attitudes. Additionally, high Scale 9 scores reflect uncertainty that these adolescents have in terms of long-term career goals, personal interests, and their preferences for various things. They are uncertain about who they are and what they want out of life. Because they have intense needs for attention and support, but are never fully satisfied, the teenager has constant fears of abandonment and rejection. Extreme measures and manipulative behaviors are often used to avoid threats of abandonment and to keep others close and involved in the adolescent's life.

In clinical settings, the elevations on Scale 9 generally represent a moderate to severe level of psychopathology. A range of clinical symptoms are possible, including depression, suicidal ideation, anxiety, and oppositional acting-out. Furthermore, clinical experiences with this scale have revealed that it is not always sensitive to the presence of borderline personality disturbances, meaning that where there is strong clinical and psychosocial data to support such a diagnosis, there may not always be a concurrent Scale 9 elevation. Given the nature of the items and the BR score conversions, it takes endorsement of several items to elevate the scale and there generally needs to be a high level of openness in the adolescent and several areas of disturbance to obtain a Scale 9 elevation. Therefore, it is useful to consider Scale 9 as a measure of overall severity of psychopathology, particularly in the area of affect regulation, identity diffusion, and instability in relationships.

SCALE CONFIGURATIONS

When considering the meaning of various MACI scale elevations that occur together or in a specific pattern, a difficulty exists in identifying an appropriate way to classify specific profile patterns. On other multiscale inventories such as the MMPI-A, for example, specific codetypes have usually been identified based on two- and three-point codetypes in which a profile is characterized based on the two or three highest scales that are within a certain number of T-score points of one another. Moreover, the MMPI interpretation literature is generally based on actuarial studies that have examined specific clinical characteristics associated with individuals who yield a particular codetype or pattern of scores. Given the very limited research base of the MACI, the configural approach to MACI interpretation must be guided by information and principles other than actuarial studies.

Because of the unique manner in which the MACI was developed, including the use of an established theoretical model, three-stage approach to test construction, and the use of BR score conversions, the interpretation of MACI Personality Patterns scale configurations is not dependent on actuarial data because the interpretive process can be guided by using theoretical principles and psychometric characteristics of the instrument. Therefore, the interpretive hypotheses outlined in this section are derived from an integration of psychometric properties, including scales that cluster together due to high correlations between them, and clinical observations based on use of the MACI in a variety of settings. In addition, interpretation will also be guided by the theoretical descriptions of various personality patterns and subtypes outlined by Millon and Davis (1994).

The following descriptions are meant to serve as hypotheses that require corroboration from other sources such as clinical interview data, the psychosocial history, and other psychological assessment instruments. Before outlining the interpretation of Personality Patterns scales, however, it is worth reviewing the general approach to interpreting MACI scales. When BR scores are elevated above 75, this denotes the presence of the features being measured by each scale, while BR scores elevated above a BR of 85 denote that the features are prominent. When two or more scales are considered in combination, their relative elevations (e.g., Scale 2A > Scale 1) are more important than the actual degree of difference (e.g., 5 BR points vs. 10 BR points) because the MACI BR scale represents an ordinal scale of measurement, not an interval or ratio scale of measurement. However, the degree of elevation becomes important when a specific scale is in the nonelevated range (i.e., BR 60–74) as opposed to the "present" range (i.e., BR 75–84) or the "prominent" range (i.e., BR 85 and above). It is important to keep these factors in mind when evaluating the relative elevations of various scales within the clusters discussed in this section.

In addition, the MACI scale clusters can be identified in several ways, including along theoretical dimensions (e.g., detached personality types) or psychometric factors (e.g., scales that correlate highly with one another, or that share several items). Some Personality Patterns scale clusters are described based on a combination of these factors as well as general clinical observations on commonly occurring scale configurations.

1-2A-2B

A common pattern that can be observed in MACI profiles is a combination of Scales 1, 2A, and 2B. When any two or all three of these scales are elevated, it represents a lack of capacity for the adolescent to experience the rewards and positive experiences that occur in life. The adolescent appears detached and uninvolved with others and is socially withdrawn and isolated. Social withdrawal and isolation will be a dominant presentation, particularly if Scales 1 and 2A are the primary scales elevated. In addition, there tends to be the expectation that nothing positive will arise out of close relationships with other people, particularly if Scales 2A and 2B are the primary scale elevations. When Scales 1 and 2B are the major scale elevations, the adolescent is likely to be lethargic, apathetic, and lacking in motivation to pursue pleasurable or productive experiences.

A common observation is that a combination of any two or all three of these scales being elevated generally reflects that the adolescent is moderately or severely depressed. When Scale 1 is the prominent elevation, there is a marked degree of apathy, low energy, and lack of vitality; the teenager may have difficulty putting how he or she feels into words, and others may see him or her as difficult to motivate. When Scale 2A is the prominent elevation, there is a pronounced sensitivity and preoccupation with stress and misfortune and the adolescent is likely to be seen as fretful and as suffering an agitated form of depression. When Scale 2B is the major elevation, a marked sense of hopelessness and futility dominate and others are likely to see the adolescent as difficult to engage.

2B-8A-8B-9

This configuration represents chronic dysphoria and depression that is manifest in a number of negative attitudes and behaviors. The adolescent exhibits intense irritability and somatic complaints that are expressed in a grumbling and sour fashion, particularly when Scales 2B and 8A are the principal elevations. In addition, strong self-defeating attitudes and intense feelings of guilt are often excessive and are a defense against the expression of resentment and hostility. While Scale 8B is a prominent elevation, there is a greater level of defensive guilt that is designed to control the expression of anger. Given intense feelings of ambivalence, the expression of anger is avoided because the teenager fears rejection and abandonment by others.

When Scale 9 is also elevated, a more severe level of psychopathology is indicated and the depression tends to be more incapacitating and chronic. The adolescent is likely to have serious identity concerns and thoughts are apt to be vague and confused due to the high level of psychic turmoil experienced by the teenager. Moreover, the moods tend to be more intense and unstable, with depression, irritability, and angry resentment the dominant emotional themes expressed. Several diagnoses may be considered, including dysthymia, borderline personality disorder, major depression, and posttraumatic stress disorder.

3-7/7-3

The major characteristics of adolescents with this two-scale configuration are passive dependence, excessive compliance with rules, deference to authority, and the deferring of one's needs to the wishes of others. In social settings, the adolescent does not appear competitive or assertive. He or she also tends to have self-doubts and to feel inadequate compared with peers or parental expectations. Adolescents with this configuration do not like to take risks and tend to be ineffective problem-solvers because of uncertainty or fears of making a mistake. Therefore, they often look to others to influence or guide what they choose to do. Adolescents with a learning disability or other long-standing academic difficulties sometimes exhibit this pattern; it may also be found in severely impaired adolescents who have a major psychiatric diagnosis (e.g., schizophrenia) that has been present for some time. The scale pattern in these cases can be interpreted as the adolescent's adaptation to chronic disability or difficulty in that they have come to view themselves as dependent on external structure and supports to cope and function effectively.

4-5/5-4

The major feature of adolescents with this MACI scale configuration is narcissism and self-centered attitudes and behaviors. There is a strong need for excitement and stimulation and the teenager has difficulty delaying gratification. Instead, they often engage in impulsive risk-taking to experience the thrill of taking chances and beating the odds. Although antisocial acting-out is not a primary motive for these adolescents, they may occasionally come into conflict with the law for reasons that are related more to their need for attention and admiration. For example, they may engage in group criminal activity to receive affirmation from peers who are on the fringe of social norms. In other cases, they may engage in assaultive or aggressive behavior if provoked by an insult or slight. However, traditional antisocial motives (e.g., greed, sadistic anger) are generally not the driving force for these adolescents.

Overall, these teenagers tend to be superficially cheerful, lively, and spirited. However, they have difficulty forming close attachments. Instead, relationships are likely to be superficial or fleeting and based more on what others can do for the adolescent, rather than on a more sensitive and sharing manner of interaction.

4-5-6A

These three scales represent a high degree of impulsive and manipulative acting-out when they are all elevated simultaneously. In addition to the personality features associated with each scale, including attention-seeking, self-centered feelings of entitlement, and manipulation of others, there also tends to be excessive risk-taking. Adolescents with elevations on all three scales rarely consider the consequences of their actions. In social interactions, they tend to be intimidating and demanding and will charm others only to achieve some self-centered goal.

4-5-7

When these three scales are elevated concurrently, a hypothesis that should be entertained is whether the adolescent is providing a socially desirable response set. These scales share items with Scale Y (Desirability), so examination of this scale is also indicated. Usually, Scale 7 is the controlling elevation in that it will be present with either or both of Scales 4 and/or 5. There is less likelihood of a socially desirable response set if Scale 7 is not elevated and Scales 4 and 5 are high. Likewise, there is less likelihood of a socially desirable response set and a greater likelihood that elevations reflect actual personality traits if the elevations are quite high (e.g., BR > 90). Chapter 4 provides a more detailed discussion about this pattern.

6A-6B-8A

This scale configuration is common among adolescents who present with conduct disorder or other forms of oppositional or antisocial acting-out. When any two or all three of these scales are elevated, it represents a hostile, abrasive, and rejecting pattern of behavior in an adolescent who is rejecting of social norms. In general, when all three scales are elevated, the adolescent uses acting-out as a major means of coping with tension. There is a predominant hostile and angry mood and close interpersonal relationships are lacking because the teenager has negative views of human nature and does not see the value of close relationships.

When Scales 6A and 6B are the primary elevations, with Scale 8A either not elevated or only moderately elevated, the adolescent tends to be much more ruthless and brutal in relationships. There is a strong tendency to seek revenge when the teenager feels wronged. Moreover, despite a capacity for rationally knowing what is right and wrong, there is a marked deficiency in the capacity to feel genuine guilt or remorse. These adolescents must constantly prove their toughness to others and will seek retribution to show their power and control.

When Scales 6B and 8A are the primary elevations and Scale 6A is either not elevated or only moderately high, the adolescent is characterized by abrasive and quarrelsome interpersonal behavior. The teenager will strive to prove independence by deliberately engaging in behavior that shows how independent and separate he or she is from parents. In some adolescents, this abrasive oppositionality may be time-limited and will lessen as the adolescent enters adulthood. For others, this pattern becomes more entrenched and part of an adult pattern of antisocial or abusive behavior that causes impairment in relationships and social adjustment.

When Scales 6A and 8A are the primary elevations, the adolescent's conduct problems are directed at actively lashing out in anger. There are deep-seated feelings of resentment over the failure of significant others to provide the privileges and rewards to which the adolescent feels entitled. The resentment results in acting-out, and the adolescent remains insensitive to the turmoil this behavior causes for others.

6B-7-8A-8B: ASSESSING DEFENSIVE PROCESSES

Each of these four scales represents one of the intrapsychically conflicted personalities outlined by Millon and Davis (1994). These four personality styles (the forceful, conforming, oppositional, and self-demeaning) correspond to adult personality disorders that are characterized in Millon's theoretical model as having marked conflict at various levels of personality functioning. For example, these personalities are ambivalent over satisfying personal self-centered needs versus acquiescing to the wishes of others; they also are conflicted over the nature of what is pleasurable and painful in various life experiences. As such, a significant level of emotional turmoil and conflict must be managed. Therefore, aside from the personality styles measured by Scales 6B, 7, 8A, and 8B, these four scales are useful for assessing the way in which the adolescent manages internal conflict. They can be used as a general gauge of defensive styles by the adolescent to cope with intrapsychic tension.

There are several ways to conceptualize defense mechanisms (Ihilevich & Gleser, 1986). According to Appendix B in *DSM-IV* (American Psychiatric Association, 1994), the Defensive Functioning Scale has been proposed as an additional Axis for further study. Defense mechanisms are defined as "automatic psychological processes that protect the individual against anxiety and from the awareness of internal or external dangers or stressors" (p. 751). Moreover, defense mechanisms help control and modulate the person's psychological reaction to emotional conflicts and stressors. The model proposed in *DSM-IV* lists 27 individual defense mechanisms and uses a level of adaptation model in which these mechanisms are grouped into seven levels according to the degree of adaptability of the defenses and the severity of distortion and dysregulation that occurs.

According to Ihilevich and Gleser (1986), defense mechanisms can be conceptualized as extensions of basic problem-solving and coping mechanisms. Problem-solving strategies are generally aimed at either changing one's self or through manipulation of the environment. Whereas problem-solving strategies are more immediate means for resolving problems, coping strategies imply there is a change in the individual through accommodation and the learning of new strategies for managing daily demands. Defense mechanisms accomplish the goal of protecting the individual through psychological processes, including the falsification of reality, illusory mastery of threat, reducing and regulating anxiety, and enhancing self-esteem. Many ways to conceptualize defense mechanisms include internalizing and externalizing defenses, which reflects the turning inward of psychic tension or the acting-out and projection of tension onto the environment, respectively. Ihilevich and Gleser define five basic defense styles: (1) turning against the object (e.g., acting-out); (2) projection; (3) principlization (e.g., intellectualization, rationalization); (4) turning against the self (e.g., self-punishment); and (5) reversal (e.g., denial, reaction-formation).

With respect to the MACI, Scales 6B, 7, 8A, and 8B are useful measures of defensive styles. In general, externalizing defenses, such as acting-out, displacement, and projection are represented in Scale 6B and 8A elevations. The internalizing defenses of self-devaluation and intrapunitive disappointment are represented in Scale 8B elevations. Defenses involving the minimization of perceived threat through denial, reaction formation, and intellectualization are represented in Scale 7 elevations.

This general view of defensive styles is helpful as a gauge to determine how the adolescent manages threat and tension. Although defense mechanisms are intrapsychic processes that are difficult to assess with self-report instruments, Scales 6B, 7, 8A, and 8B provide some information to infer how the adolescent is modulating and controlling psychological reactions to perceived threat and conflict.

SUMMARY

This chapter reviews the general characteristics and interpretation of the MACI Personality Patterns scales. The major purpose of these scales is to provide a measure of the adolescent's personality style and a context for understanding clinical concerns and syndromes. In this way, individual clinical problems and concerns are interpreted differently, depending on how the adolescent functions across situations and settings. In addition to the individual scales, various configurations of the Personality Patterns scales are analyzed, particularly those that appear to occur with the greatest frequency in clinical settings. Specific personality scales on the MACI are also presented as indices of defense styles, or the manner in which the adolescent protects him- or herself from anxiety and manages internal conflict.

CHAPTER 6

Expressed Concerns Scales

A SERIOUS challenge in developing a psychological assessment instrument for adolescents is to construct scales that assess the issues that most concern them. In the past, the primary method of assessing adolescent personality was with adult personality inventories after standardizing and norming the instrument on adolescents. A major drawback of this approach is that items and scales originally designed for adults often fail to assess concerns and attitudes that are unique to adolescents. Therefore, the MACI includes a set of eight scales that are collectively called the Expressed Concerns scales that are designed to measure attitudes and feelings that tend to be significant issues in adolescents.

It is very useful to conceptualize the Expressed Concerns scales literally as measures of what their collective name implies; they are concerns that the adolescent is expressing as troublesome areas in his or her life. Therefore, it is better to view the Expressed Concerns scales not in terms of specific objectively observable behaviors that are associated with scale elevations (although there will undoubtedly be some behavioral correlates with these scales). Rather, an elevation on one of the Expressed Concerns scales reflects the adolescent's *perception* of what he or she finds troublesome or worrisome. In the same way, the lack of an elevation on the Expressed Concerns scales, even in the face of collateral information that would suggest an elevation should be present, generally reflects the adolescent's perception that the issue is not problematic or is not something that he or she wants to discuss.

An example may help to clarify this approach to interpreting the Expressed Concerns scales. Suppose a teenager with a documented history of sexual abuse has been referred for a psychological evaluation because of poor peer relationships, anxiety, and preoccupation with sexual issues.

Furthermore, suppose the MACI profile reveals, among other things, an elevation on Scale E (Peer Insecurity), but no other elevations on the Expressed Concerns scales. The clinician might expect Scales H (Childhood Abuse), D (Sexual Discomfort), and perhaps C (Body Disapproval) to be elevated based on the history. The lack of elevation on any of these scales does not necessarily mean that there are no problems in those areas. Rather, the results in this case may mean that the adolescent does not want to deal with concerns over body image, sexual concerns, and the abuse. Instead, the adolescent is most distressed by peer rejection and the lack of support from friends. In this way, the Expressed Concerns scales are most useful as measures of what the adolescent sees as the problems he or she is experiencing. These concerns may or may not be consistent with external collateral information.

Interpretation of the Expressed Concerns scales generally follows the same principles outlined for the Personality Patterns scales. Concerns are viewed as falling along a continuum, with the BR scores reflecting the general level of concern. Again, only BR scores that equal or exceed 75 are considered clinically significant. Scores that equal or exceed a BR of 85 are considered more prominent and as scores elevate above this level, the higher BR values reflect more extreme levels of concern. With BR scores that fall between 60 and 74, the MACI Expressed Concerns scales may be viewed as potentially reflecting areas of moderate concern for the adolescent, if the MACI profile has a very low disclosure level or if scores approach the BR level of 75 (i.e., BR = 70–74). In such cases, collateral information or additional interviewing of the adolescent will be useful in clarifying the extent to which such subtle elevations are important.

In this chapter, the interpretation of elevations on the MACI Expressed Concerns scales is discussed. In the first section of the chapter, each scale is examined individually with respect to general psychometric properties and the interpretation of significant elevations (i.e., BR ≥ 75 or BR ≥ 85) on each scale. As before, the material for these discussions is drawn from the MACI manual (Millon et al., 1993), previously published material on MACI interpretation (McCann, 1997), and clinical experiences with using the MACI in a variety of settings.

The second portion of this chapter outlines major configurations and patterns of elevations typically found on these scales when using the MACI. These configurations can be classified based on common conceptual and theoretical constructs that are shared by the scales, as well as common concerns that occur among adolescents with a particular form of psychopathology or who experience a similar type of psychosocial stressor.

INDIVIDUAL SCALES

SCALE A: IDENTITY DIFFUSION

Basic Characteristics

The major purpose of Scale A is to assess concerns that adolescents may have about who they are, what they want out of life, and what may be required to achieve a set of ideals and goals. This scale is designed to evaluate the adolescent's progress from having dependent childhood attachments to achieving an independent and autonomous adult identity.

Scale A is made up of 32 items. It correlates highly in the positive direction with Scales 1 (0.64), 2B (0.54), 8A (0.64), 8B (0.54), 9 (0.73), B (0.62), and GG (0.61). There are high negative correlations between Scale A and Scales 4 (–0.57), 5 (–0.62), and 7 (–0.74). The internal consistency of Scale A is good, with an alpha coefficient of 0.79 in the development sample. Test-retest reliability is also good for Scale A, with a coefficient of 0.77. The concurrent validity of Scale A reveals high correlations with the Body Dissatisfaction (0.57), Ineffectiveness (0.60), Interoceptive Awareness (0.55), and Social Insecurity (0.58) subscales of the EDI-2. There are also significant correlations with the Beck Depression Inventory (0.60) and Beck Hopelessness Scale (0.63). There is a significant but modest correlation (0.17) between Scale A BR scores and clinicians' ratings of identity problems in adolescents from the cross-validation sample. Again, these lower correlations may reflect method variance due to what clinicians may expect on the basis of clinical history versus what the adolescent perceives to be the most troubling concerns. The lack of strict behavioral criteria, and reliance on the adolescent's perception, may render clinicians' judgments a poor criterion against which to measure the validity of the Expressed Concerns scales. Overall, the pattern of correlations with other MACI scales and collateral measures reflect general mental health and identity concerns represented in Scale A elevations.

Significant Elevations

Adolescents scoring high on Scale A will exhibit confusion and uncertainty about who they are and what they want out of life. When these teenagers look at life, they are concerned about the direction of their lives. Because of a lack of clarity about one's identity, future goals and aspirations are not clearly defined. When asked about what they want out of life, these adolescents do not have well-formulated plans for their future and seem directionless or lost. Moreover, these teenagers have difficulty describing career plans, educational goals, interests and hobbies, or values that may guide their decisions. When scores are extremely elevated, the adolescent may be difficult to engage in therapy because he or she lacks a consistent framework that might offer some perspective on what the person wants out of life or the person he or she would like to be.

Because identity formation is a major task in adolescence, Scale A tends to reflect chronic and long-standing concerns about the development of one's self. The presence of Scale A elevations tends to occur along with chronic depression, borderline personality disturbance, and very detached and socially withdrawn adolescents. Therefore, elevations are also common on Scales 1, 2B, 9, and GG.

Scale B: Self-Devaluation

Scale Characteristics

The main purpose of Scale B is to measure concerns the adolescent may have over low self-esteem, feelings of inadequacy, and self-criticism. During adolescence, there is greater pressure to compare one's self against ideals and standards that are goals for achievement and to compare one's self favorably or unfavorably with those ideals. As such, Scale B is a measure of negative self-appraisal that arises when adolescents see themselves as falling short of what they would like to be.

There are 38 items in Scale B, and the scale correlates highly with other MACI scales, including Scales 1 (0.63), 2A (0.65), 2B (0.75), 8A (0.57), 8B (0.79), 9 (0.64), A (0.62), C (0.68), H (0.53), AA (0.59), FF (0.87), and GG (0.73). There are high negative correlations between Scale B and Scales 4 (−0.72), 5 (−0.83), 7 (−0.55), and F (−0.52). The high correlations with other MACI scales show there is a strong negative self-appraisal associated with many scales on the MACI. Internal consistency for Scale B is the highest among all MACI scales and represents strong reliability with an alpha level of 0.91. The stability of Scale B is also quite good with a test-retest reliability coefficient of 0.85. The concurrent validity of Scale B reveals a significant, but modest correlation of 0.25 between Scale B BR scores and clinicians' ratings of self-devaluation tendencies in adolescents in the cross-validation sample. Criterion validity of Scale B is supported by high correlations with the Body Dissatisfaction (0.78), Ineffectiveness (0.81), Interoceptive Awareness (0.60), and Social Insecurity (0.59) subscales of the EDI-2 and with the Beck Depression Inventory (0.59) and Beck Hopelessness Scale (0.57). In general, Scale B is associated with negative self-appraisal, depressive affect, and ineffectiveness that is typically found in individuals with poor self-esteem.

Significant Elevations

High scorers on Scale B generally express feelings of dissatisfaction with their self-image. There tend to be general feelings of discontent and distress over personal inadequacy and low self-esteem. Often the adolescent is unhappy with his or her rate of progress in achieving goals and has a self-perception of incompetence or ineffectiveness that may or may not be realistic. Adolescents with Scale B elevations tend to speak openly about personal shortcomings and they find it hard to identify anything about themselves that is positive or worthy of admiration. In addition, teenagers with high scores often expect to fall short in attempts to achieve personal goals or aspirations and so they are reluctant to take on challenges or demanding tasks because they fear they will fail. Personal attributes the adolescent may express about him- or herself include being weak, inadequate, ineffective, unlikable, or unlovable.

Because low self-esteem is a common characteristic in certain personality styles and clinical syndromes, Scale B elevations are often found in depressed adolescents, abused or traumatized adolescents who feel scarred, and inhibited or passive teenagers. Therefore, Scale B elevations may also occur in a variety of profile configurations. The most common concurrent elevations tend to be Scales 2A, 2B, 3, 8B, E, AA, and FF.

SCALE C: BODY DISAPPROVAL

Scale Characteristics

Because adolescence is a time of great physical change brought on by puberty, Scale C is designed to measure discomfort and negative attitudes an adolescent may feel when examining his or her physical appearance. Therefore, this scale is designed to measure poor body image, dissatisfaction with physical appearance, and concerns over maturation.

Seventeen items make up Scale C, making it the shortest scale on the MACI except for the Modifying Indices. The scale correlates highly in the positive direction with Scales 8B (0.52), B (0.68), AA (0.90), FF (0.66), and GG (0.56). Scale C correlates highly in the negative direction with Scale 5 (−0.61). Despite being such a brief scale, relative to other MACI scales, Scale C has very good internal consistency reliability, with an alpha coefficient of 0.85 obtained in the development sample. Test-retest reliability is also good, with a stability coefficient of 0.89. Although Scale C BR scores were not correlated with clinicians' judgments of body dissatisfaction in the cross-validation sample, correlations with collateral measures are strongly supportive of criterion validity. Scale C correlates highly with the Drive for Thinness (0.68), Body Dissatisfaction (0.86), and Ineffectiveness (0.73) subscales of the EDI-2. Although assessment of concerns over body image may be problematic based on clinical observation, self-report measures show greater convergence in the expected direction. As such, Scale C appears to be a good measure of body dissatisfaction and concerns over physical appearance.

Significant Elevations

High scores on Scale C represent concerns with physical growth or maturation. Adolescents with elevations on this scale are generally unhappy with their physical appearance and are often discontented with their level of physical attractiveness and appeal to others. Although general concerns of this nature are common in adolescence, high scores on Scale C generally reflect strong concerns and worries that are causing the adolescent significant emotional turmoil. The teenager may focus on his or her worst physical features and may magnify their severity. In social situations, the adolescent may perceive him- or herself as deviant, unusual, an outcast, or inadequate based primarily on negative physical features.

Body concerns are a fairly specific symptom and tend to occur most frequently in adolescents with eating disorders, weight problems, or physical disfigurement. The most frequent concurrent elevations are on Scales AA and B. There are cases, however, where Scale C may be elevated that are characterized by more pervasive problems. Adolescents who have been physically or sexual abused, taunted by aggressive peers about their appearance, or who are confused about their identity may also have Scale C elevations.

SCALE D: SEXUAL DISCOMFORT

Scale Characteristics

The purpose of Scale D is to measure the adolescent's level of discomfort and tension over issues of sexuality and awareness of maturing sexual feelings. The scale measures immature attitudes (i.e., heightened dependency and submissiveness) and feelings of guilt or shame over sexual feelings.

Scale D has 37 items and correlates highly in the positive direction with Scales 3 (0.58), 7 (0.60), and EE (0.59) on the MACI. High negative correlations are noted between Scale D and Scales 6A (−0.64), 6B (−0.52), 8A (−0.54), BB (−0.64), and DD (−0.54). The internal consistency of Scale D is acceptable with an alpha coefficient of 0.73 in the development sample and stability of the scale is also acceptable with a test-retest reliability coefficient of 0.74. Concurrent validity data on the scale reveal a significant, but modest correlation of 0.21 between Scale D BR scores and clinicians' judgments of sexual concerns in adolescents from the cross-validation sample. Criterion validity reveals significant negative correlations between Scale D and the Family Relations (−0.44) subscale of the POSIT and the Impulse Regulation (−0.43) subscale of the EDI-2. In addition to sexual concerns, Scale D measures such factors as dependence on family, tight control of impulses, and passivity.

Significant Elevations

The major characteristic of adolescents who score high on this scale is excessive confusion or discomfort over sexual thoughts and feelings. There tend to be heightened levels of anxiety and tension over sexual impulses and the teenager often fears the expression of sexuality. In social situations and interpersonal relationships, the adolescent may be conflicted over required social roles such as asking for or accepting offers for a date or adopting a particular style of dress. In other situations, the adolescent may feel uncomfortable with discussing sexual issues that are raised in situations with peers. In addition, the adolescent tends to be anxious and worried about physical changes that occur with the onset of stronger sexual interests and the development of secondary sex characteristics. There may be constant turmoil over intrusive thoughts and feelings related to sexuality.

Given the nature of sexual concerns, as well as the composition of Scale D, elevations tend to be more common in adolescents who are inhibited, socially withdrawn, and overly rigid and conforming (i.e., Scale 2A, 3, 7, E, or H elevations). Sexual concerns may be common in adolescents who have been sexually abused or assaulted either in childhood or more recently in adolescence, although this is not necessarily true for every case of sexual abuse. These concerns may also be evident in adolescents with concerns over their sexual identity. Elevations on Scale D in adolescents with conduct disorder, problems with aggression, or negative attitudes (i.e., Scale 6A, 6B, and 8A elevations) are unusual. A secondary set of features associated with Scale D elevations pertain to immature attitudes and anxiety, because the scale is a moderate threshold scale (see Chapter 3) and elevations are possible without the endorsement of prototypic items with content involving sexual concerns. Therefore, the adolescent with Scale D elevations may express fears of having to assume a more adult role and with being autonomous and independent. There may be an overcontrol of impulses and a restricted range of emotions; however, these features are more subtle and usually underlie more overt concerns over sexuality or independence.

SCALE E: PEER INSECURITY

Scale Characteristics

Although low self-esteem is a concern in adolescence that implies negative self-appraisal relative to peers, Scale E is designed to assess concerns the adolescent has about being rejected by peers. Moreover, the scale is designed to measure the degree to which adolescents feel they do not fit in with a peer group and worry about their inability to find a secure and comfortable position in their peer group.

Scale E has 19 items, making it one of the shortest scales on the MACI. As expected, there are high correlations with other scales that reflect item overlap as well as common themes shared by several MACI scales; Scale E correlates highly with Scales 1, (0.61) and 2A (0.77) in the positive direction and with Scales 4 (−0.67) and CC (−0.54) in the negative direction. Although the scale is brief, the internal consistency of Scale E is acceptable, with an alpha coefficient of 0.75 in the MACI development sample. Test-retest reliability is the lowest among all MACI scales, with a stability coefficient of 0.57. This finding suggests that Scale E may be highly sensitive to situational changes in the extent to which the adolescent may feel accepted by peer groups. The criterion validity of Scale E reveals no significant correlations with collateral measures that assess sensitivity (e.g., social insecurity on the EDI-2). As such, Scale E appears to have adequate face and content validity. However, the lack of criterion validity may reflect the lack of an adequate criterion measure for establishing validity. When compared with clinicians' ratings of peer insecurity concerns, Scale E BR scores correlated significantly, but modestly (0.20) with clinicians' ratings. Given the low test-retest reliability and weak concurrent validity against collateral self-report measures, it may be that Scale E is measuring more transient and situational aspects of peer insecurity.

Significant Elevations

The major feature associated with adolescents who score high on Scale E is sadness and discouragement over being rejected by peers. These adolescents tend to be anxious and tense because they fear that others will ridicule or reject them. In general, there tends to be a desire to have close relationships and friendships, but the expectation of rejection often causes the adolescent to withdraw and to become isolated and estranged further from peers. There may also be a self-image of ineffectiveness and incompetence that revolves primarily around the adolescent's perception of his or her social skills.

Peer insecurity is frequently found in adolescents with very introverted and inhibited personality styles. Therefore, elevations on personality scales measuring detached styles (e.g., Scales 1, 2A, and 2B) is common. Because peer rejection is a strong factor in determining the adolescent's self-concept, there may also be elevations on Scale B, but this does not always have to occur. Also, adolescents with chronic depression and more severe personality disturbances may have Scale E elevations, particularly if there is a long history of poor social adjustment. However, the scale can also be sensitive to temporal changes in the extent to which the adolescent feels accepted by the peer group.

SCALE F: SOCIAL INSENSITIVITY

Scale Characteristics

The major purpose of Scale F is to measure the extent to which the adolescent is indifferent to the feelings and reactions of others. Hostility and anger are not major aspects of the lack of concern being measured. Rather, the scale is designed to assess the degree to which the adolescent does not care for and is unmoved by the need for give-and-take in reciprocal relationships.

There are 39 items on Scale F, and it correlates highly in the positive direction with Scales 5 (0.59), 6A (0.67), 6B (0.60), and CC (0.80). There are high negative correlations between Scale F and Scales 2A (−0.67), 3 (−0.52), B (−0.52), EE (−0.57), and FF (−0.57). The internal consistency of Scale F is very good, as the alpha coefficient in the development sample was 0.79. Test-retest reliability is also very good, with a stability coefficient of 0.83. Criterion validity of Scale F reveals that the correlation coefficient of 0.39 between Scale F BR scores and clinicians' judgments of social insensitivity was one of the highest among all MACI scales. There were also moderate correlations between Scale F and the Substance Use or Abuse (0.34) and Aggressive Behavior/Delinquency (0.32) subscales of the POSIT. Overall, the concurrent validity data and pattern of correlations with other MACI scales reveal that Scale F elevations are associated with acting-out behavior and inversely related to psychological tension and negative affect such as anxiety and depression.

Significant Elevations

Adolescents who score high on Scale F can be generally described as cool and indifferent to the feelings and welfare of others. They tend to take advantage of others to obtain some personal advantage or achieve personal goals. People view these teenagers as having very little regard for the rights or feelings of others. In some cases, the adolescent may appear cold and callous and in other cases he or she may appear manipulative and superficially cordial, but only to lull others into a false sense of security. Adolescents with Scale F elevations are generally not interested in developing warm and close relationships with others. Their ties to others are usually based on sharing similar antisocial or unempathic attitudes. However, even these relationships are not particularly strong and if personal needs can be satisfied by taking advantage of friends, the socially insensitive teenager will do so.

Given the nature of social insensitivity, Scale F elevations are often found with other scale elevations on the MACI, particularly on Scales 6A, 6B, 8A, and CC. In those adolescents whose social insensitivity is more influenced by a need for peer acceptance, Scale 4 may be the primary personality scale elevation. In some cases, Scale F can be a useful indicator of the adolescent's insight and the treatment prognosis for a particular teenager. Because it is an Expressed Concerns scale, Scale F may or may not be elevated in adolescents with a documented history of behavior that shows a clear pattern of indifference toward others and a lack of concern for the rights and feelings of people. When Scale F is not elevated and the history reveals a pattern of social insensitivity, this generally denotes a lack of insight on the part of the adolescent in which the social indifference is ego-syntonic; the adolescent does not see the need for change. When Scale F is elevated, then the adolescent is at least capable of admitting his or her insensitivity and the issue can be discussed in treatment; thus the prognosis may be relatively better, though the problem may still be difficult to change. Elevations on Scale F are common in teenagers with a diagnosis of oppositional defiant disorder or conduct disorder.

SCALE G: FAMILY DISCORD

Scale Characteristics

A common problem in adolescence is tension and conflict that arises between the teenager and his or her parents. Scale G is designed to assess the adolescent's perceptions of the extent to which parents are accepting of the teenager as well as the degree of conflict and tension in the home. Again, the scale measures what the adolescent perceives to be problematic rather than what is objectively so.

Although 28 items make up Scale G, it does not have extremely high correlations with other MACI scales. There are positive correlations between Scale G and Scales 6A (0.55) and 8A (0.52) and a negative correlation with Scale 3 (−0.56). The internal consistency of Scale G is acceptable with an alpha coefficient of 0.79 established in the development sample. Test-retest reliability is very good, with a stability coefficient of 0.89. The criterion validity of Scale G also reveals a significant, but modest correlation of 0.25 between BR scores and clinicians' judgments of family discord. Concurrent validity is also supported by a high correlation between Scale G and the Family Relations (0.55) subscale of the POSIT. This scale is one of the most frequent elevations on the MACI profile because adolescents in clinical settings often see their parents as unsupportive or their family situation as conflicted.

Significant Elevations

The major problem represented by high scores on Scale G is the adolescent's perception that family relationships are strained and lacking in support. Adolescents scoring high on this scale generally view their parents as rejecting and unsupportive, and the atmosphere at home is described as tense and full of conflict. Although conflict with parents is common among adolescents, elevations on this scale generally reflect that the adolescent feels cut off from parents with little emotional warmth or support.

Elevations on Scale G are common, but a high score alone says little about the family conflict. The personality and clinical scales need to be examined, along with the history and clinical data, to clarify the specific family problems. Some adolescents are highly sensitive to parental rejection, in which case Scales 2A, 8B, and/or B may be elevated. For other teenagers, a high Scale G score may be associated with oppositional, rebellious, and acting-out behaviors, causing Scales 6A, 6B, 8A, F, and/or CC to be elevated. Where the adolescent was abandoned and rejected by parents or subjected to early physical abuse and neglect, Scale G may be elevated along with Scale H. There are also instances in which the adolescent may have experienced early disruption in the family and was raised in residential or institutional settings. Some adolescents may come to view the institution or the "system" as their parent; thus no elevation is found on Scale G because of the adolescent's shift from viewing biological parents as family to viewing the system as family.

Scale H: Childhood Abuse

Scale Characteristics

The major purpose of Scale H is to provide a measure of the degree to which the adolescent has been subjected to some type of abuse, including physical, sexual, or emotional abuse. It is important to reiterate that the scale measures the adolescent's perception and recollection of the events, not necessarily the objective reality of those experiences. Moreover, the item content is generally designed to measure abuse in general, although one or two items are focused specifically on sexual abuse.

Scale H has 24 items, and there is a moderate level of intercorrelation with other MACI scales assessing themes of depression and self-loathing. High positive correlations are noted between Scale H and Scales 2B (0.50), 8B, (0.50), B (0.53), and GG (0.70). The reliability of Scale H is good, as internal consistency was established with an alpha coefficient of 0.83. Stability is also good, with a test-retest reliability coefficient of 0.81. In one of the cross-validation samples, a correlation of 0.43 was obtained between Scale G BR scores and clinicians' judgments of childhood abuse, which is one of the highest among all MACI scales using this external criterion. No other appropriate collateral measure was used during MACI development to establish concurrent validity, though some support was obtained with a positive correlation between Scale H and the Ineffectiveness (0.53) sub-scale of the EDI-2. In clinical settings, Scale H has been shown to be elevated even where the abuse is remote in time and not a recent stressor, suggesting that the scale is a measure of the adolescent's current thought content and perceptions of abuse, regardless of when the abuse occurred.

Significant Elevations

Adolescents who score high on Scale H generally report feelings of shame, embarrassment, or disgust over having been subjected to abuse. The nature of the abuse may be physical, sexual, or psychological; and the abuse may have been inflicted by parents, relatives, friends, or siblings. In addition, high scores generally reflect anxious rumination and self-deprecating thoughts and attitudes that are associated with the abuse.

Because Scale H does not correlate very strongly with any one MACI scale, several concurrent profile patterns are possible and the abuse must be interpreted within the context of the adolescent's personality, psychosocial history, and presenting symptoms. In general, Scale H is fairly robust in that it is sensitive to both long-standing issues related to abuse as well as more acute reactions in response to recent trauma or abuse. It is also important to recognize that the absence of an elevation on Scale H in the face of documentation of abuse can point to several alternative hypotheses. The adolescent may be denying and minimizing the abuse to avoid dealing with it. The adolescent may have resolved issues surrounding the abuse, particularly where the abuse is remote in time. Another possibility is that the adolescent is particularly resilient and has adequate psychological resources to cope with the abuse and is relatively unaffected, particularly where the abuse is recent.

SCALE CONFIGURATIONS

Analyzing combinations of MACI scale elevations requires a somewhat different approach than the use of actuarial studies as has been done with the other multiscale inventories such as the MMPI-A. As discussed in Chapter 5, the unique manner in which the MACI was developed permits clinicians to combine theory, psychometric properties, and rational analysis of item content to derive interpretive hypotheses for various scale combinations.

Interpretation of combinations involving the Expressed Concerns scales follows the same general approach outlined for the Personality Patterns scales. Elevations equal to or above a BR score of 75 generally represent the presence of the concerns being measured by each scale and BR scores that are equal to or above a BR score of 85 generally represent the concerns being prominent. Moreover, when considering two or more scales in combination, the relative elevation of each scale (e.g., Scale B > A) is of greater importance than the actual degree of difference between them (e.g., 5 BR points vs. 10 BR points) because of the ordinal BR score scaling. Again, however, the degree of relative elevation becomes important if scales fall into different ranges, such as the clinically nonsignificant range (i.e., BR < 75) versus the "present" range (i.e., BR 75–84) or "prominent" range (i.e., BR ≥ 85).

A survey of the issues assessed with the Expressed Concerns scales reveals that major themes are represented in various groups of scales. If one moves from Scale A (Identity Diffusion) across the eight scales to Scale H (Childhood Abuse), there is an apparent progression from themes involving the self to themes involving psychosocial issues. The major themes have been broken down into specific issues involving the self, others, and environmental stressors as outlined in Table 6.1. The assignment of any one scale to a particular theme is an approximation and some degree of overlap exists nevertheless.

Adolescence is a period of development involving psychological, biological, and social pressures that impact the individual. A major developmental task is the formation of a clear sense of self, an understanding of who one really is, and a degree of comfort and satisfaction with the self. Toward this end, Scales A and B have been identified as assessing *self-development*.

Another major demand of adolescence involves biological and physical changes brought on by puberty and general physical growth and maturation. Successful coping with these changes results in the adolescent having a positive view of him- or herself. Scales C and D can be conceptualized as measures of the adolescent's *self-perception*, particularly with respect to physical and biological change.

Adolescence is also a period of transition between dependence on parents and the formation of independent attachments to peers and intimate partners. Thus, social concerns and peer relationships are a critical issue to consider when assessing adolescents. Therefore, Scales E and F have the general theme of *interpersonal relationships* as the major unifying issue.

A final consideration is the impact of one's psychosocial environment as a source of either support or stress. Although adolescence is filled with

Table 6.1
Themes Associated with the Expressed Concerns Scales

Theme	Representative Scales	
Self-development	A (Identity Diffusion)	B (Self-Devaluation)
Self-perception	C (Body Disapproval)	D (Sexual Discomfort)
Interpersonal relationships	E (Peer Insecurity)	F (Social Insensitivity)
Psychosocial stressors	G (Family Discord)	H (Childhood Abuse)

stressors, family relationships and exposure to abuse are two of the more critical clinical issues. Thus, Scales G and H are conceptualized as Expressed Concerns scales that pertain to the common theme of *psychosocial stressors*.

Although these groupings of the Expressed Concerns scales help outline the major issues that are being measured and may thus facilitate interpretation, there is considerable overlap across the themes and a single scale may also involve other dimensions. Scale B (Self-Devaluation), while a measure of self-development, also involves considerable self-appraisal and could also reflect aspects of the adolescent's perception of the self. Likewise, Scale E (Peer Insecurity) reflects interpersonal concerns, but also implicates aspects of self-perception since feelings of insecurity are based in part on feelings of personal inadequacy. The four themes used in Table 6.1 to conceptualize the various Expressed Concerns scales are not independent of one another and each of the representative scales may also reflect more than one problem theme. Nevertheless, these dimensions and scale assignments are intended to serve as a conceptualizing framework for facilitating the analysis of the following scale configurations.

SCALES A AND B: SELF-DEVELOPMENT

A comparison of Scales A and B is particularly useful for examining the adolescent's success in developing a sense of identity and his or her self-appraisal. These two issues, identity and adequacy, have been discussed at length by many developmental psychologists. The best known theory on identity in adolescence is Erikson's (1968) discussion of adolescence as a period of self-development in which individuals must develop a secure sense of who they are and what they want for the future. In addition, teenagers experience inner struggles to arrive at an acceptance of values and ideals while attaining an identity. Development of the self in adolescence involves both the seeking of a coherent identity and the attainment of satisfaction about that identity.

These two issues—identity formation and self-appraisal—are key elements that can be measured with the MACI by analyzing combinations of Scales A and B. The following configurations are based on a general rule that high scores are those in a clinically significant range (i.e., BR ≥ 75) and low scores are not in the significant range (i.e., BR < 75).

High A-High B

This configuration represents feelings of being lost, directionless, and uncertain about one's future that cause the adolescent to feel inadequate and incompetent. Not only does the adolescent have a vague notion about future goals and aspirations, but these issues appear to be causing the adolescent distress that leads to poor self-esteem. The implication is that the identity diffusion may be a source of worry and concern for which the adolescent has some motivation to change. However, another concern would be that the adolescent feels unworthy of help and feels resigned to a life in which no clear goals or achievements are worthwhile.

High A-Low B

In this configuration, the adolescent lacks a clear sense of who he or she is and is uncertain about what life has in store; however, no negative self-appraisal appears to be associated with this identity diffusion. Such a pattern is common in adolescents who have chronic feelings of emptiness and a lack of direction in life, yet they do not appear to be particularly concerned. The lack of self-devaluation suggests that the adolescent is resigned or indifferent to the elusiveness of future life goals. There may also be a passive acceptance that a weak and diffuse identity is a fate that may not change.

Low A-High B

This configuration represents that the adolescent has attained some sense of who he or she is and has a general clarity about aspirations and goals. However, the teenager is experiencing high levels of dissatisfaction with his- or herself. Therefore, the general picture that emerges is an adolescent with a clear sense of who he or she is, but who is unhappy with who he or she has become. The level of discomfort generated by the self-loathing may create some motivation to change in treatment.

Low A-Low B

This configuration reveals no difficulties in the area of self-development. The adolescent has a clear sense of who he or she is and there is satisfaction with the self. This pattern may reflect satisfactory adjustment in this particular area or it may reflect denial and minimization or an ego-syntonic personality disturbance that causes no distress. A careful analysis of the clinical data and case history is therefore necessary to establish the significance of this null finding.

SCALES C AND D: SELF-PERCEPTION

This configuration is occasionally encountered particularly with adolescents who have strong feelings of self-consciousness about their physical appearance that interferes with psychosexual adjustment. It is not clear how frequently this configuration occurs; however, it reflects significant sexual concerns associated with distortion in body image. Diagnostically, this pattern may be found in sexual abuse victims who feel scarred as a result of their victimization; however, it should not be considered a diagnostic sign that abuse has actually occurred. This configuration may also occur in eating disorder populations where adolescents feel unattractive or unwanted by members of the opposite sex because of serious distortions of body image.

Although these scales are sometimes elevated together, a more common pattern emerges with Scales C and B, reflecting strong feelings of inadequacy and low self-esteem connected to body image, such as in overweight adolescents who are teased by peers (in which case Scale E may also be elevated). Scale D suggests higher levels of passivity and concerns over maturity that may or may not be associated with body image disturbances.

SCALES E AND F: INTERPERSONAL RELATIONSHIPS

It is extremely rare that these two scales would be elevated simultaneously in the MACI profile, as they are negatively correlated (−0.47). However, an examination of the configuration of these two scales provides some indication of the adolescent's sensitivity to others. Hypersensitivity to criticism and self-consciousness that interferes with feeling accepted by peers would be reflected in Scale E elevations. A lack of sensitivity and unempathic attitudes that interfere with social adjustment would be reflected in Scale F elevations.

With respect to other Expressed Concerns scales, Scale E is often associated with elevations on Scales B, and to a lesser extent Scales C and D. These scales suggest that peer rejection is associated with feelings of inadequacy, perceived physical deformity (real or imagined), and discomfort in dealing with sexual issues. Scale F tends to be elevated either in isolation or in connection with Scale G, in which case the adolescent projects blame onto family members and feels justified in taking advantage of others.

SCALES G AND H: PSYCHOLOGICAL STRESSORS

These scales are elevated together in cases where the adolescent has been subjected to parental rejection, abandonment, and abuse. The abuse may be physical, emotional, or sexual. Generally, when these scales are elevated together, there is considerable disruption in the adolescent's psychosocial environment and the teenager feels a lack of support from others. In some cases, active intervention such as hospitalization, residential placement, or some temporary supports may be required to stabilize the adolescent's support network.

SUMMARY

This chapter reviews the general characteristics and interpretation of the Expressed Concerns scales on the MACI profile. These eight scales represent a useful set of measures for assessing problems and concerns perceived by the teenager. Therefore, individual scales may or may not be elevated based on that perception, rather than objective facts or circumstances as revealed in the history or by collateral sources. In addition to the individuals scales, configurations are analyzed on the Expressed Concerns scales based on general problem themes that are assessed by each scale. Even though individual scales undoubtedly tap many themes related to the self, interpersonal relationships, and psychosocial stressors, a general framework is provided for conceptualizing these scales to facilitate interpretation. Further research is needed to examine the occurrence of various scale configurations in actual clinical settings. The framework outlined in this chapter is offered as an interpretive guide while clinicians await the arrival of future research.

CHAPTER 7

Clinical Syndromes Scales

A MAJOR goal of assessment in clinical settings is to identify fairly well-defined clusters of symptoms reflecting diagnostic syndromes that have become the focus of treatment. Adolescents rarely come into mental health treatment voluntarily, and even in situations where parents, school personnel, or some other third party initiates the referral, the presenting complaint usually focuses on a distinct problem such as anxiety, depression, suicidal ideation, or some other symptom. It is unusual that treatment would be sought out due to a "personality problem" or other problem that requires a deeper level of insight.

The Clinical Syndromes scales of the MACI are seven measures designed to evaluate problems that are fairly specific and constitute, in many cases, the reason for initiating treatment. The specific clinical problems assessed with these scales are eating disorders, substance abuse, delinquency and conduct disturbances, impulsivity, anxiety, depression, and suicidal risk. These problems were selected because of their relative importance and frequency of occurrence across clinical settings. Some of the more severe forms of psychopathology such as thought disorder, paranoid ideation, bipolar mood disturbances, and other psychotic symptoms are not assessed directly on the MACI. Adolescents with extreme forms of psychopathology will need to have these issues evaluated with other assessment techniques. However, the MACI will still provide insight into these adolescents' perception of their difficulties and will add some useful information about the personality style associated with more severe forms of psychopathology.

The MACI Clinical Syndromes scales were designed to reflect behavioral and emotional extensions of the adolescent's basic personality, but they also measure transient and changeable states and behavior that become more or less prominent depending on the circumstances. More about this issue will be raised in the next chapter on MACI profile integration. For purposes of the present discussion, it is important to recognize that the Clinical Syndromes scales are designed to measure difficulties that may fluctuate over time.

The interpretation of these seven scales follows the same general principles outlined for the Personality Patterns and Expressed Concerns scales. The clinical syndromes are viewed as falling along a continuum, with lower BR scores reflecting less psychopathology and higher scores reflecting greater intensity and severity of the symptoms. Only BR scores that equal or exceed 75 are considered clinically significant and reflect the presence of the clinical syndrome. Scores that equal or exceed a BR of 85 are considered to represent prominent clinical syndromes. When BR scores fall between 60 and 74 (inclusive), the Clinical Syndromes scales may be viewed as potentially reflecting an area of moderate concern if the MACI profile has a very low disclosure level or if the BR score on any one scale approaches the clinically significant level (i.e., BR = 70–74). Collateral information and additional assessment data are needed to clarify whether such subtle elevations are meaningful or important.

In the remainder of this chapter, the interpretation of the MACI Clinical Syndromes scales is outlined. As in previous chapters, the scales are first examined individually in terms of general psychometric properties and the clinical meaning of significant elevations (i.e., BR ≥ 75 or BR ≥ 85). The second part of this chapter outlines major configurations and patterns on the Expressed Concerns scales that are commonly found in clinical practice. Material for the discussion of individual and configural scale elevations is drawn from the MACI manual (Millon et al., 1993), previously published material on MACI interpretation (McCann, 1997), as well as clinical experiences and the theoretical literature (Millon & Davis, 1994).

INDIVIDUAL SCALES

SCALE AA: EATING DYSFUNCTIONS

Scale Characteristics

The major purpose of Scale AA is to assess the likelihood that the adolescent is suffering from an eating disorder. Symptoms of anorexia and bulimia are both represented in the items for this scale; the psychopathology associated with these disorders is also assessed, including body image disturbances, low self-esteem, and mood disturbances such as depression.

Twenty (20) items are included on Scale AA, and there are high positive correlations with Scales 8B (0.50), B (0.59), C (0.90), FF (0.60), and GG (0.53). There is a high negative correlation between Scales AA and 5 (–0.51). Internal consistency of Scale AA is excellent, with an alpha coefficient of 0.86 established in the MACI development sample. The stability of the scale is also acceptable, with a test-retest reliability coefficient of 0.78 established in a subsample of the MACI development and cross-validation samples. Criterion validity, using clinicians' judgments of eating disorders as the external criterion, was not examined for Scale AA because of the very low base rate of eating disorders in the MACI cross-validation sample. In the development sample, no relationship was found between Scale AA BR scores and clinicians' ratings of eating disorders. Using the Eating Disorders Inventory-2 (EDI-2) as an external criterion yielded very good support for the validity of Scale AA. There were high correlations between Scale AA BR scores and the Drive for Thinness (0.75), Bulimia (0.44), Body Dissatisfaction (0.88), Ineffectiveness (0.75), Interoceptive Awareness (0.65), and Impulse Regulation (0.57) subscales of the EDI-2. There was no relationship between Scale AA and measures of perfectionism or maturity fears. In general, the data support the reliability and validity of Scale AA as a measure of eating disturbances and body image concerns.

Significant Elevations

A high score on Scale AA is indicative of eating disturbances associated with anorexia and bulimia. There are also likely to be severe disturbances in body image as well as strong fears of gaining weight or getting fat. In some cases where adolescents do not necessarily have anorexic or bulimic tendencies, the scale may still be elevated if the adolescent overeats or is overweight and has strong concerns over body image. In these cases, Scale C is also likely to be elevated. Several behaviors may be encountered that reflect eating disturbances, such as laxative abuse, self-induced vomiting, or compulsive exercising.

Where there is no clear evidence of an eating disorder, a scale elevation usually reflects low self-esteem, dysphoria, and concerns over body image. These cases are rare, however, because the endorsement of prototypic items is necessary to elevate this scale. The most likely concurrent elevation on the Clinical Syndrome scales is on Scale FF, which reflects strong dysphoric mood and symptoms of clinical depression that are frequently observed in eating disorder populations. Mild elevations may occur on Scale AA if profile adjustments or corrections contribute to the BR score or if the adolescent's overeating is connected more to a general impulsive and reckless behavioral lifestyle that includes overeating as a means of self-stimulation.

Scale BB: Substance Abuse Proneness

Scale Characteristics

The major purpose of Scale BB is to provide a measure of substance abuse problems in adolescence. Item content reflects potential problems with alcohol abuse, drug abuse, or both. Whereas actual substance abuse is a major focus, the presence of secondary and tertiary items not specifically addressing substance abuse also make the scale a measure of personality and behavioral predispositions that create a heightened risk for substance abuse.

Scale BB has 35 items. High positive correlations have been observed between Scale BB and Scales 6A (0.72), 6B (0.61), 8A (0.57), 9 (0.54), AA (0.51), CC (0.59), and DD (0.65). There are high negative correlations between Scale BB and Scales 3 (−0.64), 7 (−0.67), D (−0.63), and EE (−0.71). The internal consistency of Scale BB is respectable with an alpha coefficient of 0.89 established in the MACI development sample. In addition, the stability of the scale is very high with a test-retest reliability coefficient of 0.90 found in a subsample of the MACI normative sample. Concurrent validity of Scale BB is also strong, with a correlation of 0.52 between BR scores and clinicians' judgments of substance abuse proneness among all MACI scales. In addition, there are high correlations between Scale BB and the Substance Use or Abuse (0.64) subscale of the POSIT. Overall, there is adequate support for the reliability and validity of Scale BB as a measure of substance abuse problems.

Significant Elevations

Adolescents who score high on Scale BB typically show a pattern of alcohol and/or drug abuse that has caused problems in their adjustment in one or more settings. There may be academic problems such a truancy or poor achievement related to substance abuse. Additionally, there may be family disputes and conflict over the adolescent's use of illicit substances. These teenagers typically spend large amounts of time seeking out situations where they can drink alcohol or use drugs and tend to spend most of their time with friends who are also substance abusers. The use of alcohol or drugs continues because the teenager has minimal awareness of the negative affects of such substances on his or her health and well-being, or does not care much about potential consequences.

The level of insight an adolescent has, including the extent to which he or she denies or minimizes substance abuse, undoubtedly has an impact on this scale. Therefore, the scale may not always be elevated if the history reveals a substance abuse problem because Scale BB has a high threshold in that face valid substance abuse items (i.e., prototypic items) must be endorsed to yield an elevation. Similarly, Scale BB may be elevated in a very few cases where the history reveals no evidence of substance abuse, but this tends to be unusual. Such false positive elevations occur when profile adjustments or corrections add to the final BR score to yield a clinically significant elevation when no prototypic items are endorsed.

Clinical experiences with the MACI generally reveal that Scale BB is sensitive to the attitudes and behaviors that may predispose the teenager to substance abuse problems. Elevations sometimes occur in adolescents who were raised in a family environment where one or both parents abused substances. Where the adolescent does not actively abuse substances, the Scale BB elevation can be interpreted as reflecting attitudes such as sensation-seeking, impulsivity, and defiant attitudes that create a heightened risk that may require monitoring of the adolescent's substance use over time. In Chapter 10, more is said about making sense of inconsistencies that may arise between the clinical history (i.e., positive vs. negative substance abuse) and Scale BB elevations (i.e., clinically vs. nonclinically elevated).

SCALE CC: DELINQUENCY PREDISPOSITION

Scale Characteristics

The purpose of Scale CC is to measure the extent to which the adolescent is unable or unwilling to adhere to societal norms and rules. Delinquency in this context is conceptualized as a group of behaviors, attitudes, and emotions that lead the adolescent to act out in a hostile manner or through the commission of antisocial acts.

Scale CC comprises 34 items and correlates highly in the positive direction with Scales 6A (0.81), 6B (0.60), F (0.80), BB (0.59), and DD (0.58). There are high negative correlations between Scale CC and Scales 2A (−0.62), 3 (−0.61), E (−0.54), EE (−0.73), and FF (−0.52). Internal consistency of Scale CC is acceptable, with an alpha coefficient of 0.77 found in the MACI developmental sample. The stability of the scale is also good, with a test-retest reliability coefficient of 0.80 obtained in a subsample of the MACI normative group. When compared against the external criterion of clinicians' judgments, Scale CC BR scores yielded a significant correlation (0.34) against the criterion. Concurrent validity study of Scale CC revealed significant correlations with the Substance Use or Abuse (0.44) and Aggressive Behavior/Delinquency (0.37) scales of the POSIT and a negative correlation with the Maturity Fears (−0.52) scale of the EDI-2. In a sample of 173 juvenile delinquents, Timmons-Mitchell et al. (1997) found that the mean elevation on Scale CC was above a BR of 75 for both males and females, lending further support for the validity of this scale as a measure of delinquency problems.

Significant Elevations

Adolescents who score high on Scale CC generally display problematic behaviors that have resulted in violations of the rights of others in some way. Characteristics of conduct disorder are likely to be present, including the rejection of societal norms, rule breaking, and defiant acting-out. Other likely characteristics include threatening others, lying, stealing, and a lack of empathy for others. In relationships, these adolescents tend to be hostile and threatening, particularly when self-centered needs are frustrated. When in trouble, these adolescents will usually lie to avoid punishment but they will not learn from their past difficulties.

The most common diagnosis associated with elevations on this scale is conduct disorder. However, there are other possible considerations, including substance abuse, attention deficit/hyperactivity disorder, and severe oppositional defiant disorder. However, these diagnoses are usually associated with conduct disturbances. Given item overlap and high correlations with other scales, the most common concurrent MACI elevations are found on Scales 6A and F.

SCALE DD: IMPULSIVE PROPENSITY

Scale Characteristics

The major purpose of Scale DD is to measure the extent to which the adolescent is impulsive and acts before considering consequences. There is also a view of impulsive behavior lying along a continuum of acceptable and nonacceptable behavior in society.

Twenty-four (24) items make up Scale DD. This scale correlates highly in the positive direction with Scales 6A (0.77), 6B (0.75), 8A (0.60), 9 (0.63), G (0.59), BB (0.65), and CC (0.58). High negative correlations occur between Scale DD and Scales 3 (−0.67), 7 (−0.70), D (−0.54), and EE (−0.69). Internal consistency of Scale DD is respectable, with an alpha coefficient of 0.79 established in the MACI development sample. Stability of Scale DD is also good, with a test-retest reliability coefficient of 0.78 found in a subsample of the MACI normative sample. The criterion validity of Scale DD reveals a significant but modest correlation of 0.25 between Scale DD BR scores and clinicians' judgments of impulsivity. Additional support for the validity of Scale DD was found in a positive correlation between Scale DD and the Social Skills (0.54) and Aggressive Behavior/Delinquency (0.34) subscales of the POSIT and the Impulse Regulation (0.38) subscale of the EDI-2. In addition, Timmons-Mitchell and her colleagues (1997) found that the average BR score on Scale DD exceeded 75 in female delinquents. These findings support the reliability and validity of Scale DD as a measure of impulse control problems that interfere with adequate psychosocial adjustment.

Significant Elevations

The major characteristic of adolescents who score high on this scale is the tendency to act out without much provocation. They tend to have poor control over their behavior and have difficulty in areas such as sexual or aggressive acting-out. In general, there is little concern or thought about the adverse consequences of their actions. If problematic sexual or aggressive behavior is not evident in the clinical history, then other problems with impulsivity are likely to be identified such as excessive risk-taking, sudden temper tantrums, fighting, stealing, or other impulsive action. Another characteristic associated with elevations is that others tend to view the teenager as temperamental because sudden emotional outbursts trigger acting-out. The parents of these adolescents are likely to complain about the teenagers' lack of judgment.

Although this scale is associated with many different forms of impulsive behavior, clinical experiences have shown that it has a rather firm ceiling: it takes the endorsement of many items to elevate the scale. Scale DD has a high threshold in that the endorsement of face-valid items pertaining to impulsivity is required to obtain a clinical elevation. Therefore, if the adolescent is unwilling to admit to being impulsive or acting without thinking, the scale will not be elevated although the history might reveal evidence of impulsive acting-out.

SCALE EE: ANXIOUS FEELINGS

Scale Characteristics

The major purpose of Scale EE is to measure persistent anxiety and tension that impair the adolescent's sense of well-being and ability to relate socially and function adaptively. Symptoms of anxiety are generally cognitive forms of anxiety such as indecisiveness, rumination, social fears, and hypersensitivity.

There are 42 items on Scale EE. High positive correlations have been found between Scale EE and other MACI scales, including Scales 3 (0.74), 7 (0.55), and D (0.59). High negative correlations have been found with Scales 6A (–0.82), 6B (–0.66), F (–0.57), BB (–0.71), CC (–0.74), and DD (–0.69). Internal consistency of Scale EE is acceptable, with an alpha coefficient of 0.75 found in the MACI development sample, and test-retest reliability has been established with a stability coefficient of 0.85. Concurrent validity for Scale EE is supported with a significant correlation of 0.30 found between BR scores and clinicians' judgments of anxiety. Using collateral measures, additional support for the validity of Scale EE was obtained with a positive correlation between the Maturity Fears (0.49) subscale of the EDI-2. It is important to note that there was no relationship between Scale EE and the Beck Anxiety Inventory (0.10), suggesting that aspects of anxiety measured by each of these measures are not represented in the other. Overall, a review of Scale EE item content and the data on concurrent validity suggests that Scale EE measures cognitive worry as well as social fears and concerns.

Significant Elevations

The adolescent who scores high on Scale EE has strong fears and worries that something bad may happen. Feelings of tension and apprehension generally are due to the expectation that harmful or unpleasant events are about to take place. The adolescent is uneasy and has significant difficulty relaxing and enjoying life. Although physical symptoms of anxiety are not well represented in the item content, adolescents with high Scale EE scores are generally seen by others as tense, agitated, or prone to worry. Excessive rumination may interfere with concentration, and in social situations the adolescent has difficulty relaxing. Many aspects of daily life may be disrupted or restricted due to the adolescent's persistent fears and worries.

Elevations on Scale EE appear to be common, particularly for adolescents who are in situations where they are unclear as to the outcome. Examples include acute hospitalization, residential placement, and placement by the courts. However, elevations also can occur when the adolescent has strong anxiety, worries, or fears that are part of a more definite condition, such as an anxiety disorder, social phobia, personality disorder, or adjustment disorder with anxiety. In general, Scale EE is useful as a measure of either situational anxiety or pervasive feelings of worry and rumination.

SCALE FF: DEPRESSIVE AFFECT

Scale Characteristics

This scale is designed to measure feelings of sadness, discouragement, and dejection that are common in depressed adolescents. Other associated features such as low self-esteem, apathy, and hopelessness are also assessed. A major goal of this scale is to measure symptoms associated with a depressive disorder.

Scale FF has 33 items. High positive correlations have been found between this scale and others on the MACI, including Scales 1 (0.56), 2A (0.62), 2B (0.70), 8B (0.70), 9 (0.53), A (0.51), B (0.89), C (0.66), AA (0.60), and GG (0.71). Negative correlations have been found between Scale FF and

Scales 4 (–0.67), 5 (–0.75), F (–0.57), and CC (–0.52). The internal consistency of Scale FF is excellent, with an alpha coefficient of 0.89 found in the MACI development sample. Stability of the scale is also very good in that a test-retest reliability coefficient of 0.81 was found in a subsample of the MACI normative sample. Concurrent validity of Scale FF is also good when compared against collateral measures. High correlations were observed between Scale FF BR scores and the Body Dissatisfaction (0.68), Ineffectiveness (0.73), Interoceptive Awareness (0.52), and Social Insecurity (0.63) subscales of the EDI-2, as well as the Beck Depression Inventory (0.59) and the Beck Hopelessness Scale (0.59). A moderate correlation of 0.31 also was found between Scale FF BR scores and clinicians' ratings of depressive affect. Overall, there is support for the validity of Scale FF as a general measure of depressed affect.

Significant Elevations

Adolescents who score high on this scale are sad and report high levels of dysphoric mood. They are generally apathetic and lack vitality, and often report low energy and fatigue. Many symptoms of clinical depression are more likely to be present as scores become markedly elevated. Then, there are feelings of guilt, a loss of confidence, ineffectiveness in solving problems, and hopelessness about the future. In addition, high scores reflect social withdrawal, diminished interest in pleasurable activities, agitation, and worry. In social situations, the adolescent is apt to feel inadequate and less interesting than peers. Among family members, the adolescent may feel like a burden or unwanted.

The common diagnoses associated with Scale FF elevations are adjustment disorder with depressed mood at lower elevations and dysthymia or major depression at higher elevations. A survey of items on this scale can help the clinician identify the more salient features of depression such as low self-esteem, hopelessness, or general dysphoria.

SCALE GG: SUICIDAL TENDENCY

Scale Characteristics

This scale is a critical measure on the MACI because it measures a clinical problem with a potentially life-threatening impact. Scale GG is designed to measure thoughts about self-harm, suicide, or a wish to be dead that the adolescent may be experiencing. A clearer understanding of these problems can be derived by interpreting any elevation within the context of other scale elevations.

Twenty-five (25) items make up Scale GG. High positive correlations have been observed between this scale and Scales 2B (0.68), 8A (0.61), 8B

(0.63), 9 (0.61), A (0.61), B (0.73), C (0.56), H (0.70), AA (0.53), and FF (0.71). High negative correlations have been obtained between Scale GG and Scales 4 (−0.53), 5 (−0.66), and 7 (−0.61). The internal consistency of this scale is very good, with an alpha coefficient of 0.87 established in the MACI development sample. In addition, the stability of Scale GG was highest among all MACI scales over a 3- to 7-day period with a test-retest reliability coefficient of 0.91. Against the external criterion of clinicians' judgments of suicidal tendency there was a correlation of 0.24 with Scale GG BR scores. Concurrent validity has also been supported by high correlations between Scale GG and the Body Dissatisfaction (0.69), Ineffectiveness (0.77), Impulse Regulation (0.54), and Social Insecurity (0.74) subscales of the EDI-2, as well as the Beck Depression Inventory (0.67) and Beck Hopelessness Scale (0.65). Overall, there is support for the validity of Scale GG as a measure of hopelessness, poor problem-solving, and suicidal ideation.

Significant Elevations

Adolescents with high scores on this scale admit to having suicidal thoughts and, in some cases, definite plans. However, much of the item content reflects passive suicidal ideation such as the perception that others would be better off if the teenager was not around. Other associated features that are represented in high scores include hopelessness, a lack of purpose or direction in life, ineffective problem-solving and stress management, and feelings of guilt.

Although no research yet exists on the utility of this scale in predicting an actual suicide attempt, the higher the score the more active intervention that must be undertaken. When scores are markedly elevated (i.e., BR > 85), the clinician should more actively assess suicidal plans. Chapter 10 provides more specific recommendations for evaluating suicide risk and intervening when suicidal risk is deemed to be high.

SCALE CONFIGURATIONS

As noted, there is no large scale actuarial study on the MACI that would permit an analysis of common codetype and scale configurations. Therefore, when considering common scale patterns on the Clinical Syndrome scales, the most useful approach is to examine common themes that are assessed across different scales. For example, Scales AA and BB are similar in that they evaluate clinical symptoms associated with addictive or appetitive disturbances. Eating disorders and substance abuse problems both involve disturbed patterns of consumption, of food and illicit substances, respectively. Nevertheless, the correlation between Scales AA and BB is very small (0.15) and thus the likelihood of concurrent elevations on these two scales is likely to be small, as they appear to be measuring independent clinical phenomena.

A second and more useful approach to evaluating Clinical Syndromes scales elevations is to group these scales into two general categories. Three scales, BB, CC, and DD, appear to be measuring some form of behavioral or conduct disturbance that involves impulsivity, acting-out, and sensation-seeking as common characteristics. A second group of scales, EE, FF, and GG, measure some aspect of disturbance in mood or emotional experience such as anxiety, depression, and suicidal ideation. Support for this general grouping of the MACI Clinical Syndrome scales is found in Chapter 8, where common configurations are derived according to the intercorrelation of all scales on the instrument. Also, this grouping has face validity when one considers the general nature of what each scale is measuring. Therefore, two broad Clinical Syndromes scale patterns are discussed in this section: (1) Behavioral Problems represented by Scales BB, CC, and DD; and (2) Mood Disturbances represented by Scales EE, FF, and GG.

The same general approach used for interpreting configurations on the Personality Patterns and Expressed Concerns scales is recommended for the Clinical Syndromes scales. Scale elevations are considered to be clinically significant when they equal or exceed a BR of 75, and elevations are considered to be markedly elevated when they equal or exceed a BR of 85. In addition, the relative elevation of a particular scale in relation to other scales is more important than the actual difference between two scales (i.e., 5 BR points vs. 10 BR points). However, the exception to this general principle is when one scale falls in the present range (i.e., BR = 75–84) or prominent range (i.e., BR ≥ 85) compared with another scale.

SCALES BB-CC-DD: BEHAVIORAL PROBLEMS

The major clinical problems represented in this cluster of scales include impulsivity, acting-out as a defense, risk-taking behaviors, and a disregard for social norms or conventional forms of behavior. When Scales BB and CC are elevated concurrently, the adolescent is likely to exhibit severe problems with acting-out, antisocial conduct, and maladjustment in academic and interpersonal settings that are exacerbated by substance abuse. For some adolescents, the alcohol or drug use may be a major causal factor of conduct problems, whereas in other cases the substance abuse may be just one of several behaviors that are part of a general lack of respect for conventionality. In addition, alcohol or drugs may facilitate acting-out as a defense by reducing inhibitions or producing transient periods of heightened grandiosity, fearlessness, and entitlement (particularly if psychostimulants are used).

There is a stronger correlation between Scales BB and DD than there is between Scales BB and CC. Therefore, concurrent elevations on BB and DD are common and reflect a disinhibited, impulsive, and risk-taking attitude that does not necessarily result in antisocial or delinquent behavior. Other forms of addictive behavior such as gambling, daredevil acts, and recklessness may nevertheless cause problems in the adolescent's functioning in a variety of areas.

When Scales CC and DD are both elevated, there is strong evidence of antisocial acting-out that tends to be poorly planned. The adolescent does not think about the consequences of his or her actions and has much difficulty learning from his or her mistakes. Because the adolescent must be willing to admit to problems with impulsivity, these scales may not be elevated if the adolescent has poor insight or is unwilling to admit to problems of this nature.

When Scales BB, CC, and DD are all elevated, a strong core of impulsive, reckless, and delinquent acting-out is likely to be manifest in several areas of the adolescent's functioning. All three scales correlate highly in the negative direction with Scale EE. These adolescents tend to feel little anxiety or worry about their behavioral problems, which creates a strong obstacle for treatment since there is likely to be no psychological discomfort to motivate change. Any anxiety that is reported is likely to be situational and related to being placed in a setting where the adolescent does not want to be, such as detention, a hospital, or temporary placement.

SCALES EE-FF-GG: MOOD DISTURBANCES

The major features associated with this cluster of Clinical Syndromes scales are significant emotional turmoil, such as anxiety, depression, hopelessness, and suicidal ideation. When Scales EE and FF are elevated together, the adolescent is reporting emotional upheaval that involves agitation, rumination, and confusion. In many respects, the diagnostic picture tends to be an agitated depression in which the adolescent experiences overt turmoil. This pattern represents general psychological maladjustment that may be either situational due to extremely difficult circumstances or a more chronic and pervasive problem. When the emotional distress is pervasive, there are likely to be several elevations across the MACI profile, including several Personality Patterns and Expressed Concerns scales. Elevations on Scales EE and FF that are due to situational stressors tend to be associated with a specific and defined personality style or the absence of any other significant elevations in the MACI profile.

Concurrent elevations on Scales EE and GG appear to be unusual, given that these two scales are uncorrelated (−0.09). The more common configuration is concurrent elevations on Scales FF and GG. This pattern is associated with strong feelings of hopelessness and despair that result in suicidal ideation and rumination. The adolescent is likely to have strong feelings of guilt over personal transgressions that may be exaggerated or otherwise based on distortions of self-image. A heightened risk of suicidal acting-out is often present, requiring assessment of the content of the adolescent's thoughts, plans, and accessibility to methods for trying to end one's life.

SUMMARY

This chapter reviews the psychometric properties of the Clinical Syndromes scales on the MACI as well as the interpretive significance of high scores on each scale. The seven scales in this section of the MACI profile measure disturbances in behavior, emotional expression, and social adjustment that tend to take the form of a specific syndrome or disturbance which is often the initial focus of treatment. The chapter also includes an overview of major clusters of the Clinical Syndromes scales organized around two general themes: behavioral problems and mood disturbances. Although the MACI measures clinical syndromes that are prominent in adolescent populations—eating disorders, substance abuse, juvenile delinquency, impulsiveness, anxiety, depression, and suicidal propensity—other forms of serious mental disturbance are not represented, such as psychotic, bipolar, and paranoid disturbances. Therefore, the MACI Clinical Syndromes scales are useful for evaluating moderate levels of psychopathology. In Chapter 8, an interpretive strategy will be outlined along with ways of integrating all components of the MACI profile into a meaningful and useful description of the adolescent's functioning.

CHAPTER 8

Integrating the MACI Profile

THE ADVANTAGE of using multiscale inventories such as the MACI is that they provide broad coverage of psychopathology, permitting applications in a variety of settings. The challenge several scales create is the integration of configurations to arrive at a useful interpretation. The MACI is divided into four distinct sections: Modifying Indices, Personality Patterns, Expressed Concerns, and Clinical Syndromes. As a result, some structure and organization can be applied to integrating the MACI profile.

There are no clear-cut rules to follow when integrating the MACI profile, but the essential guiding principle is that the same clinical syndrome or concern an adolescent has takes on different meaning depending on the specific personality style of the adolescent. An elevation on Scale BB (Substance Abuse Proneness) generally implies that the adolescent has difficulty controlling his or her use of drugs or alcohol and that substance abuse has created problems in the adolescent's life. When this elevation is accompanied by elevations on Scales 2A (Inhibited) and E (Peer Insecurity), for example, the substance abuse must be interpreted with these issues in mind. The adolescent may use illicit substances to cope with high levels of social anxiety or to gain acceptance from peers. On the other hand, an adolescent with elevations on Scales 6A (Unruly), 6B (Aggressive), and CC (Delinquent Predisposition) may abuse substances as an act of defiance against parents or to lessen inhibitions further to facilitate antisocial acting-out. Specific MACI scale elevations must be interpreted in light of other elevations in the profile.

Another factor that affects MACI interpretation is the issue of frequent concurrent elevations on multiple scales that are due to factors such as item overlap, measurement of similar constructs, and response style. The inexperienced MACI user may be confused by seeing multiple elevations on several scales, such as a profile with significant elevations on Scales 2A, 2B, 8A, 8B, and 9. Frequently, the question is raised: "Does that mean the adolescent really has all of those personality styles?" The most reasonable answer to this question is that some of these patterns may be due to shared items, but the profile may also represent other clinically meaningful factors such as mood disturbances, high levels of psychopathology, and the presence of several different personality traits or clinical symptoms.

In this chapter, strategies for integrating the MACI profile are outlined. First, however, it is necessary to outline an interpretive strategy for the instrument. By providing a stepwise approach to interpretation, of which profile integration is one step, the MACI user can organize statements derived from the test results in an organized fashion. Next, common scale patterns are provided for each of the MACI scales, including the most likely and least likely concurrent elevations. This information provides some perspective on configurations that emerge based primarily on the intercorrelation of the scales; these intercorrelations reflect item overlap as well as the measurement of similar constructs by different scales. Finally, various approaches to integrating the profile are discussed to assist placing each of the scale configurations within a meaningful context that takes into account the specific characteristics of the adolescent being evaluated.

AN INTERPRETIVE STRATEGY

The MACI manual outlines a sequential approach to interpreting the test that advocates several strategies, including the interpretation of single-scale elevations, analysis of scale configurations within a specific section of the profile, and integration of the sections with one another (Millon et al., 1993). The accuracy of these strategies for yielding useful information on the adolescent depends on the appropriate use of the MACI and the validity of the individual test results.

In previous chapters, the meaning of single-scale elevations and configurations was outlined. This previous material can be of assistance in conducting preliminary steps to MACI interpretation. The latter portion of this chapter provides useful information on integrating the parts of the MACI profile.

There are four basic steps to interpreting the MACI in clinical settings. Each of these steps is carried out sequentially before each subsequent step. In other words, the first step is necessary before the second step can be carried out; the second step forms the necessary basis for the third step, and the third step proceeds before the final step of profile integration takes place.

STEP 1: REVIEW PATIENT INFORMATION

The first step to carrying out MACI interpretation is to analyze the clinical and demographic characteristics of the adolescent who has taken the MACI. Specific features such as the gender and age of the adolescent are important from a practical standpoint, since these two variables define whether the MACI was given appropriately and direct which BR conversion tables are to be used for converting MACI raw scores into BR scores.

Other pieces of information must be reviewed as part of the initial MACI interpretive process. Most important, the MACI should not be interpreted without a context in which case history is available and there is access to clinical information that provides an assessment of symptoms that are present and absent. This information is necessary because in some cases the MACI results are consistent with the history or clinical presentation, and in a few instances there may be inconsistency between the test results and the adolescent's clinical presentation. There are cases where the clinician needs to determine why the MACI results may or may not match the history. Therefore, clinical and background information is needed. Although blind interpretation of the MACI is sometimes an interesting exercise, whereby the test results are interpreted without access to any information about the adolescent to see whether the final interpretation matches the history, this approach should not be used in clinical settings. An understanding of the case history, clinical data, and referral context is a necessary part of MACI interpretation and should precede other steps in the interpretive process.

STEP 2: ASSESS PROFILE VALIDITY

The second step of MACI interpretation is to determine whether the resulting profile is both reliable and valid. There are two parts to assessing profile validity: (1) evaluating the consistency and reliability of item endorsement, and (2) evaluating the accuracy or validity of responding. Chapter 4 outlines the critical stages and procedures involved in evaluating MACI profile validity. In particular, the Reliability Index (Scale VV) and examination of Scales Y and Z for concurrent elevations are useful for determining the consistency of MACI responding and identifying response sets such as random, irrelevant, and confused responding that can affect the reliability of the MACI. Likewise, Scales X, Y, and Z are used to evaluate the accuracy of the adolescent's self-reports. Response sets characterized by honesty, denial, exaggeration, malingering, and other forms of dissimulation are evaluated first before proceeding to the next phase of interpretation.

STEP 3: ANALYZE PROFILE SECTIONS

Once a determination has been made that the MACI profile is valid, the next step in the interpretive process is to undertake an analysis of the different sections of the profile. There are three sections: Personality Patterns, Expressed Concerns, and Clinical Syndromes—discussed in Chapters 5, 6, and 7, respectively. The material in these chapters can be used to conduct two basic analyses: an interpretation of individual scale elevations and typical scale configurations within each section of the profile. This third step provides the MACI user with basic information on the meaning of scale elevations and configurations that can be used in the final stage of profile integration.

STEP 4: PROFILE INTEGRATION

This final step in MACI interpretation rests on the assumption that particular scales take on different significance and meaning depending on factors such as the context of the evaluation, the response style used by the adolescent when completing the instrument, and the adolescent's personality style. Although an analysis of single scale elevations and configurations within a particular profile section provides useful information, a more accurate and useful approach is to consider the meaning of elevations and configurations within the context of the entire profile. Moreover, other factors such as item overlap and high interscale correlations may affect the integration of sectional components of the MACI profile. In the remainder of this chapter, this final interpretive step is outlined in greater detail.

COMMON PATTERNS ON THE MACI PROFILE

It is helpful to recognize that certain MACI profile patterns emerge because common traits, symptoms, or clinical problems are being tapped by more than one scale. For example, impulsive acting-out is the major psychological construct being measured by Scale DD, but this construct is also a significant feature of unruly personality as measured by Scale 6A. Likewise, an adolescent with concerns over the formation of a clear identity will likely obtain an elevation on Scale A, but this issue is also a symptom of borderline personality disturbances as measured by Scale 9. There is overlap across MACI scales because certain traits and symptoms are shared by various personality styles and clinical concerns. Therefore, many MACI items are shared by more than one scale.

As a result of both item overlap and the conceptual similarity between particular personality traits, expressed concerns, and clinical syndromes, many MACI scales are highly correlated. Consequently, many MACI profiles may reflect certain expected patterns because of the influence of these high correlations. Recognizing these common patterns facilitates MACI profile integration because some of the patterns that emerge may reflect a major clinical problem or psychological dimension of the adolescent's functioning that happens to be measured, in part, by multiple scales.

To identify common MACI profile patterns, the correlations among MACI scale scores were examined in Appendix E of the MACI manual (Millon et al., 1993). For each of the individual scales, the correlations with other MACI scales were examined to identify the specific Personality Patterns, Expressed Concerns, and Clinical Syndromes scales that are likely to also be elevated when that particular scale is elevated. A correlation of 0.60 or higher was selected as the criterion for identifying scales that correlate highly with one another. A correlation at this level means that about a third of the variance in a score is shared by the two scales. The assumption is that concurrent elevations between two MACI scales correlating that highly are likely to be quite common. In Table 8.1, the common MACI patterns are presented. When a blank line exists under a particular scale group, this denotes that no scale in that group correlated with the target scale at or above the selected criterion correlation of 0.60. For example, Scale 1 (Introversive) correlates at or above the 0.60 level with Scales 2A, A, B, and E; however, it does not correlate with any of the Clinical Syndromes scales at or above the criterion level. Neither Scale G nor H correlates that highly with any of the other MACI scales.

Another application of the correlations among MACI scales is to identify those scales that are not likely to be elevated concurrently. In this way, unusual or very uncommon profiles can be identified. Using the same approach as previously outlined, the correlations among MACI scale scores from Appendix E in the manual were examined to identify scales that correlate highly in the *negative* direction. The assumption again is that two scales that correlate highly in the negative direction (i.e., −0.60 or higher) are unlikely to be elevated in the same MACI profile. However, since none of the MACI scales correlate −1.00 with any other MACI scale, it is theoretically and clinically possible, though unlikely, that two negatively correlated scales could be elevated in the same MACI profile. In Table 8.2, the individual MACI scales are presented with the other scales that are not likely to be elevated when that particular scale is elevated. For example, because Scale 6B correlates −0.60 or higher with Scales 3, 7, and EE, one could expect that any MACI profile with an elevation on one of these three scales when Scale 6B is also elevated would be unusual and worthy of careful analysis.

Some examples of how Tables 8.1 and 8.2 can be utilized may assist in their clinical application. Suppose a clinician working in an acute inpatient

Table 8.1
Common Concurrent Elevations for Individual MACI Scales

Scale	Common Elevations		
	Personality Patterns	Expressed Concerns	Clinical Syndromes
Modifying Indices			
X. Disclosure	2B, 8A, 8B, 9	A, B	FF, GG
Y. Desirability	5, 7	—	—
Z. Debasement	2B, 8B, 9	A, B	FF, GG
Personality Patterns			
1. Introversive	2A	A, B, E	—
2A. Inhibited	1	B, E	FF
2B. Doleful	8A, 8B, 9	B	FF, GG
3. Submissive	7	—	EE
4. Dramatizing	5	—	—
5 Egotistic	4	—	—
6A. Unruly	6B	F	BB, CC, DD
6B. Forceful	6A	F	BB, CC, DD
7. Conforming	3	D	—
8A. Oppositional	2B, 9	A	DD
8B. Self-Demeaning	2B	B	FF, GG
9. Borderline Tendency	2B, 8A, 8B	A, B	DD, GG
Expressed Concerns			
A. Identity Diffusion	1, 8A, 9	B	GG
B. Self-Devaluation	1, 2A, 2B, 8B	A, C	FF, GG
C. Body Disapproval	—	B	AA, FF
D. Sexual Discomfort	7	—	—
E. Peer Insecurity	1, 2A	—	—
F. Social Insensitivity	6A, 6B	—	CC
G. Family Discord	—	—	—
H. Childhood Abuse	—	—	—
Clinical Syndromes			
AA. Eating Dysfunctions	—	C	FF
BB. Substance Abuse Proneness	6A, 6B	—	DD
CC. Delinquency Predisposition	6A, 6B	F	—
DD. Impulsive Propensity	6A, 6B, 8A, 9	—	BB, CC
EE. Anxious Feelings	3	—	—
FF. Depressive Affect	2A, 2B, 8B	B, C	AA, GG
GG. Suicidal Tendency	2B, 8A, 8B, 9	A, B, H	FF

Table 8.2
Unlikely Concurrent Elevations for Individual MACI Scales

Scale	Unlikely Elevations		
	Personality Patterns	Expressed Concerns	Clinical Syndromes
Modifying Indices			
X. Disclosure	5, 7	—	—
Y. Desirability	—	—	—
Z. Debasement	4, 5, 7	—	—
Personality Patterns			
1. Introversive	4, 5	—	—
2A. Inhibited	4, 5	F	CC
2B. Doleful	5	—	—
3. Submissive	6A, 6B	—	BB, CC, DD
4. Dramatizing	1, 2A	B, E	FF
5. Egotistic	1, 2A, 2B, 8B	A, B, C	FF, GG
6A. Unruly	3	D	EE
6B. Forceful	3, 7	—	EE
7. Conforming	6B, 8A, 9	A	BB, DD, GG
8A. Oppositional	7	—	—
8B. Self-Demeaning	5	—	—
9. Borderline Tendency	7	—	—
Expressed Concerns			
A. Identity Diffusion	5, 7	—	—
B. Self-Devaluation	4, 5	—	—
C. Body Disapproval	5	—	—
D. Sexual Discomfort	6A	—	BB
E. Peer Insecurity	4	—	—
F. Social Insensitivity	2A	—	—
G. Family Discord	—	—	—
H. Childhood Abuse	—	—	—
Clinical Syndromes			
AA. Eating Dysfunctions	—	—	—
BB. Substance Abuse Proneness	3, 7	D	EE
CC. Delinquency Predisposition	2A, 3	—	EE
DD. Impulsive Propensity	3, 7	—	EE
EE. Anxious Feelings	6A, 6B	—	BB, CC, DD
FF. Depressive Affect	4, 5	—	—
GG. Suicidal Tendency	5, 7	—	—

treatment setting has administered the MACI to an adolescent admitted following a suicide gesture. The resulting profile reveals an expected elevation on Scale GG that is quite high, and the resulting profile shows elevations on Scales 2B, 3, and 8B on the Personality Patterns scales, Scale B on the Expressed Concerns scales, and Scale FF on the Clinical Syndromes scales. The information in Table 8.1 helps clarify some issues by noting that the elevations on Scales 2B, 8B, B, and FF reflect a chronic depression characterized by low self-esteem (Scales 8B and B), hopelessness (Scales 2B and FF), and long-standing feelings of unhappiness (Scales 2B and 8B). Therefore, a general depressive disturbance is being tapped that has both characterological and acute clinical manifestations. However, the Scale 3 elevation, which is not expected based on the information in Table 8.1, suggests that the adolescent's depression and resulting suicide gesture may be related in some way to frustrated dependency needs or the failure of some external support to provide the adolescent with nurturance and guidance.

The next example references the information in Table 8.2. Suppose that a clinician is working in a residential setting for delinquent adolescents who have been placed by the court. In one case, an initial psychological screening with the MACI yields a profile in which there are elevations on Scales 6A, 6B, and 8A among the Personality Patterns scales and the only other elevation is on Scale EE. As Table 8.2 indicates, the Scale EE elevation is unusual, yet it is meaningful when one places it within the context of the adolescent's personality style and the context of the evaluation. Rather than interpret the Scale EE elevation as indicative of an anxiety disorder, the elevation most likely represents situational tension and anxiety over placement in an adolescent who is otherwise cold and uncaring, and who acts out.

A useful strategy for identifying common and rare MACI profile patterns would be to collect a large number of profiles across several settings. In this way, the actual frequency with which a particular configuration occurs allows clinicians a means of identifying how common or rare certain MACI profile patterns are. Until such large-scale studies are conducted, the data in Tables 8.1 and 8.2 are offered as a parallel method for identifying common and uncommon patterns in the MACI profile.

APPROACHES TO PROFILE INTEGRATION

There are no clearly defined rules to provide the MACI user with a standard method for integrating the profile. In general, McCann (1997) has suggested that the best tools for integrating the profile include "sound clinical experience, an understanding of the underlying theory and diagnostic criteria upon which the MACI is based, a clear understanding of the psychometric properties of the test, and a good working knowledge of the adolescent being evaluated" (p. 382). Although these factors will facilitate profile integration, it is also helpful to have some concrete guidelines to follow when integrating the MACI profile.

In this section, a number of specific guidelines are offered for combining the scales in the four major sections (i.e., Modifying Indices, Personality Patterns, Expressed Concerns, and Clinical Syndromes) of the MACI profile. Unlike the interpretive strategy outlined earlier, these guidelines are not presented in a fixed sequence that should be rigidly followed, although they are presented in such a way that more important and basic considerations are discussed first.

CHECKING FOR RESPONSE STYLE INFLUENCES

The level of openness an adolescent displays when completing the inventory will affect the overall profile elevations. Similarly, socially desirable response sets and attempts to exaggerate or feign disturbance will have an impact on the MACI results. Therefore, a basic consideration is to evaluate the extent to which such factors are represented in the entire profile. Low disclosure levels tend to result in profiles with no clinical elevations and response styles tend to produce distinct profile patterns. The information in Table 8.1 and Chapter 4 will facilitate this process.

USING THE PERSONALITY PATTERNS AS AN ANCHOR

The Expressed Concerns and Clinical Syndromes scales tend to take on different significance and meaning depending on the adolescent's personality style. Therefore, it is often useful to use the Personality Patterns scales as an anchor for establishing a context within which other scales can be interpreted. For example, an elevation on Scale FF generally reflects depressed mood, hopelessness, ineffectiveness, and social withdrawal that are indicative of a depressive disturbance. A Scale FF elevation would represent something different in a submissive (Scale 3) and inhibited (Scale 2A) adolescent as opposed to an oppositional (Scale 8A) adolescent. In the former case, the depression would reflect sadness due to rejection from others and the failure to obtain support and nurturance. In the latter case, the depression would represent an emotional response to being misunderstood and treated unfairly.

A similar approach can be used with the Expressed Concerns scales. Elevations on Scale G represent family conflict and discord. In an unruly (Scale 6A) and forceful (Scale 6B) adolescent the Scale G elevation would represent conflict over the adolescent's rejection of parental limits and rebellion. In an inhibited (Scale 2A) and self-demeaning adolescent (Scale

8B), the Scale H elevation would reflect concerns over feeling rejected by the parents and experiencing a lack of support and validation.

Recognize Appropriate Prevalence Rates

In certain settings and populations of adolescents where the MACI is utilized, particular profile patterns and scale elevations are likely to occur with greater frequency. If the clinician is using the MACI with a particular group of adolescents, such as substance abusers, sexually victimized youth, eating disorders, or juvenile delinquents, some MACI configurations will be more common based on the clinical features associated with that particular diagnostic group. Moreover, certain scale elevations would be expected based on the setting and diagnosis. For example, substance abuse treatment settings, residential treatment for juvenile offenders, adolescent inpatient units, and adolescents with learning disabilities are all likely to have varying prevalence rates of certain disturbances that will affect the clinician's expectations. The broader range of experience a clinician has in using the MACI across settings and populations, the more skilled he or she will become in identifying meaningful profile patterns.

Identifying Common Dimensions Across Scales

As noted, the fact that items are shared across MACI scales is less a psychometric weakness of the instrument and more a representation of clinical reality. Many clinical syndromes represent acute exacerbations of underlying personality traits, and expressed concerns reflect subjective concerns related to clinical disturbances or social problems arising from the adolescent's interaction with others. Symptoms such as depression, substance abuse, impulsivity, or anxiety can reflect characterological disturbances in some ways. Therefore, concurrent elevations on several MACI scales may reflect these factors. In the previous section, common and uncommon patterns on the MACI profile were provided to assist the clinician with identifying common problems and clinical features that may produce multiple elevations across the different sections of the profile.

SUMMARY

The MACI profile is unique in delineating four major groups of scales that measure significant issues such as response style, personality patterns, concerns subjectively experienced by the adolescent, and clinical syndromes that suggest a particular diagnosis. In this chapter, strategies are presented for integrating the Modifying Indices, Personality Patterns, Expressed Concerns, and Clinical Syndromes scales. A four-step interpretive strategy is provided to help integrate and organize material presented in previous chapters. In addition, MACI scale combinations are presented based on an analysis of the correlations between scales; both common and uncommon profile patterns are identified. Finally, strategies are provided for integrating the MACI profile. Although there are no standard rules or guidelines for integrating the profile, clinicians are likely to find the results most useful if several features are taken into account, including the context in which the evaluation takes place, the theory and diagnostic criteria on which the MACI is based, a sound understanding of the test's psychometric properties, and a broad range of clinical experiences with adolescents.

CHAPTER 9

Special Diagnostic and Assessment Issues

BECAUSE CLINICIANS are continuously learning more about the adolescent as time progresses, psychological assessment in clinical settings is not static and diagnostic hypotheses are frequently modified as more information is obtained. Another feature of the assessment process is that any one assessment procedure or technique does not stand alone as the definitive factor for a particular diagnosis or clinical feature of the individual. Because the clinician relies on several sources of information, including interviews, collateral informants, other psychological assessment techniques, and case records, psychological assessment is necessarily integrative. The clinician must take many pieces of data from different sources and bring them together to draw a meaningful and useful conclusion.

Many times, the clinical data are consistent with one another and are supportive of a particular diagnosis, dynamic formulation, or treatment recommendation. However, not all data are easily synthesized and integrated into a clear diagnostic picture. Moreover, although most clinicians would agree that psychological assessment is integrative, most would also agree that little information is available in the professional literature to direct exactly how to integrate clinical data and psychological testing results.

Clinicians who use the MACI to assess adolescent personality and psychopathology, may encounter several issues when integrating it with other known information. This chapter focuses on these special diagnostic and assessment issues. A particularly important, yet interesting phenomenon is the MACI profile that does not describe or fit with what is known about the adolescent based on clinical interview or the case history. These "poor fit" profiles sometimes occur with any self-report instrument and ways to understand such findings are explored in this chapter. A second area of integrating MACI data with other sources of information is using the test with other assessment instruments. Two major personality assessment techniques used with adolescents are the MMPI-A and Rorschach; strategies for combining the MACI with these two instruments are also explored. A third area where MACI results must be interpreted in light of other data has to do with demographic factors and other individual variables, such as gender, race, and educational background. Finally, information contained in the MACI computer-generated interpretive reports can raise significant challenges for the MACI user.

A common theme shared by "poor fit" profiles, multiple psychological test integration, effects of individual variables, and computerized test interpretation is that they all present challenges for the MACI user in one way or another. Various strategies are discussed for resolving interpretive dilemmas and making sense of often confusing or conflicting data.

THE "POOR FIT" PROFILE

McCann (1997) has noted that in most cases where the MACI is utilized, the results are likely to provide accurate information on the adolescent's functioning. However, the MACI is prone to some of the limitations that are inherent in self-report instruments. Information obtained from self-report psychological tests can sometimes be distorted by response sets, the adolescent's poor insight into his or her difficulties, biased or distorted perceptions of one's self or others, or a wish to portray one's self as how one wants to be seen rather than how one actually is. Thus the clinician may occasionally find the MACI profile fails to fully capture the clinical symptoms or personality style revealed in the interview and history. As noted by McCann, "It is tempting to discard the MACI results as inaccurate or useless" when the test results are at odds with what is actually known about the adolescent (p. 383).

Although profile adjustments are implemented to control some of the distortions that can occur with MACI profiles, some distortions cannot be corrected by these adjustments. Nevertheless, by carefully analyzing the clinical context in which the distorted MACI results were obtained and by characterizing the distortion that is believed to have occurred, the clinician can usually obtain some useful information from MACI results that appear on the surface to be at odds with the history and clinical presentation. These types of MACI result represent poor-fit profiles.

A useful starting point for analyzing these profiles is to first characterize the distortion that is thought to have occurred. There are three basic manifestations of distorted MACI results. The first is when a specific MACI scale is expected to occur and the results show that the scale is not elevated; in the language of diagnostic accuracy statistics, such results represent a false negative test finding. An example would be a juvenile offender with a history of aggressive acting-out, manipulation of others, and a lack of empathy toward others who does not obtain an elevation on Scale F (Social Insensitivity) or an adolescent inpatient with a recent suicide attempt who does not elevate Scales FF (Depressive Affect) or GG (Suicidal Tendency). A second manifestation of distorted MACI results would be the elevation of a specific MACI scale when the history or clinical presentation would suggest no problem in the particular area. In the language of diagnostic accuracy statistics, these test results would be characterized as false positive findings. For example, an adolescent with no history of substance abuse obtains an elevation on Scale BB (Substance Abuse Proneness) or an adolescent with no history of juvenile delinquency or conduct problems obtains an elevation on Scale 6A (Unruly). A third manifestation of distorted MACI results occurs when the overall profile configuration reflects psychopathology that is not supported by the history or clinical presentation. For example, elevations on Scales 6A (Unruly), 6B (Forceful), 8A (Oppositional), F (Social Insensitivity), CC (Delinquent Predisposition), and DD (Impulsive Propensity) might suggest a severe conduct disturbance in an adolescent with no significant history of legal difficulties or major conduct problems.

Once the specific distortion in MACI results has been characterized, the next step is to analyze why the poor-fit results were obtained. Although no clear rules exist for classifying poor-fit profiles, several reasons have proved to be meaningful and interpretively useful in clinical practice. A possible factor in producing a distorted MACI profile is a socially desirable response set. As noted in Chapter 4, a few personality scales, such as 4, 5, and 7, overlap with Scale Y (Desirability) and thus elevations or scale configurations involving two or more of these scales, especially Scale 7, can be viewed as a socially desirable response set. If the adolescent does not present clinically as particularly conforming, egotistic, or dramatic, this hypothesis might be entertained to explain the profile.

Distortions in MACI results can also occur when an adolescent adopts a response set in which symptoms are intentionally or unintentionally exaggerated or when there is a severe level of psychopathology. Scales that reflect emotional turmoil or general psychological maladjustment can be elevated in such cases. Specific scales include 2A (Inhibited), 2B (Doleful), 8B (Self-Demeaning), 9 (Borderline Tendency), A (Identity Diffusion), and B (Self-Devaluation). Thus, elevations on these scales, particularly when they occur together, often reflect excessive psychological difficulties that may represent an exaggerated self-report style associated with either a deliberate attempt to feign symptoms or extreme forms of psychopathology such as severe personality disorders, major affective disturbances, or dissociative disorders.

Another possible reason for obtaining MACI results that do not fit with the clinical or background information on an adolescent is that the results reflect how the adolescent wants to be seen, rather than how he or she actually is. This response to taking the MACI sometimes occurs in adolescents who are sophisticated or defensive and who are effective at portraying themselves in a particular way. Moreover, because many MACI items are face valid, what is being measured by each is sometimes clear to the teenager taking the test. Thus, an acting-out adolescent who has been restricted either by incarceration or hospitalization may want to appear cooperative, compliant, and self-assured. Hence, elevations on Scale 3 (Submissive) or 7 (Conforming) may sometimes be obtained in adolescents whose history suggests the opposite. In such instances, the MACI results could be interpreted as representing the personality style the adolescent wants to portray to the examiner, not his or her genuine self.

A third common source of distortion in MACI results involves an interesting phenomenon. It has been observed in clinical settings that some MACI results reflect a behavioral reaction or adjustment to psychosocial stressors, trauma, or other circumstances, rather than preexisting personality propensities. Examples of the environmental factors that can produce poor-fitting MACI profiles include severe trauma, recent attachment and identification with a peer group that has specific norms, and reactive dependence and self-deprecation in response to a chronic lack of achievement. An adolescent female who had been the victim of a recent date rape provided a MACI profile that was suggestive of severe antisocial behavior and conduct disturbances, with elevations on Scales 6A (Unruly), 6B (Forceful), 5 (Egotistic), 8A (Oppositional), F (Social Insensitivity), and CC (Delinquent Predisposition). The psychosocial history revealed, however, that this teenager had no history of legal troubles; moreover, her conduct at home had always been somewhat oppositional and she was described as "strong-willed" by her parents. However, she was always manageable. It was only following the date rape that her conduct became uncontrollable and severely problematic. In this case, the MACI results were not interpreted as indicative of an antisocial adolescent with severe conduct disturbance. Rather, the MACI was viewed as a reaction to the rape trauma in which the adolescent identified with characteristics of her aggressor. More specifically, as treatment progressed, it was uncovered that her perception was that if she was more assertive, aggressive, self-confident, and less sensitive to others, she could protect herself from any similar attack or try to manage the situation differently to prevent being victimized. Thus, although the MACI interpretive report suggested an antisocial, criminally oriented personality, the results instead represented a reaction to psychosocial trauma.

This type of distortion can also occur if the adolescent has recently become strongly allied with a particular peer group. In these instances, the MACI profile may represent fairly recent changes in clinical status or personal attitudes that may not be particularly representative of the teenager's long-standing personality style. Instead, the endorsement of specific MACI items may have been guided by attitudes and values that have been adopted by the teenager in response to strong identification with a particular peer (e.g., boyfriend or girlfriend) or peer group (e.g., gang).

A final source of distortion in MACI results may reflect personality patterns, expressed concerns, or clinical symptoms that have arisen in response to chronic or long-term difficulties. For example, severely disabled or chronically ill adolescents may produce elevations on Scale 3 (Submissive) or 8B (Self-Demeaning) because of self-perceptions that one is dependent on others, inadequate, or ineffective. Such findings might be interpreted not as premorbid personality traits or manifestations of recent symptomatology; they may instead reflect understandable reactions to chronic and long-standing aspects of this lifestyle or defined by the disability or mental illness.

Regardless of why a MACI profile occasionally represents a poor fit with the clinical data and history, such results tend to be exceptions rather than the rule. Depending on the setting in which one works, some forms of distortion may be more common than others. Nevertheless, poor-fit profiles do not necessarily reflect inadequacies with the MACI as a test or the specific application, assuming that standard administration procedures have been observed. Rather, poor-fit profiles reflect the challenges that arise with self-report test results in general. Specific rules and guidelines for analyzing problematic MACI profiles are elusive and obtaining useful and meaningful information from such profiles requires careful attention to the clinical data, case history, context in which the MACI was administered, and the specific profile generated by the adolescent. As McCann (1997) has noted, it is generally useful to ask the following question when faced with puzzling MACI results: "Why did *this* adolescent produce *this* profile under *these* circumstances?" (p. 383). By observing the issues previously discussed, useful information can usually be obtained from those uncommon and unusual MACI profiles that appear at first glance to be either slightly or completely inaccurate.

INTEGRATING THE MACI WITH OTHER ASSESSMENT INSTRUMENTS

The proliferation of many assessment instruments and treatment methods in clinical psychology has brought considerable attention to the problem of integrating divergent theoretical approaches. A substantial literature has evolved in the past several years on integrating approaches to doing psychotherapy (Garfield, 1995; Norcross & Goldfried, 1992). In the field of personality assessment, Ganellen's (1996) work with the Rorschach and MMPI-2 has advanced the understanding of how to integrate diverse assessment instruments. Despite these advances, however, much remains unknown about the ways in which the data from different assessment instruments can be combined to provide a thorough and clinically useful description of the individual's psychological functioning.

There are several ways to integrate psychological tests, and these have been summarized by Acklin (1993). At one level, the clinician can merely list the findings that have been obtained on a test-by-test basis. Although this approach strives for comprehensive assessment, little actual integration takes place. Another approach is to compare scales or scores on different tests that purport to measure the same thing. A third level of integration is the use of constructs such as defense mechanisms, affect controls, self-concept, thought processes, and the like to examine different data sets to see if particular themes emerge. Finally, another approach to integration is the use of a theory to integrate and examine information from different tests and data sources. Overall, Acklin notes that data are integrated and interpreted in terms of their meaning with respect to the individual being examined. Moreover, Weiner (1993) argues that data from different tests should be used to generate hypotheses and findings about the person rather than to confirm or disconfirm data from other tests. Thus, integration of assessment instruments must be done with a unifying framework of constructs or theory in mind and with the goal of describing the unique aspects of the person being evaluated.

There is no established body of literature that has examined the empirical relationship between the MACI and other instruments. The two instruments that appear to be of greatest interest are the MMPI-A and Rorschach because they are the most popular personality assessment measures used with adolescent populations. Therefore, the following discussion focuses on the issues that clinicians may face when combining the MACI with one of these other instruments in an assessment battery.

MMPI-A and the MACI

A survey of psychological test usage in evaluations on adolescents revealed that the MMPI was the 6th most frequently used instrument and the MAPI was the 12th most frequently used test (Archer, Maruish, Imhof, & Piotrowski, 1991). This study by Archer and his colleagues was undertaken prior to publication of the MMPI-A (Butcher et al., 1992) and the MACI (Millon et al., 1993). Nevertheless, it seems highly probable that the MMPI-A and MACI are the two most commonly used self-report psychological instruments used in clinical assessments of adolescents.

Although there may be some reluctance to use two self-report, multi-scale inventories in the same evaluation, a body of literature has emerged with the MMPI and MCMI in adult evaluations that demonstrates how clinical assessments can be refined with these two objective personality measures (Antoni, 1997). Rather than viewing the MMPI and MCMI as competitors, this research shows that these two instruments can contribute different types of data that can be combined in a complementary fashion. The MMPI is based on a normal sample and provides a measure of clinical and personality functioning against the normally distributed T-score scale, whereas the MCMI provides a measure of functioning against the clinically based BR-score transformation. In addition, the MMPI provides direct coverage of Axis I-based symptomatology, whereas the MCMI is designed specifically for measuring Axis II-based pathology.

There are many reasons to expect that the MMPI-A and the MACI could complement each other, in the same way as the adult versions of these instruments. For example, the MACI has specific scales designed to measure personality styles that are representative of Axis II disturbances in *DSM-IV*; the MMPI-A is not designed to measure specific personality styles. On the other hand, the MMPI-A has scales measuring more severe forms of psychopathology such as paranoia, formal thought disorder, and manic symptoms, whereas the MACI does not have scales designed to measure such clinical problems. Therefore, the MMPI-A and MACI have the potential to be combined nicely in clinical assessments to complement one another, perhaps even more so than the adult versions of these instruments.

Despite the potential for combining the MMPI-A and MACI, there are impediments to such a practice. For example, there is a complete lack of published research on the combined use of the MMPI-A and MACI. Neither the MMPI-A nor the MACI manual report any data on the relationship between these two instruments. Whereas Antoni (1997) reviews almost a dozen studies on the relationship between MMPI and MCMI scales and code types in adults, there are no studies on MMPI-A and MACI relationships. Therefore, no research base exists for developing a framework for combining these two instruments in clinical practice. Another major impediment to combining the MMPI-A and MACI has to do with the special demands of the adolescent population when undergoing psychological evaluations. Any clinician who has worked with teenage populations recognizes that they can be a challenge to evaluate because of resistance and oppositional attitudes. Thus, as a practical matter, it is often difficult to get adolescents to cooperate with examination procedures. The demands of completing a 478-item inventory such as the MMPI-A *and* a 160-item inventory such as the MACI are quite formidable. Many adolescents are resistant to completing 638 items, even over several sessions, and many may instead opt to complete the shorter inventory as a compromise. It may be that this heavy demand of completing so many items has hindered research on the combined use of the MMPI-A and MACI. As a practical matter in clinical settings, there is a great deal of resistance by adolescents to complete both instruments and clinical experience has revealed that many adolescent subjects refuse to complete both instruments in a timely manner. In many respects, the shorter MACI is more acceptable to the average adolescent in a clinical setting.

Although combined use of the MMPI-A and MACI may be more useful in forensic settings, where the adolescent may have some motivation to co-operate with the examination and there are stronger grounds for the clini-cian to justify heavy testing to establish a broad database, there are more limitations in clinical settings. The need to accomplish a more rapid as-sessment and build a working alliance, as well as reduce early confronta-tion and resistance makes the MACI a more attractive option with adolescents. Although some strategies for combining the MMPI and MACI (Antoni, 1997) may be extended to the MMPI-A and MACI, research is needed to clarify the extent to which this extrapolation is accurate and useful.

Rorschach and the MACI

Although there is no literature on the relationship between MACI scales and Rorschach data, a handful of studies on the MAPI and Rorschach provide some empirical data that can inform the process of MACI and Rorschach interpretation. Overall, the relationship between MAPI and Rorschach data is very modest, which is consistent with research demonstrating weak relationships between the Rorschach and MMPI in adolescent samples (Archer & Kristnamurthy, 1993). Again, however, these weak relationships do not necessarily reflect poor validity of one instrument as opposed to the other. Rather, the combination of self-report instruments with projective techniques may yield complementary and additive data on the person being assessed. In fact, the Rorschach, despite being the frequent target of criticism and scorn by some, has good psychometric properties that are commensurate with those of other personality assessment instruments (Atkinson, 1986; Parker, Hanson, & Hunsley, 1988).

One study by Hart (1991) examined the relationship between the Ego-centricity Index of the Rorschach Comprehensive System (Exner, 1993) and selected scales from the MAPI. The Egocentricity Index is a measure of the extent to which an individual focuses on the self. There was no sig-nificant relationship with most of the MAPI scales examined. There was a modest correlation of 0.25 between the Egocentricity Index and the Sociable scale on the MAPI, which is the precursor to Scale 4 (Dramatizing) on the MACI. When predicting Scale 4 scores on the MAPI, the Egocentricity Index and the number of responses on the Rorschach resulted in a multiple regression correlation of 0.43. These results might be expected to extend to the MACI because of the high correlation between Scale 4 on the MAPI and Scale 4 on the MACI (0.74). Nevertheless, this study provides very modest support for the relationship between self-focus as measured by the Rorschach and dramatizing personality traits.

In another study on MAPI and Rorschach relationships, Watson and Pantle (1993) found no direct relationship between Rorschach reflection responses and significant elevations on Scales 5 and 6 on the MAPI. However, two groups of depressed adolescents who were distinguished from one another on the basis of whether or not a reflection response was present differed significantly on Scale 5, which is the MACI precursor to the Egotistic scale. Again, there is modest support for a relationship between Rorschach and MAPI measures of narcissism. These findings may also extend to the MACI, given the high relationship between MAPI Scale 5 and MACI Scale 5 (0.84).

One other study by Trenerry and Pantle (1990) examined the relationship between MAPI profile configurations and Rorschach variables. One significant finding was that adolescents who gave one or more Vista (V) response showed elevations on Scale 2 (Inhibited) of the MAPI. In addition, high rates of Vista responses were associated with the following MAPI profiles: 2-8/8-2, 4-8/8-4, and 4-5/5-4. Therefore, a painful process of introspection and self-examination represented in Rorschach Vista responses was associated with MAPI profiles that reflect intense emotional discomfort, negative self-appraisal, and self-absorption. These findings provide support for some of the relationships between specific MAPI codetypes and painful intrapsychic experiences that can be explained by theoretical constructs widely used in Millon's theory.

On a more practical level, Dorr (1997) has summarized general strategies for integrating Rorschach and MCMI-III data that can easily be applied to the integration of Rorschach and MACI data. The first step involves interpreting each instrument independently, while ignoring information from any other measure. A second step consists of integrating clinical and psychosocial data and refining individual test interpretations in light of this data. Next, the clinician combines all sources of data into a refined test interpretation that provides a unified picture of the individual's personality. Any inconsistencies observed in different tests are resolved by creatively analyzing and explaining why such differences exist. Finally, the clinician explains inconsistencies between the data by formulating hypotheses that serve an explanatory purpose.

A key component in the approach for integrating Rorschach and MACI data summarized by Dorr (1997) is the formulation of a "complete and unified picture of the personality" (p. 82). An advantage of the theoretical model that underlies the MACI is the formulation of eight distinct domains of personality that represent both functional and structural components of personality: expressive acts/behavior, interpersonal conduct, cognitive style, object representations, self-image, regulatory mechanisms, and morphologic organization. Each of these domains was briefly discussed in Chapter 1, and Appendix A provides the major descriptors for these domains for each personality style measured on the MACI.

The domains provide a useful framework for integrating the Rorschach and the MACI as the following examples illustrate. Suppose an adolescent has prominent elevations on Scales 1 (Introversive) and 2A (Inhibited) of the MACI. An important diagnostic question is the extent to which the adolescent is lacking strong interpersonal interest as opposed to experiencing strong interpersonal sensitivity. The Rorschach can be useful in addressing this question by examining such factors as the amount of human content (pure H) in the record and the extent to which the adolescent is preoccupied with some painful self-examination (Vista, Form Dimension), which would be more common in the self-conscious inhibited, as opposed to isolated inhibited style. In this case, Rorschach data would be useful in making important distinctions between personality styles that share similar features.

In another example, suppose an adolescent has extremely restricted emotional displays. A question might arise as to whether this represents a functional aspect of personality that is part of the adolescent's interpersonal conduct or whether it represents a more structural aspect of the adolescent's mood and temperament. Again, the MACI and Rorschach can be combined to generate data that help to resolve this issue. Data from the MACI represent the adolescent's self-reports of his or her subjective experiences and behavioral tendencies. The Rorschach provides data on structural aspects of the adolescent's capacity for control and how he or she typically manages affect. Together, they can suggest whether the adolescent's constricted emotions represent situational and transient modes of coping or more pervasive and stable aspects of functioning.

As noted by Dorr (1997), there are no clear guidelines for integrating individual pieces of data and integration must therefore take place at the level of the person. The theory outlined by Millon that forms the foundation on which the MACI was constructed offers a useful framework for integrating MACI and Rorschach data at the level of the person by outlining different domains of personality that reflect different aspects of the same person. Much research is needed on MACI and Rorschach relationships. Studies that have been conducted with the MAPI and Rorschach need to be replicated using the MACI and much remains to be learned about the complementary ways to use these two instruments.

EFFECTS OF INDIVIDUAL VARIABLES

A key consideration when interpreting the results from any psychological test is the impact of extraneous factors. Specific variables that may have a potential effect include gender, age, ethnicity, socioeconomic status, and other demographic factors. The ethical use of psychological assessment instruments dictates that psychologists remain cognizant of how such extraneous variables impact on test results.

On the MACI, two variations in converting raw scores to BR scores are designed to control for two extraneous factors. The first variation involves separate conversion tables for males and females to control for the influence of gender on MACI scores. The second variation is separate conversion tables for 13- to 15-year-olds and 16- to 19-year-olds to control for the influence of age on MACI scores resulting from developmental differences between younger and older adolescents.

Although these procedures are designed to reduce the impact of extraneous variables, other factors such as race, ethnicity, and clinical setting may potentially influence how MACI scores are interpreted. Moreover, independent research is necessary not only to explore the effect of additional variables but to also provide additional information on whether the separate BR conversions for gender and age effectively eliminate the influences of these extraneous variables. There are no studies in the published literature on the impact of race or ethnicity on MACI scores. One study has examined gender differences that may exist between males and females in legal settings despite the presence of different norms for males and females.

A comparison of the mental health needs of male and female offenders in a juvenile justice population was made by Timmons-Mitchell et al. (1997). The MACI scores of 121 male and 52 female juveniles were compared. There were no differences in age or race between the male and female groups of offenders. There were also no differences between the two groups in the number of felonies committed and a comparison of diagnoses between the two groups with the *Diagnostic Interview for Children and Adolescents (DICA)* revealed no significant differences between them. The exception to this latter finding was that males had a significantly greater number of substance abuse disorder diagnoses. Moreover, females had a longer period of incarceration and had completed less formal schooling.

Overall, Timmons-Mitchell and her colleagues found that although male and female juvenile offenders exhibit delinquency patterns on the MACI (i.e., elevations on Scales 6A, E, and CC), females showed evidence of greater reporting of mental health needs than males. Females scored significantly higher on 13 MACI scales: X, 6A, 6B, 8A, C, E, G, H, AA, BB, CC, DD, and GG, whereas males scored significantly higher on four MACI scales: 1, 3, 7, and EE. Although this study represents only one data set on gender differences on the MACI, it suggests that female juvenile delinquents may be more willing to disclose their clinical problems and to admit mental health problems on the MACI.

Other than this one study on gender differences, there is no other published data on the impact of individual variables on MACI results. Thus, many questions about the impact of individual variables must be answered in future research.

COMPUTERIZED TEST INTERPRETATION

With the remarkable advances in computer technology over the past several decades, there has been an increase in the range of applications of computers in all aspects of life. In clinical personality assessment, automated computer scoring and interpretation have resulted in a reduction of time that clinicians have to invest in scoring and interpreting psychological test instruments. There are both advantages and disadvantages of computerized test interpretation, as any innovations that can facilitate certain procedures are also capable of being misused.

The advantages of computerized psychological testing include greater efficiency of scoring, reduction of clerical errors, and the ability to employ actuarial procedures that have been shown to be superior to subjective clinical judgment (McCann & Dyer, 1996). There are limitations to the use of computerized test interpretation including the failure to tailor individualized reports to the individual being examined, the pathological tone of reports, and the encouragement of passive assessment practices whereby clinicians rely excessively on the computer-generated report without actively questioning the results or testing alternative hypotheses.

Computer-generated narrative reports written by the test author, Theodore Millon, are available for the MACI. The manner in which these computerized narrative reports were derived is outlined in Millon et al. (1993). During the process of development of the MACI, the most common profile configurations were identified and descriptive narratives for these profiles were written using ratings made by the clinicians evaluating adolescents in the MACI normative sample as well as the clinical theoretical model on which the MACI is based (Millon, 1981, 1990; Millon & Davis, 1994).

The MACI interpretive reports available from the test publisher, NCS Assessments, are arranged according to a format outlined in the manual that consists of 11 sections or components. There is a cover page followed by a graphic profile of the MACI scales and a listing of the raw and BR scores for each scale. Next, the narrative report begins with a brief discussion of the limitations and restrictions of the MACI, including the contexts where the instrument is appropriate. To provide an individualized context for the report, demographic information is then summarized, followed by a description of the probable reliability and validity of the adolescent's self-reports. The next three major sections of the report provide detailed narrative interpretations of the Personality Patterns, Expressed Concerns, and Clinical Syndromes scales. The last three sections of the report provide a listing of noteworthy responses, which are items with critical content that may require more careful analysis, a listing of possible *DSM-IV* diagnoses, and a section on treatment planning based on information from the MACI profile. A sample MACI interpretive report is provided in Figure 9.1.

There are some advantages to using the MACI interpretive reports in clinical settings. In one study on the MAPI computer-generated reports, Rubenzer (1992) found that the MAPI reports were rated as accurate as reports generated by therapists and nursing staff for adolescent inpatients, but the MAPI reports were viewed as offering more specific interpretations and being of higher quality of writing than traditional clinical reports. Although these findings were obtained using the MAPI reports, they are likely to apply to the MACI as well, given that the MAPI and MACI reports were both written by the test author. Nevertheless, because accuracy of the reports in Rubenzer's study was based on ratings of mental health professionals having some familiarity with the clinical functioning of the adolescents being assessed, there is some support for the accuracy of the Millon generated interpretive reports.

The use of interpretive reports in clinical settings also creates some potential problems. Because the MACI manual does not report the operating characteristics of positive and negative predictive power for the scales, clinicians cannot judge the relative accuracy of the diagnoses provided in the MACI report. The probability of a diagnosis being accurate cannot be determined in the same way that diagnostic formulations in the MCMI-III reports are determined. Also, the use of computerized interpretive reports in forensic settings has been criticized by McCann and Dyer (1996) because statements in the reports must be confirmed by collateral information, and the inclusion of unsubstantiated hypothetical statements may be a source of confusion and conflict in forensic settings. Moreover, computer reports foster passive test interpretation that should be avoided in both clinical and forensic settings. Therefore, although MACI computerized interpretive reports may be of some use in clinical settings for generating diagnostic hypotheses and treatment planning strategies, their use should be conservative and judicious and should not replace sound clinical judgment and critical analysis of testing results.

MACI™

Clinical Interpretive Report

Theodore Millon, PhD

ID Number 5516

Female

Age 15

High School Sophomore

1/06/98

Figure 9.1   Sample MACI Interpretive Report. Copyright © 1993 DICANDRIEN, INC. All rights reserved. Published and distributed exclusively by National Computer Systems, Inc. (NCS). Reproduced with permission by NCS.

MACI™
ID 5516

PERSONALITY CODE: 6A6B**45*8B8A//GF**-*-//CCDD**-*-//
VALID REPORT   DATE: 1/06/98

CATEGORY		SCORE		PROFILE OF BR SCORES				DIAGNOSTIC SCALES
		RAW	BR 0	60	75	85	115	
MODIFYING	X	395	67					DISCLOSURE
INDICES	Y	12	65					DESIRABILITY
	Z	4	43					DEBASEMENT
	1	11	30					INTROVERSIVE
	2A	9	22					INHIBITED
	2B	13	39					DOLEFUL
	3	32	42					SUBMISSIVE
	4	50	76					DRAMATIZING
PERSONALITY	5	47	75					EGOTISTIC
PATTERNS	6A	55	106					UNRULY
	6B	31	88					FORCEFUL
	7	34	45					CONFORMING
	8A	30	74					OPPOSITIONAL
	8B	33	74					SELF-DEMEANING
	9	16	44					BORDERLINE TENDENCY
	A	14	42					IDENTITY DIFFUSION
	B	17	33					SELF-DEVALUATION
	C	9	28					BODY DISAPPROVAL
EXPRESSED	D	17	30					SEXUAL DISCOMFORT
CONCERNS	E	8	43					PEER INSECURITY
	F	45	86					SOCIAL INSENSITIVITY
	G	20	87					FAMILY DISCORD
	H	8	31					CHILDHOOD ABUSE
	AA	8	21					EATING DYSFUNCTIONS
	BB	25	53					SUBSTANCE-ABUSE PRONENESS
	CC	38	93					DELINQUENT PREDISPOSITION
CLINICAL	DD	30	93					IMPULSIVE PROPENSITY
SYNDROMES	EE	20	43					ANXIOUS FEELINGS
	FF	11	42					DEPRESSIVE AFFECT
	GG	6	23					SUICIDAL TENDENCY

CONFIDENTIAL INFORMATION FOR PROFESSIONAL USE ONLY

Figure 9.1   (Continued).

The MACI report narratives have been normed on adolescent patients seen in professional treatment settings for either genuine emotional discomforts or social difficulties and are applicable primarily during the early phases of assessment or psychotherapy. Distortions such as exaggerated severity may occur among respondents who have inappropriately taken the MACI for essentially educational or self-explanatory purposes; in a school counseling setting, the MAPI guidance report is likely to be more relevant and provide a more suitable picture of the psychological and vocational traits of this teenager. Inferential and probabilistic, this report must be viewed as only one aspect of a thorough diagnostic study. Moreover, these inferences should be reevaluated periodically in light of the pattern of attitude change and emotional growth that typifies the adolescent period. For these reasons, it should not be shown to patients or their relatives.

INTERPRETIVE CONSIDERATIONS

In addition to the preceding considerations, the interpretive narrative should be evaluated in light of the following demographic and situational factors. This 15-year-old female is currently in the tenth grade. In the demographic portion of the test, she did not identify any specific problems that are troubling her. The response style of this adolescent showed no test-taking attitudes that would significantly distort MACI results.

The BR scores reported for this adolescent have been modified to account for the minor self-enhancing response tendencies shown by the elevation of Scale Y (Desirability) over Scale Z (Debasement).

PERSONALITY PATTERNS

This section of the interpretive report pertains to those relatively enduring and pervasive characterological traits that underlie the personal and interpersonal difficulties of this adolescent. Rather than focus on specific complaints and problem areas, to be discussed in later paragraphs, this section concentrates on the more habitual, maladaptive methods of relating, behaving, thinking, and feeling.

This adolescent has resentful and suspicious attitudes and an impulsive and socially irritable manner. She takes pride in being assertive, bold, and self-reliant. Her prideful unsentimentality hides a deep insecurity about her self-worth and is employed as a pose to counteract anticipated humiliation and rejection. Deeply felt resentment toward family and authorities is projected outward, precipitating frequent verbal squabbles, personal antagonisms, and possibly both peer and legal difficulties. Others are seen as belligerent and antagonistic, thus justifying her defensive posture.

Although self-recriminating at times, feeling she deserves punishment, she is guided by the principle that one must outwit others before they outwit and dominate you. Closeness to others and displays of weakness are seen as potentially fatal concessions that must be counteracted by acting either cool and independent or rash and blunt. She may exhibit an impulsive willingness to court danger

Figure 9.1 (Continued).

and risk harm and is notably fearless in the face of threats and punitive action. Punishment only reinforces her rebellious, provocative, and defiant attitudes. Frank antisocial behavior, particularly alcoholism, drug difficulties, or sexual acting out, may have become prominent. Achievement failures and social irresponsibilities are typically justified with boastful arrogance and frank prevarications.

This young woman is touchy and jealous. She is brooding and resentful, and she thinks other people are malicious. Easily provoked, she may express impulsive and unanticipated outbursts. She may distort the incidental remarks of others into major insults. Some of her aggressive postures may be as much a matter of fantasy as of reality. Nevertheless, the desire to provoke or to intimidate others stems from her need to overcome feelings of inner weaknesses and to vindicate past injustices. No less significant is her tendency to seek out risks and put herself in personal danger.

EXPRESSED CONCERNS

The scales in this section pertain to the personal perceptions of this adolescent concerning several issues of psychological development, actualization, and concern. Because experiences at this age are notably subjective, it is important to record how this teenager sees events and reports feelings, not just how others may objectively report them to be. For comparative purposes, her attitudes regarding a wide range of personal, social, and familial matters are contrasted with those expressed by a broad cross section of teenagers of the same sex and age with psychological problems.

Detached and coolly impersonal, this young woman shows little empathy or desire to maintain close ties with others. The difficulties and troubles people experience are viewed either critically or harshly by this typically indifferent adolescent, who would not be inclined to be helpful even if others were in clear need.

The normal turbulence of family relationships in early adolescence is greatly magnified in the case of this young woman. She finds her family both a source and a focus of tension and conflict. Moreover, there is a general feeling of estrangement and a lack of mutual understanding. Conflicts within the home appear to take up much of her emotional energy and are likely to be a central focus of her expressed difficulties.

CLINICAL SYNDROMES

The features and dynamics of the following distinctive clinical syndromes are worthy of description and analysis. They may arise in response to external precipitants, but are likely to reflect and accentuate enduring and pervasive aspects of this young woman's basic personality makeup.

Rebellious acts and social noncompliance or both are indicated in the protocol of this young woman, who is highly erratic, irritable, and negativistic in mood. Her

Figure 9.1 (Continued).

delinquent tendencies are a statement of resentful independence from the constraints of conventional life and a means of disjoining her conflicts and liberating her uncharitable impulses toward others. Likely to be brought to the attention of authorities, her acts of assertive defiance have undertones of self-destruction, and her angry noncompliance is displayed with a careless indifference to its consequences.

This driven and precipitate young woman has periods of unconstrained energy, hyperdistractibility, and flights of ideas in which intense and contrary thoughts and energies are discharged recklessly. She exhibits restlessness and impulsivity in an erratic sequence characterized by both exploitive and hostile facets. One moment she may present a saucy and seductive manner; minutes later, incited by either an inner stimulus or an outer provocation, she may become thoughtlessly enraged and heedlessly belligerent. These quickly discharged impulses intensify her difficulties in an ever-increasing spiral of vicious circles within family and other social settings.

NOTEWORTHY RESPONSES

The client answered the following statements in the direction noted in parentheses. These items suggest specific problem areas that the clinician may wish to investigate.

Acute Distress

109. I get very frightened when I think of being all alone in the world. (True)
125. Lately, little things seem to depress me. (True)
133. Lately, I feel jumpy and nervous almost all the time. (True)
160. I probably deserve many of the problems I have. (True)

Dangerous Ideation

76. Too many rules get in the way of my doing what I want. (True)
78. I will sometimes do something cruel to make someone unhappy. (True)
97. I sometimes get pleasure by hurting someone physically. (True)
157. I enjoy starting fights. (True)

Emotional Isolation

20. It is not unusual to feel lonely and unwanted. (True)
119. Others my age never seem to call me to get together with them. (True)

Anorexic Tendency

65. I'm supposed to be thin, but I feel my thighs and backside are much too big. (True)

Bulimic Tendency

11. Although I go on eating binges, I hate the weight I gain. (True)

Drug-Abuse Inclination

No items.

Figure 9.1 (Continued).

Alcohol-Abuse Inclination

No items.

Childhood Abuse

14. I feel pretty shy telling people about how I was abused as a child. (True)

DIAGNOSTIC HYPOTHESES

Although the diagnostic criteria used in the MACI differ somewhat from those in the DSM-IV, there are sufficient parallels to recommend consideration of the following assignments. More definitive judgments should draw upon biographical, observational, and interview data in addition to self-report inventories such as the MACI.

Axis II: Personality Disorders, Traits, and Features

Although traits and features of personality disorders are often observable in adolescents, the data from the MACI should not be used to assign diagnostic labels without additional clinical information. Even when assigned, diagnostic labels tend to be less stable for adolescents than for adults. The traits listed below are suggested by the MACI results and may be important adjuncts to the diagnostic process.

Antisocial and Aggressive/Sadistic Personality Traits with Histrionic and Narcissistic Features

Axis I: Clinical Syndromes

The following list contains suggested clinical syndromes and other conditions relating to the DSM-IV that may be a focus of clinical attention.

> 312.8 Conduct Disorder
> > Also consider: 313.81 Oppositional Defiant Disorder
> > or V71.02 Childhood or Adolescent Antisocial Behavior
> 312.9 Disruptive Behavior Disorder NOS
> V61.20 Parent-Child Relational Problem

PROGNOSTIC AND THERAPEUTIC IMPLICATIONS

This adolescent is apt to be increasingly testy in therapy, acting annoyed, sarcastic, and resentful, most probably agreeing to therapy under the pressure of family or legal difficulties. She may be in trouble as a consequence of aggressive or abusive behavior at school or as a result of incessant quarrels and brutality within her family. Rarely does she experience guilt or accept blame for the turmoil she causes. To her, a problem can always be traced to another person's stupidity, laziness, or hostility. Even when she accepts some measure of responsibility, she may feel defiance and resentment toward the therapist for trying to point this out. She may also seek to challenge, test, bluff, and outwit the therapist. Looking to blame others for her discomfort, she expects that things will not work out well with authorities, such as a therapist.

Figure 9.1 (Continued).

She may seem to be spoiling for a fight, and she may appear to enjoy tangling with the therapist to prove her will and test her powers. She evinces an omnipresent undertone of anger and resentment, a persistent expectation that the therapist may be devious and hostile. Because these moods and expectations endure, she may repeatedly distort the incidental remarks and actions of the therapist so that they appear to deprecate and vilify her. She may persist in misinterpreting what she sees and hears, magnifying minor slights into major insults and slander. These actions demand that the therapist restrain impulses to react with disapproval and criticism. An important step in building rapport with this teenager is to see things from her viewpoint. Therefore, the therapist must convey a sense of trust and a willingness to develop a constructive treatment alliance. A balance of professional authority and tolerance is necessary to diminish the possibility that this teenager will impulsively withdraw from treatment.

Drugs may modulate both the threshold and the intensity of her reactivity. Such changes may minimize the frequency and depth of her hostile feelings and thereby decrease some of the self-perpetuating consequences of her aggressive behavior. Less confrontive cognitive approaches may provide this teen with opportunities to vent her anger; once drained of venom, she may be led to explore her habitual feelings and attitudes, and she may be guided into less-destructive perceptions and outlets than before. Exploratory and insight-oriented procedures are unlikely to prove beneficial unless a thorough reworking of her aggressive strategies seems mandatory. Behavioral methods geared to increasing restraint and control may be usefully pursued. As far as group methods are concerned, this youth may disrupt therapeutic functions. On the other hand, she may become a useful catalyst for group interaction and may appear to gain more constructive social skills and attitudes.

Figure 9.1 (Continued).

SUMMARY

Several extraneous factors can potentially impact the accuracy of psychological test results. Some of these factors characterize the adolescent being evaluated, such as demographic variables, whereas others define the particular nature of the test (e.g., self-report inventory) or the specific setting in which it is used. In this chapter, special diagnostic and assessment issues are discussed for use of the MACI in clinical assessment. Among these issues are the challenges presented by MACI profiles that do not appear at first glance to accurately reflect what is known clinically about an adolescent; these poor-fit profiles are discussed in terms of how the clinician can derive helpful information from the test results. Another challenge is raised when the clinician must integrate MACI test results with the findings from other test instruments; the MMPI-A and Rorschach are two commonly used instruments that can complement the MACI to produce an integrated assessment of the adolescent. Two other issues, the effect of individual variables such as gender or ethnicity and computer-assisted test interpretation, are discussed with respect to use of the MACI in clinical settings. As with other issues discussed earlier, more research is needed on many of these topics.

CHAPTER 10

Clinical Applications

CLINICIANS OFTEN confront diverse diagnostic issues in clinical work with adolescents. In some instances, these issues are broad in range and cover an array of clinical problems, particularly in general inpatient or outpatient settings. In other instances, the diagnostic concerns may pertain to a relatively narrow set of issues such as the assessment of adolescents with a specific disturbance (e.g., substance abuse) or in a specific setting (e.g., juvenile detention center). Although the MACI is useful for assessing a broad range of clinical syndromes and personality characteristics across settings, certain issues create unique challenges.

In this chapter, some of the more significant diagnostic issues are reviewed for clinical use of the MACI with various types of psychopathology. Seven major applications have been selected for coverage based on their relative importance in general clinical practice: (1) suicide risk assessment, (2) disruptive behavior disorders, (3) learning disabilities, (4) child abuse, (5) personality disorders, (6) substance abuse, and (7) psychosis. Although this is not an exhaustive list, these clinical applications are where some of the more common questions arise or difficult challenges emerge.

The major focus of the chapter is to highlight some of the more difficult diagnostic issues, such as how to analyze MACI scales and items to make sense of confusing test results, such as a scale elevation (or lack of elevation) when the case history would suggest otherwise. Where there is published research on a particular clinical issue, the results are discussed in a manner that will assist with MACI interpretation. In addition, the limitation of using the MACI for some clinical issues is also discussed so that the test results are not extended into inappropriate areas and clinicians will not have unrealistic expectations as to how the MACI can be helpful in a particular case.

SUICIDE RISK ASSESSMENT

The problem of adolescent suicide is a major issue that clinicians face in working with adolescent populations. Historical trends over a span of several decades reveal that adolescent suicide rates wax and wane, with the suicide rate of youths in the 1910s being comparable to the rate in the 1970s (Berman & Jobes, 1991). Over the past 30 years, however, there has been a steady increase in the rate of adolescent suicide.

The challenge for the clinicians assessing an adolescent who has been referred for treatment or admitted for inpatient care for suicide-related symptoms is to assess the degree of risk for completed suicide and make appropriate treatment recommendations. What makes suicide risk assessment such a difficult task is that there is no homogeneous profile of a suicidal adolescent and unpredictable situational factors have an impact on suicidal behavior. Moreover, there is a wide range of suicidal behaviors that have varying levels of intensity and risk, including ideation, gestures without intent, threats, and intentional planning of bringing about one's own death.

Given the challenges of assessing suicide risk, it is not surprising that psychometric instruments have been shown to be inaccurate in predicting suicide. Berman and Jobes (1991) cite several studies that show psychological questionnaires and scales render a high number of false positive findings and no one measure or instrument has been shown to be a reliable and accurate predictor of suicide. Moreover, no studies currently exist on use of the MACI with suicidal adolescents and thus it is unknown as to how the instrument would fare as a predictor of suicide, although research on other instruments suggests that the MACI would be prone to providing high numbers of false positive and false negative diagnoses.

What distinguishes the MACI from other multiscale instruments or broad-based personality assessment instruments, such as the MMPI-A or Rorschach, is that the MACI has a specific measure of adolescent suicide risk in Scale GG (Suicidal Tendency). Therefore, the MACI can provide clinically useful information in assessing an adolescent's suicide risk, although this scale has not been empirically evaluated independently as a predictor of suicide. The MACI should be viewed as providing information that must be integrated into a more complete clinical assessment of suicide risk that includes multiple sources of information.

The MACI can be used in adolescent suicide risk assessment by organizing test results around a framework of critical risk factors that must be evaluated in a proper risk assessment. Berman and Jobes (1991) outline seven general themes that encompass the risk factors associated with adolescent suicide: (1) A negative personal history—including stressful life events, narcissistic injury, negative role models, family history of suicide, etc.; (2) Psychopathology and negative personality attributes—depression, aggression, impulsivity, low frustration tolerance, etc.; (3) Stress—rejection, humiliation, abuse, etc.; (4) Breakdown of defenses—emotional dysregulation, rigidity, irrationality, thought disturbance, heightened anxiety, substance abuse, etc.; (5) Social and interpersonal isolation and alienation—lack of attachments, poor social supports, etc.; (6) Self-deprecatory ideation, dysphoria, and hopelessness; and (7) Method availability, accessibility, and knowledgeability—access to weapons, intent to kill self, etc.

In light of these factors, the assessment of suicide risk includes an evaluation of imminent risk factors such as depression, borderline personality disturbances, psychosis, crisis response, aggression and impulsivity, and substance abuse. In addition, the clinician must evaluate specific issues such as the adolescent's suicidal thought content, intent, plans, and access to a means of carrying out suicide. Other important factors include psychopathology, personality disturbances, and coping resources, as well as the adolescent's capacity to cooperate and comply with a treatment plan.

Given both the focused and broad-range assessment requirements when evaluating the potentially suicidal adolescent, the MACI can be particularly useful for each of these components. Nearly every scale on the MACI will be useful for broad-based assessment issues such as the severity and range of psychopathology, degree of breakdown in defenses and coping, personality disturbances, and other wide-ranging concerns. Scales 1, 2A, 2B, and E provide information on the degree of social isolation and lack of social support. Scales 2B, 8B, and B provide information on self-deprecating thoughts and hopelessness; Scales 2B, EE, and FF provide information on the extent of depression and anxiety. Also, Scales 6A, 6B, 8A, and DD provide measures of aggressive and impulsive propensities.

For specific issues concerning suicidal ideation, intent, and planning, Scale GG is the most useful measure on the MACI. Because this scale has not been empirically tested as a predictive measure, the clinician must use Scale GG as additional information to supplement the interview and history. There are two levels at which the scale can be interpreted in clinical assessment: at the BR score level and at the item level. A BR score above 75 on Scale GG means that the adolescent has scored in the clinically significant range and a further assessment is warranted to determine the adolescent's actual risk. The higher the BR score, the higher the risk and at extreme levels (i.e., above a BR of 85), there is a significant presence of suicidal ideation and/or intent that requires active clinical intervention. This intervention may range from more frequent sessions with the adolescent and the involvement of supports to acute inpatient hospitalization.

Because Scale GG can potentially yield a false negative (i.e., BR < 75 in a case where there are suicide indicators), the clinician using the MACI is also strongly encouraged to examine individual item responses on Scale GG when the adolescent is being evaluated for potential suicide risk. In Table 10.1, the 25 items comprising Scale GG have been listed and grouped according to major dimensions of suicide risk. Scale GG items address six major dimensions: suicidal plans/attempts, suicidal ideation, pessimism/hopelessness, negative self-appraisal, lack of social support and isolation, and a history of child abuse. These factors closely match at least five of the seven general risk factor themes outlined by Berman and Jobes (1991). In addition, the first seven items in Table 10.1 have been marked with an asterisk (*) because they represent MACI items that have content in which suicide or thoughts of death are measured directly. These items are listed on the MACI computerized interpretive report when they are endorsed in the appropriate direction to alert the clinician that these responses should be explored in greater detail with the adolescent. For those clinicians who use hand scoring or the profile-only computer scoring, these first seven items in Table 10.1 should be examined individually when interpreting MACI results in cases where suicide risk is being evaluated.

The MACI can be useful in suicide risk assessment by providing broad-based data on factors such as psychopathology and negative personality attributes that constitute risk factors. Moreover, Scale GG BR scores and individual item responses provide relevant information on factors that are specific to suicide risk, such as hopelessness, suicidal ideation, a history of prior attempts, and lack of social support. Although this information is clinically useful, the MACI should not be used in isolation to assess suicidal risk because there is no research on its predictive validity in this area. Because the MACI is a self-report instrument, it is prone to limitations. Some adolescents who have strong intentions of killing themselves may deny risk factors on interview and fail to respond to the MACI face valid items, thus requiring other sources of information. In fact, one finding with adults using the adult version of the Millon inventories suggests that socially desirable response patterns in the profile suggesting denial and minimization are a risk factor when there has been recent suicidal behavior (McCann & Gergelis, 1990). Some adolescents, on the other hand, may feel comfortable admitting certain symptoms or behaviors, such as a previous suicide attempt (e.g., MACI item #123), on a self-report instrument rather than on direct clinical interviewing. Therefore, the MACI can provide information not available from other sources. The MACI can supplement, but must never replace, a thorough and multimethod approach to evaluating suicide risk in adolescents.

Table 10.1
Item Composition of Scale GG (Suicidal Tendency)

Suicide Planning/Attempt

* 54. I sometimes get so upset that I want to hurt myself seriously. (3)
*123. I have tried to commit suicide in the past. (3)
*156. I've given thought to how and when I might commit suicide. (3)

Suicidal Ideation

* 16. I think everyone would be better off if I were dead. (2)
* 88. Killing myself may be the easiest way of solving my problems. (3)
* 95. No one really cares if I live or die. (2)
*107. More and more often I have thought of ending my life. (3)

Pessimism/Hopelessness

19. I guess I'm a complainer who expects the worst to happen. (1)
43. Things in my life just go from bad to worse. (2)
110. Good things just don't last. (1)
136. Many other kids get breaks I don't get. (1)
147. My future seems hopeless. (2)

Negative Self-Appraisal

25. So little of what I have done has been appreciated by others. (2)
26. I hate the fact that I don't have the looks or brains I wish I had. (1)
84. I sometimes feel very unhappy with who I am. (1)
112. I'd like to trade bodies with someone else. (1)
127. There are times I wish I were someone else. (1)
140. I don't like being the person I've become. (1)

Lack of Support and Isolation

34. I often feel as if I'm floating around, sort of lost in life. (1)
64. I often feel sad and unloved. (2)
85. I don't seem to enjoy being with people. (1)
89. I sometimes get confused or upset when people are nice to me. (1)

History of Child Abuse

14. I feel pretty shy telling people about how I was abused as a child. (1)
55. I don't think I was sexually molested when I was a young child. (1)
129. I'm ashamed of some terrible things adults did to me when I was young. (1)

Note. All items except #55 are scored when endorsed in the True direction. Item weights appear in parentheses. An asterisk (*) represents items with content involving suicide or death. Copyright © 1993 DICANDRIEN, INC. All rights reserved. Published and distributed exclusively by National Computer Systems, Inc. (NCS). Reproduced with permission by NCS.

DISRUPTIVE BEHAVIOR DISORDERS

In *DSM-IV*, the group of disturbances referred to collectively as the disruptive behavior disorders include conduct disorder, oppositional defiant disorder, and attention-deficit/hyperactivity disorder (ADHD). Although each of these disturbances is distinct from the others, considerable comorbidity exists between them and several general symptoms are common among them. Impulsivity, acting-out, noncompliance with external demands, and angry temper tantrums are frequently seen in the disruptive behavior disorders.

As with many types of psychopathology, clinicians need assessment measures that can provide diagnostic information for designing treatment plans. There is no research on use of the MACI with ADHD; however, some research is beginning to appear in the published literature on use of the MACI with juvenile offenders, a population with high rates of conduct disorder and oppositional defiant disorder. Scales 6A, 6B, E, and CC on the MACI are most relevant to the assessment of conduct disturbances in adolescents. In addition, Scale DD is a nonspecific measure of disruptive behavior disturbances that consist of impulsive acting-out. Scale 8A (Oppositional) is another MACI scale that is very useful in assessing disruptive behavior disorders; however, Scale 8A is not a direct measure of oppositional defiant disorder. Despite the scale's name, the construct for the design of the scale was the negativistic personality disorder, not oppositional defiant disorder. Nevertheless, similarities between these two diagnostic entities results in Scale 8A measuring some aspects of both, such as noncompliance, a propensity to exhibit sour moods and temper tantrums, and a feeling of being misunderstood by others.

A study by Timmons-Mitchell, Brown, Underwood, Johnston, and Schulz (1996) examined how the MACI could be used to assess the mental health needs of male juvenile offenders and male patients in a mental health setting. Although this study had a very small sample size, some interesting findings emerged. Males in the juvenile justice system scored significantly higher on Scales Y, 2B, H, BB, and EE. These findings suggest that while male offenders attempt to portray a more socially desirable response set, they also report significantly higher problems associated with chronic depression, substance abuse, a history of childhood abuse, and anxiety.

In a study with a larger sample, Timmons-Mitchell and her colleagues (1997) studied the mental health needs of incarcerated juvenile delinquents with a high prevalence of conduct disorder and ADHD. The MACI profiles of male and female juvenile offenders were compared and the results yielded significant differences between males and females. There were significantly higher scores for females than males on Scales X, 6A, C,

E, G, H, AA, BB, CC, DD, and GG. Males scored significantly higher on Scales 3 and 7. The MACI profiles of female offenders appeared more delinquent than males and showed greater levels of externalizing behavior, as opposed to males who were less disclosing and appeared more passive and internalizing, though they still scored in the clinically significant range on scales reflecting delinquency problems (Scales 6A, F, and CC).

Although these studies by Timmons-Mitchell and her colleagues represent a small number of investigations, they provide clinically useful information. They support the validity of MACI scales that are designed to identify disruptive behavior disturbances (i.e., Scales 6A, F, CC, and DD) and they illustrate how the MACI can be used to evaluate the mental health needs of adolescents in the juvenile justice system or with disruptive behavior disorder diagnoses.

LEARNING DISABILITIES

The identification of learning disability in an adolescent is based on establishing a level of achievement in one or more areas of academic skill (e.g., reading, spelling, math, etc.) that falls significantly below the adolescent's intellectual capabilities. Standardized intellectual and psychoeducational tests have direct relevance when diagnosing learning disabilities. One may therefore question if a multiscale personality inventory such as the MACI has any place in the evaluation of learning disability. There is no research on the MACI as a measure of learning disability tendencies and there is no reason to expect any research would produce findings that indicate the MACI can identify learning disability, since the theory and construction of the MACI was directed toward personality assessment and the evaluation of clinical syndromes, not psychoeducational difficulties.

Nevertheless, the psychosocial functioning of adolescents with learning disabilities is an important factor that must be considered when conducting evaluations of this sort. A body of research on the self-concepts, peer relationships, and social behavior of learning-disabled students points to important factors that must be considered in any remediation plan or psychosocial intervention. For example, learning-disabled students have negative self-perceptions, are sometimes rated less favorably than peers, and often misinterpret social cues that all create problems in interpersonal relationships (Cook, 1979; Knoff & Paez, 1992). Therefore, the MACI may be a useful instrument to complement the psychoeducational assessment of learning-disabled students by providing a measure of psychosocial functioning and adjustment.

There are no studies on use of the MACI with learning-disabled students, but one study on the MACI's predecessor, the MAPI, provides some important insights. Knoff and Paez (1992) examined the relationship between the MAPI and Personality Inventory for Children among learning-disabled students and found that the mean MAPI profile had no clinically significant elevations, although the Family Rapport scale approached clinical levels. Although Knoff and Paez speculate their MAPI findings may reflect adaptive functioning in learning-disabled students or that the test might be insensitive to problems in this population, a close examination of their data suggests an alternative and more likely reason for the lack of any significant mean elevation in the MAPI profile. The sample used by Knoff and Paez produced a mean profile with very large standard deviations across all scales. This finding suggests that MAPI profiles for learning-disabled students are heterogeneous and meaningful results tend to be hidden when many profiles are averaged. The implication of these results for using the MACI with learning-disabled students is that there are likely to be many different MACI profiles among learning-disabled students. Some profiles may reflect relatively normal and adaptive psychosocial functioning; other profiles may reflect peer insecurity and withdrawal (e.g., Scales 1, 2A, and E), aggressive and impulsive tendencies (e.g., Scales 6A, 8A, and DD), or dysphoria and self-doubt (e.g., Scales 2A, 8B, B, and FF).

Another important issue is that some learning-disabled students, particularly those with reading problems, may have difficulty completing the MACI due to the sixth-grade reading level required to complete the test. As an alternative, the MACI can easily be read to the adolescent because of the test's short length or an audiotape administration can be used: the test's publisher, NCS Assessments, offers an audiotape of the MACI items for oral administration to those adolescents with reading difficulties.

CHILD ABUSE

The social problem of physical and sexual abuse is significant among children and adolescents. Some research suggests that about 25% to 30% of girls and 10% to 15% of boys are subjected to sexual abuse at some time before adulthood (Elliott & Briere, 1995; Finkelhor, Hotaling, Lewis, & Smith, 1989). Additionally, 10% to 20% of children and adolescents are physically abused by parents or guardians to the point of physical injury (Briere, 1992). In a survey of high school students, Singer, Anglin, Song, and Lunghofer (1995) found that a substantial number of adolescents are exposed to violent stressors, including the witnessing of violence and being forced into sexual acts against one's will.

To address the issue of abuse, the MACI includes Scale H (Childhood Abuse) to measure the adolescent's concerns in this area. In addition, many of the MACI scales are likely to be useful in assessing adolescents who have been exposed to abuse trauma. As noted by Briere (1996), clinical symptoms associated with exposure to trauma in adolescents include anxiety, depression, anger, posttraumatic stress disorder symptoms, dissociative symptoms, and sexual concerns. On the MACI, several scales can be used to assess many of these features, including scales for anxiety (Scale EE), depression (Scales 2B and FF), anger (Scales 6B and 8A), and sexual concerns (Scale D). The full range of posttraumatic stress and dissociative symptoms is not adequately covered on the MACI, although Scales A (Identity Diffusion) and 9 (Borderline Tendencies) represent associated difficulties such as concerns over one's identity and overwhelming emotion. The MACI will provide useful information about many of the psychological effects of exposure to trauma, but alternative assessment measures such as structured interviews or the *Trauma Symptom Checklist for Children* (for adolescents up to age 16; Briere, 1996) will be useful supplementary measures for more severe symptoms such as posttraumatic stress disturbances (e.g., flashbacks, reexperiencing of the trauma) and dissociation.

MACI assessment of child abuse can utilize interpretation of Scale H at two levels: at the full-scale level using BR scores and at the individual item level. Research on the diagnostic accuracy of Scale H for identifying child abuse victims is lacking. However, a review of the item content of this scale supports a general clinical observation that Scale H appears to be sensitive in identifying an adolescent who has been the victim of abuse *when the adolescent is willing to acknowledge his or her abuse;* the scale appears to be sensitive to both recent and past abuse. The major focus of Scale H items appears to be measurement of an adolescent's current subjective concerns about abuse that may have occurred at some time in the past.

Of the 24 items making up Scale H, only five have content that deals with actual child abuse. These items are listed on Table 10.2, and it is important to recognize several characteristics associated with them. First, one will notice that each of these items asks about abuse that may have occurred in the past. Items ask about something that was done to the adolescent "as a child"

Table 10.2
MACI Items with Child Abuse Content

14. I feel pretty shy telling people about how I was abused as a child. (T)
55. I don't think I was sexually molested when I was a young child. (F)
72. I hate to think about some of the ways I was abused as a child. (T)
129. I'm ashamed of some terrible things adults did to me when I was young. (T)
137. People did things to me sexually when I was too young to understand. (T)

or when he or she was "young." Therefore, the focus of Scale H items appears to be abuse that occurred in the past. A second aspect of the items in Table 10.2 is that some ask about sexual abuse (Items 55 and 137), whereas others refer to general or nonspecific abuse (Items 14, 72, and 129). Therefore, Scale H is designed to measure general themes of abuse as well as sexual abuse in particular. Furthermore, the five items in Table 10.2 represent all the prototypic items for Scale H; however, it is theoretically possible for an adolescent to endorse all five items in the scored direction and still not obtain a clinically significant BR score elevation on the scale. If all five items were endorsed, this would contribute 15 raw score points (3 points × 5 items) to Scale H. For all BR score conversion tables, this raw score value results in a BR score that is below a score of 75, assuming that no secondary or tertiary items are endorsed and no profile adjustments are made. Although this pattern may be rare, the example highlights the need for MACI users to survey the responses to these five items for possible child abuse themes, since an adolescent may feel more comfortable admitting a history of abuse on an impersonal self-report instrument than during a face-to-face clinical interview.

ASSESSING PERSONALITY DISORDERS

The diagnosis of personality disorders in adolescents is a clinical issue that has been marked with controversy and confusion. According to *DSM-IV* (American Psychiatric Association, 1994), personality *traits* are "enduring patterns of perceiving, relating to and thinking about the environment and oneself that are exhibited in a wide range of social and personal contexts" (p. 630); when traits become "inflexible and maladaptive and cause significant functional impairment or subjective distress" (p. 630) they are said to constitute personality *disorders.* The *DSM-IV* notes that personality disorder diagnoses can be applied to adolescents in unusual instances where maladaptive personality traits are particularly pervasive and are not limited to the distinct developmental pressures of adolescence. Therefore, the *DSM-IV* provides that the features of a personality disorder must be present for one year before a personality disorder diagnosis can be made in a person under the age of 18; antisocial personality disorder, by definition, cannot be made in persons under this age.

A major reason for the controversy surrounding personality disorder diagnoses in adolescents has to do with the long-term stability of these diagnoses in adolescent populations. On the one hand, a body of literature supports the fact that personality disorder diagnoses can be made in adolescents with a fairly good degree of interrater reliability (Johnson et al., 1995; Marton et al., 1989). Moreover, the work of Johnson and her colleagues has shown patterns of avoidant and borderline personality disorder in the families of adolescents with these personality disorders, supporting the validity of such diagnoses in teenagers. However, major issues arise when long-term stability of personality disorder diagnoses is examined in adolescents. Several researchers have found that rates of personality disorder were lower in young adults who had been previously given a personality disorder diagnosis in adolescence (Mattanah, Becker, Levy, Edell, & McGlashan, 1995; Rey, Morris-Yates, Singh, Andrews, & Stewart, 1995).

In light of this research, it would seem that a personality disorder diagnosis may be warranted in some cases where the adolescent's functioning has been impaired by persistent and pervasive maladaptive personality traits, whereas in other cases an adolescent's maladaptive traits may lack the long-term stability required for a personality disorder diagnosis. The MACI is based on a theoretical model that recognizes these problems because the Personality Patterns scales have names reflecting an intermediate level of severity between normal personality variants and definite *DSM-IV* personality disorders. Thus, Scale 5 is labeled Egotistic, rather than confident (the normal variant) or narcissistic (the personality disorder), as an intermediate level of severity. Moreover, unlike the adult version of the Millon inventories, the MCMI-III, the MACI manual does not report specific diagnostic classification statistics such as sensitivity, specificity, positive predictive power, and negative predictive power. The lack of attention given to diagnostic classification statistics underscores the need to exercise caution when using the MACI as a strict diagnostic measure of personality disorders. On the other hand, it is unfortunate that such diagnostic efficiency statistics are unavailable from the standpoint that clinicians cannot establish the likelihood of a MACI interpretive report diagnosis being accurate, and those working in settings where such statistics are useful (e.g., forensic consultation) must rely on other sources of information.

Nevertheless, personality disorder diagnoses in adolescents are permissible (with the exception of antisocial personality disorder), so long as they are made judiciously and cautiously. Moreover, the MACI can be useful for informing the diagnostic process to determine whether a personality style is present in a particular adolescent. However, the MACI will be of greatest assistance for helping to generate hypotheses for further investigation or to confirm or disconfirm hypotheses generated from other sources such as collateral informants, structured interviews, and the psychosocial history.

SUBSTANCE ABUSE

There is a high prevalence rate of substance abuse disturbances among both community and clinical populations of adolescents (Greenbaum,

Prange, Friedman, & Silver, 1991; Reinherz, Giaconia, Lefkowitz, Padis, & Frost, 1993). The significance of this problem in adolescent populations makes it important to have some means of assessing potential substance abuse problems in clinical settings. On the MACI, Scale BB is the major scale for evaluation of substance abuse problems.

Aside from data provided in the MACI manual, there is independent support for the validity of Scale BB as a measure of substance abuse and the use of the MACI for evaluating adolescents with substance abuse problems. Grilo, Fehon, Walker, and Martino (1996) compared MACI scores of adolescent inpatients with and without substance use disorders. Diagnoses were assigned using *DSM-III-R* criteria and were based on consensus agreement of a multidisciplinary treatment staff. There were no differences on age, grade level, gender, ethnicity, or global assessment of functioning between adolescents with substance use disorders ($n = 44$) and those without substance use disorders ($n = 61$). Nor were there differences between the two groups with respect to depressive or anxiety disorder diagnoses; however, there were significantly more disruptive behavior disorder diagnoses in the group of adolescents with substance use disorders. Grilo and his colleagues found independent support for the validity of Scale BB in that the substance use disorder group scored significantly higher on Scale BB than the nonsubstance use disorder group. More importantly, the mean BR score for the substance use disorder group was in the clinically significant range (mean BR = 75.8), whereas the mean BR score for the nonsubstance use disorder group was in the average range (mean BR = 50.9).

Other significant differences were also found by Grilo and colleagues (1996) between adolescents with and without substance use disorders. There was evidence of significantly greater externalizing behaviors in adolescents with substance use disorders. In particular, this group scored significantly higher on Scales 6A, 6B, E, BB, and CC. The nonsubstance use disorders group scored significantly higher on Scales 2A, 3, D, and EE, reflecting greater anxiety, submissiveness, and inhibited personality traits. In light of the diagnostic differences between the two groups, the MACI was able to accurately reflect the higher levels of disruptive behavior disturbances in the substance-abusing adolescent group.

In actual clinical practice, the MACI user is faced with having to interpret Scale BB results in light of information obtained from the adolescent's history and clinical presentation. When assessing substance abuse problems, it is extremely important to have collateral information about the adolescent's substance use patterns from independent sources such as parents, school records, or other independent sources. In addition, the clinician should conduct a detailed interview to evaluate the patterns and associated problems of the adolescent's substance use. Together, the clinical interview and collateral information form a critical piece of data in establishing the possible presence of a substance abuse problem. In addition, the clinician has the results from Scale BB on the MACI as another piece of important data.

The adolescent's history of substance use and Scale BB results can be analyzed to help answer questions the clinician may have about the MACI results. Table 10.3 provides a standard 2 × 2 diagnostic table in which Scale BB elevations are compared against the history. There is likely to be very little concern when there is agreement between Scale BB results and the clinical data. When Scale BB is elevated and the history reveals evidence of a substance abuse problem, the MACI results represent a true positive—the test results confirm the history that the adolescent has a problem with substance abuse. When Scale BB is not elevated and the history does not reveal any potential substance abuse problems, the MACI results represent a true negative—the test results confirm the history that the adolescent does not have a problem with substance abuse.

The interpretive challenges arise when the results from Scale BB do not match with what has been uncovered from collateral interviews and the history. In Table 10.3, this inconsistency is represented by either a false negative (i.e., Scale BB is not elevated when the history suggests that it should be) or false positive (i.e., Scale BB is elevated and the history reveals that it should not be). There are some strategies to help make sense of these conflicting results.

Before outlining these strategies, it may be useful to first discuss why false negative and false positive Scale BB results might occur. False negative Scale BB results might arise when the adolescent denies substance abuse on self-report instruments and the collateral sources have independently verified problems with substance use. Another potential reason for false negative Scale BB results is that the adolescent, although willing to admit *some* substance use, minimizes the extent or severity of the problem by endorsing a few items on Scale BB but the number has been insufficient to elevate Scale BB into the clinical range. An alternative reason for a false negative result on Scale BB is that the adolescent's self-reports are accurate and the collateral sources have provided speculative, biased, or inaccurate perceptions as to the adolescent's substance abuse. Parents

Table 10.3
Diagnostic Decision Table for MACI Scale BB

History of Substance Abuse	Scale BB Clinically Elevated	
	Yes	No
Yes	True Positive	False Negative
No	False Positive	True Negative

sometimes attribute erratic behavior in their teenagers to substance abuse because it represents an obvious excuse; for example, some parents have said during collateral interviews, "My kid must be using drugs because he never acted this way before." On further questioning, the parents are unable to provide concrete examples where they have observed substance abuse in their child. In this latter example, the problem lies with the clinical criterion against which Scale BB is compared and thus the MACI results reflect the more accurate finding.

There are several reasons for obtaining false positive results on Scale BB as well. One possibility is that the adolescent has endorsed most of the secondary and tertiary items on the scale that reflect such problems as impulsivity, conduct problems, and sensation seeking; however, some of the face valid substance abuse items are not endorsed. In this case, there may nevertheless be modest Scale BB elevations in the clinically significant range that reflect these secondary characteristics rather than active substance use. Another reason for a false positive finding on Scale BB is that the elevation may represent an adolescent who is prone to substance abuse but who is not actively using drugs or alcohol. Clinical experiences have revealed that some adolescents who have been raised in families where heavy substance abuse was present or where there was exposure to adults who had a substance-abusing lifestyle will score high on Scale BB even if they do not use drugs or alcohol. These elevations can be interpreted as representing heightened risk for future substance abuse and would suggest that ongoing monitoring of substance use patterns would be part of the treatment plan. Finally, another reason for false positive results on Scale BB would be a poorly informed collateral source. In these cases, the adolescent is willing to admit substance abuse, whereas the clinical history was unable to reveal any potential problems.

In light of the reasons for potential conflict between Scale BB results and the clinical history, the clinician can employ some strategies to resolve any suspected inconsistencies that may arise. An important step is to carefully scrutinize the reliability and accuracy of the collateral information. It would be important to make sure that reports of substance abuse problems are based not on speculation but on specific examples. A second useful strategy is to examine the face valid prototypic items on Scale BB to determine the extent to which scores comprise face valid items. In Table 10.4, the 10 MACI items that make up the Scale BB prototypic items and that represent all the face valid substance abuse items on the test are listed. Both drug and alcohol abuse are represented in the content of Scale BB items: five of the items (8, 40, 75, 120, and 134) deal with drug abuse, and five of the items (22, 30, 57, 90, and 152) deal with alcohol abuse. When the clinician suspects that Scale BB results do not match the clinical presentation, an examination of the individual responses from

Table 10.4
MACI Substance Abuse Items

---

8. I would never use drugs, no matter what.

22. Drinking seems to have been a problem for several members of my family.

30. When I have a few drinks I feel more sure of myself.

40. I used to get so stoned that I did not know what I was doing.

57. I can hold my beer or liquor better than most of my friends.

75. I've gone through periods when I smoked pot several times a week.

90. Drinking really seems to help me when I'm feeling down.

120. There have been times when I could not get through the day without some pot.

134. I used to try hard drugs to see what effect they'd have.

152. When we're having a good time, my friends and I can get pretty drunk.

---

these 10 items may be undertaken to determine the number of items the adolescent has or has not endorsed. This approach can be useful for helping to establish whether the adolescent is responding to the face valid questions that pertain to substance abuse.

PSYCHOSIS

The presence of psychotic symptoms in an adolescent reflects serious impairment in psychological functioning. The reasons for an adolescent developing psychotic symptoms (e.g., confused thinking, delusional thought content, hallucinations, and disorganized behavior) include heavy substance abuse, acute stress reactions, and development of chronic mental illness such as schizophrenia. Regardless of the specific reasons for the presence of psychosis in an adolescent, one of the limitations of the MACI is that it does not have a specific scale for measuring psychotic symptoms. Therefore, other assessment procedures such as structured interviews, collateral reports, the Rorschach, and the MMPI-A are more useful for evaluating these symptoms directly.

Nevertheless, the MACI has some useful applications in the assessment of psychotic adolescents. The two most significant applications are measuring specific impairment in personality functioning associated with psychosis and the adolescent's subjective experience of his or her illness.

Specific disturbances in psychological functioning are associated with many forms of psychosis such as schizophrenia. For example, the negative symptoms of schizophrenia involve such features as emotional flattening, interpersonal isolation, and a lack of motivation (Andreasen, 1985; Andreasen & Flaum, 1991). These features are represented in the detached personality styles, including schizoid and avoidant types, that have a theoretical connection to schizophrenia (Millon & Davis, 1994), since severely decompensated detached personalities are more prone to develop schizophrenic symptomatology. Therefore, Scales 1 and 2A on the MACI can measure the negative symptoms of emotional flattening, social withdrawal and isolation, and lack of motivation. Moreover, Scales E (Peer Insecurity) and EE (Anxious Feelings) may reflect associated features of psychosis, including psychomotor agitation and interpersonal hypersensitivity. It is extremely important to note, however, that these scales are not diagnostic signs of psychosis. Rather, they can clarify the nature of pathology present once the diagnosis of psychosis has been confirmed from other sources.

The MACI also can provide some assessment of the psychotic adolescent's subjective experience or reaction to serious forms of psychopathology. Some adolescents with psychotic symptoms may have serious confusion about their identity and future direction, in which case Scales A and B may be elevated. Other adolescents experiencing psychosis may have poor behavioral controls and will lash out unexpectedly, in which case Scales F and DD may show some elevations. Many chronic schizophrenic or severely disabled adolescents may come to view themselves as overly dependent on the mental health system, parents, or other supports to provide structure in their lives. Repeated hospitalizations and failure at conventional roles may result in the adolescent having a poor self-image in which he or she feels inept at functioning more independently. Scales 3, 8B, or B may reflect these concerns; chronically disturbed adolescents sometimes yield an elevation in which one or more of these scales constitute the major profile configuration.

The MACI must not be used as the major assessment tool for establishing a diagnosis of psychosis since this type of pathology is not represented in the array of MACI scales. Other assessment techniques must be used to evaluate this more severe form of psychopathology. Nevertheless, the MACI may provide useful information on associated features such as particular areas of personality dysfunction or the adolescent's subjective experiences resulting from chronic mental illness.

SUMMARY

The test of any psychodiagnostic assessment instrument's utility lies in the extent to which it can provide clinically useful information in varied settings and with diverse diagnostic groups. In this chapter, application of the MACI to a variety of settings and diagnostic issues is discussed. The

MACI is reviewed in terms of its use in evaluating suicide risk, disruptive behavior disorders, adolescents with learning disabilities, child abuse, personality disorders, substance abuse, and psychosis. Scales are discussed with respect to specific issues and strategies for using both BR scores and individual item responses. For many applications, the MACI will be of most use for evaluating the adolescent's subjective experiences as well as his or her reaction to individual stressors or conditions. In a few cases, such as substance abuse, child abuse, and suicide risk, the MACI has some potential uses in identifying potential problems, particularly when the test is interpreted at the item level. However, more independent research is needed to evaluate the full spectrum of applications the MACI may have in clinical settings.

CHAPTER 11

Treatment Planning with the MACI

ONE OF the goals of clinical assessment is to have a practical understanding of the problems that brought a particular individual to the attention of the mental health professional. The identification of specific symptoms and the formulation of a diagnosis are among the major products of assessment. In clinical settings, however, the enumeration of symptoms and the deriving of a specific diagnosis are only intermediate steps. The assessment process should naturally lead to treatment and disposition planning. Another critical decision is the specific interventions to be utilized. Diagnosis offers little direction if the sole purpose of rendering one is to describe the individual's symptomatology. Linking diagnosis to treatment and disposition planning maximizes the true value of psychological testing.

Another criticism of diagnosis that has arisen in the past is that it does little to inform the treatment process. At one time, it seemed as though regardless of the presenting symptomatology, a patient was evaluated and the clinician began a course of treatment based more on his or her training and experience and less on the specific needs of the patient. Thus, one clinician might use a long-term, psychoanalytic oriented therapy with his or her patients or another would opt for behavioral conditioning and so on. In recent years, however, there has been considerable progress in the area of psychotherapy integration. This movement is based not on eclecticism where only bits and pieces of one form of therapy are borrowed and used but on true therapy integration that examines how different treatment approaches can complement one another.

The integrative theoretical model of personality and psychopathology developed by Millon offers a useful framework for conceptualizing treatment planning. As documented in a book by Retzlaff (1995), the domain-oriented approach to personality permits the integration of different forms of psychotherapy. Recall that Millon organizes personality around eight domains: expressive acts, interpersonal conduct, cognitive style, object representations, self-image, regulatory mechanisms, morphologic organization, and mood/temperament. In addition to providing comprehensive coverage of personality functioning, these eight domains also represent different aspects of the person that are specific targets of change in various kinds of psychotherapy. As Table 11.1 illustrates, each domain can be targeted by a specific technique or approach to psychotherapy. For example, expressive acts may be targeted using specific behavior therapy techniques such as assertiveness training, counterconditioning, or social skills training. Although the domain approach to conceptualizing the level at which a particular method of psychotherapy is directed, the domain model also serves as a nice framework for thinking about how a team-oriented approach to treatment operates. For example, the psychiatrist who prescribes medication to a difficult borderline patient is directing change at the biophysical level of mood/temperament, while the individual psychotherapist may be using a cognitive-behavioral approach at the phenomenological level of cognitive style and the behavioral level of expressive acts.

Table 11.1
Therapeutic Interventions Targeting Specific Personality Domains

Personality Domain	Relevant Therapeutic Approach
Behavioral Level	
Expressive acts	Behavior therapy; conditioning
Interpersonal conduct	Group, marital, family, or interpersonal therapy
Phenomenological Level	
Cognitive style	Cognitive-behavioral therapy; rational-emotive therapy
Object representations	Object relations therapy
Self-image	Psychoanalytic self-psychology; client-centered therapy
Intrapsychic Level	
Regulatory mechanisms	Ego analysis; psychoanalytic psychotherapy
Morphologic organization	Psychoanalysis; psychoanalytic psychotherapy
Biophysical Level	
Mood/Temperament	Psychopharmacological treatment; relaxation training; experiential therapy

As an adjunct to treatment, group therapy may address problems in the interpersonal conduct domain.

The domain-oriented approach to conceptualizing personality can help direct treatment in many ways. It can be used to guide MACI interpretation in the development of practical and effective treatment plans. This chapter outlines how the MACI can be used in treatment planning. The organization of this presentation is based on the three major sets of scales on the MACI profile: Personality Patterns, Expressed Concerns, and Clinical Syndromes. However, the most useful approach to treatment planning involves an appraisal of these three sets of scales in reverse order. When the MACI scales are to be used for treatment planning, the clinician should start with the Clinical Syndromes scales first, followed by the Expressed Concerns scales, and finally the Personality Patterns scales.

The rationale for this approach is based on the data in each section of the MACI profile. Each of the Clinical Syndromes scales provides information on clinical symptoms that can have adverse consequences for the adolescent's immediate well-being. Therefore, the approach outlined here recommends that the Clinical Syndromes scales be used first to prioritize treatment interventions and recommendations for disposition. Once an approach to treatment is begun, the Expressed Concerns scales can help position the therapist as to the salient issues the adolescent finds most troubling. These scales are a gauge of the teenager's phenomenological experiences as to what he or she finds troubling, whether or not external reality supports problems in these areas. The Expressed Concerns scales can guide development of a working relationship by suggesting topics the adolescent may be willing to discuss. Finally, the Personality Patterns scales indicate the major disruptions in functioning that are likely to be manifest and can help position the therapist once again to target treatment in the domain in which there is the greatest level of disturbance.

The following recommendations are based on the assumption that the MACI profile is valid for the specific case. That is, the Modifier Indices have been analyzed and response biases, if present, are not of sufficient intensity as to invalidate the test results. Additionally, it is assumed that the MACI profile, even if technically valid, does not represent one of the less common poor-fit profiles discussed in Chapter 9. To use the MACI properly when developing treatment plans, the test results must be reliable and valid.

CLINICAL SYNDROMES SCALES: PRIORITIZING INTERVENTIONS

The Clinical Syndromes scales are a useful place to begin treatment planning with the MACI because the difficulties assessed by these scales can potentially have a severe impact on the adolescent's functioning and they often require close scrutiny. As such, these scales can be used to prioritize treatment interventions. In Table 11.2, the Clinical Syndromes scales have been listed in order of decreasing priority. This listing is based primarily on the relative level of threat to the adolescent's physical well-being and treatment interventions are thus based accordingly.

An elevation on Scale GG takes highest priority because it reflects suicidal tendencies which raise the possibility of a life-threatening situation. As noted in Chapter 10, Scale GG cannot be used to predict suicidal behavior. Nevertheless, when this scale is elevated, clinical interventions should be directed at the targeted problem of suicidal behavior first. One approach may merely be to assess the level of suicidal risk more thoroughly to determine the relative level of intent, planning, and access to lethal means. Other treatment interventions may include increasing the frequency of outpatient sessions, involving family supports, crisis and supportive interventions, and contracting with the adolescent around suicide issues. In some cases, more intrusive interventions may be warranted, such as acute inpatient hospitalization to resolve the immediate risk factors for suicide. Scale GG elevations suggest high priority for further assessment and acute treatment interventions to resolve life-threatening factors.

The next level of priority is an elevation on either Scale AA or BB. These two scales measure clinical symptoms associated with appetitive disturbances such as eating disorders and substance abuse. The risks associated with these conditions involve physical or medical damage that can result from not eating, bingeing and purging, or abusing drugs and alcohol. If these problems continue over time, then the physical and medical complications can, in some instances, become life threatening (e.g., metabolic problems from starving one's self; drug overdose). An elevation on either of these scales should direct the clinician to examine the severity of the clinical symptoms and their impact on the adolescent. In addition, a referral for

Table 11.2
Prioritization of Interventions Using the Clinical Syndromes Scales

Scale	Level of Priority	Implication
1. GG	Very High	Possibly life-threatening
2. AA and BB	High	Physical and medical risks; possibly life threatening if severe or chronic
3. EE and FF	Moderate–High	Psychic discomfort; impairs functioning if severe
4. CC and DD	Moderate	Behavioral controls weak; episodic; can lead to restrictions on freedom; tends to be chronic

medical consultation may also be indicated to make sure any physical conditions are being treated properly. Psychological treatment recommendations may also include referral to specialized programs such as inpatient eating disorders units, alcohol or drug detoxification, or residential substance abuse treatment. These treatment programs may be undertaken concurrently with individual psychotherapy as an adjunct intervention or may be administered first before addressing long-term characterological issues.

Elevations on Scales EE and FF are considered to be at a moderate to high level of priority. These scales represent psychic discomfort in the form of anxiety and depression that can be mild to moderate symptoms associated with other disturbances or they may represent more severe symptoms of a primary anxiety or mood disorder. The major impact of these symptoms can range from modest impairment in functioning, such as difficulty concentrating or discomfort in certain situations, to more severe disruptions, such as social withdrawal or an inability to perform academically. Therefore, interventions may range from supportive psychotherapy and targeted problem-solving to referrals for medication and specific treatments for anxiety or depression (e.g., cognitive-behavioral therapy; interpersonal therapy). Typically, these symptoms are not immediately threatening to the adolescent's physical integrity unless they are associated with suicidal risk, eating disorders, or substance abuse. However, symptoms such as anxiety, sleep impairment, or appetite suppression can be severe and may require pharmacological intervention.

Finally, elevations on Scales CC and DD can be viewed as reflecting a moderate level of severity and therefore fall last in the priority levels listed in Table 11.2. These two scales reflect poor behavioral controls and are generally associated with characterological disturbances that can lead to restrictions of the adolescent's freedom. Moreover, these clinical difficulties tend to be chronic and may require structured interventions such as group home or residential placement. In other cases, legal provisions may mandate outpatient treatment as part of probation.

A special note is necessary about Scale DD (Impulsive Propensity). Although this scale is placed with Scale CC at the bottom of the prioritization listed in Table 11.2, this was done because Scales CC and DD are often elevated together. However, Scale DD elevations may suggest higher levels of priority if the adolescent's impulsivity involves behaviors that are more risky or dangerous. For example, if Scale DD was also elevated along with Scale GG, this would reflect suicidal tendencies associated with impulsivity, thus requiring very high priority being given to the adolescent's lethality risk. Likewise, impulsive behavior that involves quasi-suicidal behavior without clear suicidal intent (e.g., playing Russian roulette for fun; playing "chicken" on railroad tracks) would also raise the level of priority given to Scale DD elevations. The clinician must exercise clinical judgment that includes consideration of the complete behavioral presentation. The priorities given to the Clinical Syndromes scales in Table 11.2 are meant to serve as general guidelines and not as a strict decision-tree that must be followed in each and every case.

EXPRESSED CONCERNS SCALES:
BUILDING RAPPORT

As noted, the Expressed Concerns scales of the MACI serve as measures of the specific difficulties or concerns *as the adolescent sees them, not as external reality might suggest.* Therefore, these eight scales represent measures of the phenomenological experiences of the teenager and may thus be viewed as a representation of what the adolescent is willing to admit as being problematic in his or her life.

Because of the nature of these scales, adolescents are usually willing to admit there are problems in a particular area of their life when an Expressed Concerns scale is elevated for that particular problem. For example, if Scale G (Family Discord) is elevated, the adolescent is likely to agree that things are not good at home if the clinician asks about this issue. Likewise, an elevation on Scale D (Sexual Discomfort), generally means that the adolescent is willing to admit that he or she has some concerns about sexual issues.

On the other hand, when any of the Expressed Concerns scales are not elevated, two possible meanings can be attributed to the MACI results. Of course, one possibility is that the adolescent does not experience a problem in that area. A low score on Scale A or C, for example, may mean that the adolescent does not have concerns about his or her identity or body image, respectively. Another possible meaning of a low score on the Expressed Concerns scales is that the adolescent does not see or will not admit to a particular issue being problematic, even if there are problems in that area. An adolescent with a history of using others and acting-out in an unempathic fashion may not have elevated Scale F (Social Insensitivity) because he or she does not see the behavior as something about which there should be any concern.

Consequently, the Expressed Concerns scales can be useful as a starting point in therapy for developing rapport with the adolescent. A working alliance is more likely to build if adolescent and therapist have areas of agreement where productive discussions can occur. The adolescent is likely to feel understood and accepted if the therapist asks about problems that are meaningful to the teenager. Confrontation about problems the adolescent is unwilling to discuss or admit is likely to dampen efforts at a working relationship, especially in the initial phases of psychotherapy. The following case example illustrates these issues in greater detail.

A female adolescent was referred for treatment after her oppositional and defiant behaviors at home began to escalate. She was extremely non-compliant and verbally abusive to her parents and sister and her grades had been declining over several months. As her psychosocial history was being taken, it was learned that she had been sexually assaulted by a man in her neighborhood and that she had refused to tell anyone but her mother. On the MACI Expressed Concerns scales, she had an elevation on Scales F (Social Insensitivity) and G (Family Discord). One might have expected elevations on Scales D (Sexual Discomfort), B (Self-Devaluation), and perhaps H (Childhood Abuse), given the history and clinical presentation. Indeed, her mother provided support during collateral interviews that these areas were problematic. However, the adolescent was very resistant to discussing her sexual assault with the therapist. Therefore, she was initially given feedback about her MACI profile, particularly the elevations on Scales F and G. She admitted that she sometimes found herself being "too hard" on her sister and mother and she also saw her father as insensitive and aloof, thus explaining the elevation on Scale G. These issues became the initial focus of therapy, and the sexual assault issues were set aside during this phase. Focusing only on those issues, she was willing to discuss and not pressing her to talk about those issues she did not want to address, facilitated the therapeutic alliance, and the sexual assault issues were addressed once she felt ready to deal with them.

This example illustrates how the Expressed Concerns scales can be used to find common areas of discussion between adolescent and therapist. The real challenging cases involve those in which clear problems brought the adolescent in for treatment but there is a low level of disclosure on the MACI and no Expressed Concerns scales are elevated. Usually, these adolescents project blame onto others, such as family members or teachers and this can usually be viewed as a starting point. It is sometimes useful to acknowledge that the adolescent does not see him- or herself as having any problems. However, it is sometimes productive to ask the adolescent what others might say about the reasons for the teenager's referral for therapy.

PERSONALITY PATTERNS SCALES: IDENTIFYING SALIENT PATHOLOGY

The Personality Patterns scales provide information on the adolescent's consistent pattern of thoughts, emotions, behavior, and ways of relating to others that are relatively stable and serve functional purposes of helping the adolescent cope. There are two major approaches to using these scales in treatment planning. One approach is to help position the therapist in directing therapeutic interventions in a way that the adolescent is most likely to accept. Psychotherapy is an interpersonal process in which the adolescent's salient personality traits will be manifest. Therefore, certain interventions are either more or less likely to be accepted by the adolescent depending on his or her personality; for example, empathic understanding and accurate mirroring of feelings will be more effective with the grandiose egotistic adolescent than would confrontation. The second approach to using the Personality Patterns scales is to identify the more salient domains of disturbance that an adolescent is likely to be expressing. Everly (1995) has outlined the most prominent disturbances in personality domains that are manifest for specific personality disorders. Using Everly's approach, the MACI Personality Patterns scales can identify areas of disturbance that may be most problematic. The most salient pathology for a specific personality style is not necessarily the area of most disturbance; rather, salient pathology reflects the types of disturbances that are most readily apparent in the adolescent's functioning.

A complete discussion of treatment planning with the Millon inventories is beyond the scope of this chapter. An excellent source is the text by Retzlaff (1995) that outlines a tactical approach to treating personality disorders using Millon's domain-oriented approach to personality with the MCMI-III. This section includes a brief discussion of how each Personality Patterns scale on the MACI may be used for treatment planning. This discussion is derived from the work of Everly (1995) and Retzlaff. For a more detailed discussion of the domain-oriented approach to treatment planning using Millon's theory, the reader is encouraged to consult these works.

SCALE 1 (INTROVERSIVE)

The most salient disturbances reflected in Scale 1 elevations are in the domains of mood/temperament and interpersonal conduct. Therefore, treatment may need to be directed at the apathetic mood and unengaged interpersonal behavior that the adolescent will manifest. From a treatment perspective, the adolescent may be hard to engage because there is little motivation to change and a lack of interest in relating to others, including the therapist. Regular and dependable contact with the adolescent may help to foster a connection with the therapist. It is likely to be very difficult to engage the introversive adolescent in group therapy.

SCALE 2A (INHIBITED)

The alienated self-image of the inhibited teenager is one of the most salient areas of disturbance. The adolescent expects criticism and rejection and withdraws socially to avoid the discomfort of rejection. Clarification and empathic understanding tend to work well because these techniques minimize the likelihood that the adolescent will feel judged or criticized by the therapist. As a therapeutic alliance is built, the therapist may then work with the adolescent to introduce other interventions, such as group therapy or cognitive-behavioral treatment of social phobic symptoms that can change the feelings of alienation.

Scale 2B (Doleful)

Chronic feelings of melancholia, hopelessness, and pessimism characterize the doleful adolescent, and elevations on Scale 2B reflect mood/ temperament as the most salient pathology. The major clinical difficulties that need to be addressed include chronic depression such as a dysthymia or depressive personality. Use of medication to treat targeted symptoms of depression may be useful. Cognitive-behavioral therapy for depression and interpersonal therapy are also recommended approaches for individual psychotherapy.

Scale 3 (Submissive)

The most salient clinical pathology revealed by Scale 3 elevations is in the domain of interpersonal conduct. The adolescent's submissiveness and excessive need for reassurance and guidance are likely to lead to underachievement and an inability to function more autonomously. Treatment can thus be directed at encouraging more independence and efficacy at making decisions for one's self. This treatment can involve focused problem-solving, group and family therapy, and insight-oriented approaches.

Scale 4 (Dramatizing)

Disturbed interpersonal conduct tends to be the most salient domain of pathology represented in Scale 4 elevations. The adolescent is attention-seeking and actively manipulates others and situations to get attention and approval. In treatment, the dramatizing adolescent is likely to engage quickly because therapy provides attention. However, important topics are often avoided or denied, and in group treatment the adolescent is likely to monopolize the conversation. The goals of treatment should thus include developing more appropriate methods for seeking attention and gently raising the adolescent's awareness of how his or her behavior affects others.

Scale 5 (Egotistic)

The most salient domain of pathology represented in Scale 5 elevations is likely to be the grandiose and admirable self-image the adolescent has of him- or herself. Because there is a need for praise and special treatment, confrontational approaches in psychotherapy are not likely to work well. Also, interpretation and other attempts at increasing insight are likely to be ineffective. The admirable self-image requires mirroring and empathic understanding to facilitate the working alliance, and the therapist is likely to feel as though he or she is in a constant struggle to earn the adolescent's respect. In group treatment, the egotistic adolescent will tend to distance him- or herself from the group and will feel above the other members.

Scale 6A (Unruly)

Disturbances in expressive acts and cognitive style are the major domains of pathology for unruly adolescents. Thus, Scale 6A elevations will point to impulsivity and deviant attitudes as the major areas of focus for treatment. Antisocial personality disturbances are among the most difficult to treat. With adolescents, the focus will need to be on focused strategies for changing impulsive acting-out and modifying deviant attitudes. Behavioral and cognitive-behavioral strategies may be useful, as would structured interventions such as court mandated compliance with treatment or residential placement to structure the adolescent's environment.

Scale 6B (Forceful)

The most salient disturbances revealed by Scale 6B elevations are likely to be in the domain of mood/temperament and interpersonal conduct. The adolescent is characterized as hostile and abrasive and derives satisfaction from intimidating, coercing, or humiliating others. These factors create several impediments to treatment and Scale 6B elevations have been observed in clinical practice to be one of the strongest negative treatment indicators on the MACI. Therapeutic interventions are likely to be met with a resistant or combative stance. Structured interventions such as residential placement have been shown to provide regular opportunities for confrontation and targeted problem-solving that may have some impact.

Scale 7 (Conforming)

A constricted cognitive style is the most salient domain of pathology that is reflected in Scale 7 elevations on the MACI. The adolescent tends to be rigid and stubborn, and in some cases there is denial and minimization of problems. If the adolescent has some psychological strengths, such as good stress tolerance or average intelligence, the use of confrontation may be useful. Also, cognitive therapy strategies that point out the evidence for specific problems in the teenager's life may also prove helpful.

SCALE 8A (OPPOSITIONAL)

The most salient domains of disturbance reflected in Scale 8A elevations are self-image and interpersonal conduct. The adolescent sees him- or herself as discontented, and in relationships there are prominent contrary and oppositional behaviors. Treatment goals would therefore reflect the need to develop a more balanced and stable self-image and alternative problem-solving strategies that are less oppositional and more adaptive. The use of assertiveness training and focused problem-solving are likely to be of benefit in achieving these goals.

SCALE 8B (SELF-DEMEANING)

An undeserving self-image and dysphoric mood are the major pathological domains represented in Scale 8B elevations on the MACI. The adolescent will exhibit guilt, unhappiness, and self-debasing attitudes; treatment goals should thus reflect the need for change in these areas. Pharmacological treatment may be warranted if depression is a major aspect of the presentation. Also, cognitive-behavioral treatment and group therapy may be useful for gently challenging the adolescent's distorted view of the self. Cognitive distortions about the self may also be pointed out in a gentle fashion.

SCALE 9 (BORDERLINE TENDENCIES)

The most salient domains of disturbance revealed in Scale 9 elevations are mood/temperament and interpersonal conduct. The adolescent will display a labile mood in which there is much instability and a lack of predictability to emotional presentation. Also, the adolescent will engage in paradoxical and highly changeable behaviors in relationships. Treatment goals should reflect the need for greater stability in mood and more stable and adaptive interpersonal behavior. Specific interventions may include pharmacological agents, long-term psychodynamic psychotherapy, and cognitive-behavioral strategies aimed at specific symptoms such as self-injurious behavior and periods of depression or anxiety.

SUMMARY

The MACI is useful for assessing clinical problems and concerns in adolescence and for providing insight into the personality dynamics that underlie diagnostic issues in adolescents who present for mental health treatment. Because of the underlying theory on which the MACI is based, test results can be conceptualized and applied in many ways to the clinical task of treatment planning. This chapter uses three of the major sections of the MACI profile to organize an approach to treatment planning. The Clinical Syndromes scales are viewed as a way of prioritizing treatment interventions and to assist in recognizing specific clinical problems that may require more immediate attention. The Expressed Concerns scales are discussed as a useful set of data to help build rapport in therapy by identifying problems the adolescent is willing and able to recognize. Finally, the Personality Patterns scales are each reviewed individually in terms of the salient types of pathology elevations may represent; this approach may assist the clinician in identifying relevant treatment goals and suitable interventions. Overall, the MACI is useful not only as a diagnostic instrument, but also as a tool to construct an organizing framework for treatment goals and strategies.

Clinical Domains for Personality Patterns

The following tables represent descriptions that apply to the clinical domains for each personality pattern measured by the MACI. At the behavioral level are two attributes: behavioral expression and interpersonal behavior. The phenomenological level has three attributes: cognitive style, self-image, and object representations. At the intrapsychic level are two attributes: regulatory mechanism and morphologic organization. Finally, the biophysical level is represented by mood/temperament. Each of these attributes or domains is described in Chapter 1. Functional attributes are those with an (F) in front; these represent dynamic processes encompassing interactions between the person and the psychosocial environment. Structural attributes are those with an (S) in front; these represent deeply embedded and relatively enduring memories, attitudes, and conflicts that guide life experiences. In addition to describing the personality prototypes, the tables in this appendix can be used as additional interpretive guides.

Table A.1
Scale 1: Introversive

Behavioral Level:

(F)   Lethargic—low energy; lack of vitality; deficits in expressiveness and spontaneity.

(F)   Aloof—indifferent and remote; possesses minimal human interests; few close relationships.

Phenomenological Level:

(F)   Impoverished—communication is easily derailed; loses its sequence of thought or is conveyed via a circuitous logic.

(S)   Complacent—minimally introspective; impervious to emotional qualities of personal life.

(S)   Undifferentiated—experiences are poorly distinguished; percepts, memories, drives and conflicts remain blurred.

Intrapsychic Level:

(F)   Intellectualization—describes experiences in matter-of-fact, mechanical manner; attention given to formal aspects of events.

(S)   Meager—an intrapsychic barrenness exists; inner structural pattern noted best by its sterile order and limited coordination.

Biophysical Level:

(S)   Flat—weak affectionate or erotic needs; unable to experience in depth, either pleasure, sadness, or anger.

Table A.2

Scale 2A: Inhibited

Behavioral Level:

(F)   Guarded—scans environment for potential threats to security; anxiously overreacts to innocuous events.

(F)   Aversive—experiences social pain/anxiety; distrust leads to distancing; seeks acceptance but anticipates derogation.

Phenomenological Level:

(F)   Distracted—the upsurge from within of irrelevant and digressive ideation upsets thought continuity and interferes with social communications.

(S)   Alienated—sees self as isolated and rejected; devalues own achievements.

(S)   Vexatious—intense and conflict-ridden affects and memories are easily reactivated; has limited avenues of need gratification.

Intrapsychic Level:

F)   Fantasy—turns excessively to imagination; inner reveries safely discharge emotional impulses.

(S)   Fragile—inner structures comprise a precarious complex of tortuous emotions; few adaptive resources; short of fantasy escape or psychic decompensation.

Biophysical Level:

(S)   Anguished—feels constant undercurrent of tension, sadness and anger; vacillates between desires, fears and numbness.

Table A.3
Scale 2B: Doleful

Behavioral Level:

(F)   Disconsolate—forlorn, somber, heavy-hearted, dispirited, discouraged, sense of permanent hopelessness.

(F)   Defenseless—feels vulnerable, unshielded, needs other to be nurturant and protective, fears abandonment and desertion.

Phenomenological Level:

(F)   Pessimistic—defeatist, fatalistic attitudes, expects the worst, despairing of the future.

(S)   Worthless—valueless to self or others, barren, sterile, sees self as contemptible.

(S)   Forsaken—representations of past are depleted or devitalized, drained of their richness or joy.

Intrapsychic Level:

(F)   Asceticism—engages in self-denial, self-punishment, self-tormenting, believes that one should be deprived of pleasure.

(S)   Depleted—scaffold of structures is markedly weak; exhausted capacity to initiate action and regulate affect, impulse, and conflict.

Biophysical Level:

(S)   Melancholic—woeful, gloomy, tearful, joyless, morose, worrisome, low spirits.

Table A.4
Scale 3: Submissive

Behavioral Level

(F)   Incompetent—lacks functional skills; avoids self-assertion; withdraws from adult responsibilities.

(F)   Submissive—is compliant, placating, conciliatory; subordinates needs to nurturing figure.

Phenomenological Level

(F)   Naive—reveals a Pollyanna attitude toward interpersonal difficulties, watering down objective problems and smoothing over troubling events.

(S)   Inept—views self as weak, fragile, inadequate; lacks self-confidence.

(S)   Immature—unsophisticated ideas, incomplete memories, childlike impulses.

Intrapsychic Level

(F)   Introjection—firmly devoted to another; jettisons any independent view in favor of those of others.

(S)   Inchoate—marked deficits in defensive mechanisms and regulatory controls; underdeveloped adaptive capabilities.

Biophysical Level

(S)   Pacific—warm, tender, noncompetitive; timidly avoids social conflicts.

Table A.5
Scale 4: Dramatizing

Behavioral Level

(F) Affected—is overreactive; exhibits theatrical responsiveness; has penchant for excitement.

(F) Flirtatious—solicits praise, attention, and approval; is seductively exhibitionistic.

Phenomenological Level

(F) Flighty—integrates experiences poorly, resulting in scattered learning and thoughtless judgments.

(S) Sociable—views self as gregarious, stimulating, pleasure oriented, attractive, and charming.

(S) Shallow—inner world consists of superficial or insubstantial affects, memories, and conflicts.

Intrapsychic Level

(F) Dissociation—presents changing sequence of social facades; does not integrate unpleasant experiences.

(S) Disjoined—internal structures and controls are scattered and unintegrated; thoughts, feelings, and actions kept disconnected.

Biophysical Level

(S) Fickle—displays short-lived, dramatic emotions; can get enthused or angered or bored easily.

Table A.6

Scale 5: Egotistic

Behavioral Level

(F) Arrogant—flaunts conventional rules; disregards personal integrity; is indifferent to rights of others.

(F) Exploitive—feels entitled; is unempathic; takes others for granted, without reciprocating.

Phenomenological Level

(F) Expansive—is minimally constrained by objective reality; takes liberties with facts and often lies to redeem self-illusions.

(S) Admirable—confidently exhibits self; acts self-assured; displays achievements.

(S) Contrived—consists of illusory ideas and memories; values and attitudes are refashioned as need arises.

Intrapsychic Level

(F) Rationalization—is self-deceptive; justifies socially inconsiderate behaviors; offers facile alibis.

(S) Spurious—defenses are flimsy and transparent; conflicts are dismissed and failures are redeemed.

Biophysical Level

(S) Insouciant—exhibits air of nonchalance and imperturbability; is buoyantly optimistic or cooly unimpressionable.

Table A.7
Scale 6A: Unruly

Behavioral Level

(F)   Impulsive—is impetuous and restless; seems short-sighted, incautious, failing to plan or heed consequences.

(F)   Irresponsible—untrustworthy and unreliable, failing to meet obligations; engages in duplicitous or illegal behaviors.

Phenomenological Level

(F)   Deviant—is disdainful of traditional ideals and contemptuous of conventional rules.

(S)   Autonomous—enjoys and values being unfettered by social restraints and personal loyalties.

(S)   Rebellious—revengeful attitudes and restive impulses driven to subvert establishment ideals and mores.

Intrapsychic Level

(F)   Acting-Out—offensive thoughts and malevolent actions are rarely constrained; without guilt.

(S)   Unbounded—low thresholds for impulse discharge; few subliminatory channels; intolerant of frustration.

Biophysical Level

(S)   Callous—is insensitive, unempathic, coldblooded; ruthless indifference to others' welfare.

Table A.8
Scale 6B: Forceful

Behavioral Level

(F) Fearless—is attracted to challenge and risk, seems thick-skinned and undeterred by pain.

(F) Cruel—gains satisfaction in intimidating and humiliating others; is verbally abusive and physically brutal.

Phenomenological Level

(F) Dogmatic—exhibits a broad-ranging authoritarianism, social intolerance, and prejudice.

(S) Competitive—presents tough, domineering, power-oriented image.

(S) Pernicious—possesses strongly driven aggressive energies and malicious attitudes.

Intrapsychic Level

(F) Isolation—detached from impact of own destructive acts; views objects of violation impersonally.

(S) Eruptive—surging, powerful, and explosive aggressive and sexual energies overwhelm modulating controls.

Biophysical Level

(S) Hostile—exhibits excitable and pugnacious temper; is mean-spirited, fractious and persecutory.

Table A.9
Scale 7: Conforming

Behavioral Level

(F)   Disciplined—is highly regulated and perfectionistic; maintains well-organized lifestyle.

(F)   Respectful—shows unusual adherence to social conventions; is polite and formal in personal relationships.

Phenomenological Level

(F)   Constricted—constructs world in terms of rules, regulations, and schedules and hierarchies; is unimaginative, indecisive, and notably upset by unfamiliar or novel ideas and customs.

(S)   Conscientious—sees self as industrious, reliable, meticulous, and efficient.

(S)   Concealed—only socially approved affects and attitudes are allowed conscious awareness.

Intrapsychic Level

(F)   Reaction Formation—presents thoughts and behaviors diametrically opposite inner, forbidden feelings.

(S)   Compartmentalized—psychic structures are rigidly organized and partitioned into distinct constellations.

Biophysical Level

(S)   Solemn—emotions are under tight control; is unrelaxed, tense, joyless, grim.

Table A.10
Scale 8A: Oppositional

Behavioral Level

(F)   Stubborn—exhibits procrastination, inefficiency, and contrary behaviors; resists expectations and undermines pleasures of others.

(F)   Contrary—assumes conflicting and changing roles in relationships; e.g., is assertive and then acquiescent.

Phenomenological Level

(F)   Negativistic—has a misanthropic view of life, expressing disdain and caustic comments toward those experiencing good fortune.

(S)   Discontented—sees self as misunderstood and unappreciated, but also pessimistic and disgruntled.

(S)   Oppositional—possesses a mix of dissident impulses, conflicting memories and countervailing inclinations.

Intrapsychic Level

(F)   Displacement—discharges resentments by substitute means, such as acting perplexed or forgetful.

(S)   Divergent—defensive maneuvers are directed toward incompatible goals; fulfillment of one need often nullifies another.

Biophysical Level

(S)   Irritable—is touchy, resentful, petulant, and fretful; easily annoyed or frustrated by others.

Table A.11
Scale 8B: Self-Demeaning

Behavioral Level

(F) Abstinent—refrains from exhibiting pleasure or attractiveness; places self in inferior light or abject position.

(F) Deferential—is self-abasing, servile, and obsequious; accepts undeserved blame and criticism.

Phenomenological Level

(F) Inconsistent—experiences contrasting emotions and conflicting thoughts toward self and others, notably love, rage, and guilt.

(S) Undeserving—sees self as worthy of being shamed and humbled; focuses on worst personal features.

(S) Debased—possesses a complex of disparaged past memories and recently discredited achievements.

Intrapsychic Level

(F) Exaggeration—recalls past injustices and anticipates future disappointments as a means of raising distress.

(S) Inverted—reversal of pain-pleasure polarity results in undoing of affect and intention; e.g., antithetical and self-sabotaging acts.

Biophysical Level

(S) Doleful—frequently forlorn, plaintive, and mournful; appearance designed to induce guilt in others.

Table A.12
Scale 9: Borderline Tendency

Behavioral Level

(F) Precipitate—displays abrupt, endogenous shifts in drive state; show sudden, unexpected, impulsive outbursts.

(F) Paradoxical—although needing affection, is unpredictably contrary, manipulative, and volatile.

Phenomenological Level

(F) Capricious—vacillating and contradictory reactions are evoked in others by virtue of one's behaviors, creating, in turn, conflicting and confusing social feedback.

(S) Uncertain—experiences the confusions of an immature, nebulous, or wavering sense of identity.

(S) Incompatible—possesses excess of perplexing memories, enigmatic attitudes, antithetical emotions, and opposing strategies for conflict resolution.

Intrapsychic Level

(F) Regression—retreats readily to developmentally earlier levels of anxiety tolerance, impulse control, and social adaptation.

(S) Diffused—internalizations lack clarity and distinctness; permeability of boundaries blurs unrelated memories and affects.

Biophysical Level

(S) Labile—shifts from depression to excitement interspersed with spells of anger, anxiety, or euphoria.

The Effect of Item Weights on MACI Scale Elevations

The present analysis was performed to examine the impact of item weighting on relative scale elevations by examining contributions made to scores by each of the three levels of item weight: prototypic (3 raw score points), secondary (2 raw score points), and tertiary (1 raw score point). The specific questions addressed were: (1) Is it possible to obtain clinically significant scale elevations on the MACI if none of the most diagnostically significant items (i.e., prototypic) are endorsed; (2) Are prototypic items alone sufficient to yield clinically significant elevations on the MACI; and (3) Is it possible to obtain clinically significant elevations on MACI scales with secondary and tertiary items only?

To identify the item composition of each MACI scale and the relative impact various items have on BR score elevations, information contained in the MACI manual (Millon, Millon, & Davis, 1993; Appendixes B and C) was subjected to analysis to identify characteristics for each scale. Using Appendix B in the MACI manual, descriptive statistics were identified, including the number of items per scale and the number of prototypic, secondary, and tertiary items per scale. Using this information, the raw score distribution for each scale was calculated by multiplying the number of prototypic items by 3, the number of secondary items by 2, and the number of tertiary items by 1 and then summing these three values to obtain a maximum possible raw score for each scale. In addition, the raw score contribution made by each group of items to the total raw score was computed.

The first two questions to be explored were whether or not a clinically significant elevation is possible when only prototypic items are endorsed and when no prototypic items are endorsed. To answer these questions, it was necessary to convert the relative raw score contribution of each item type into base rate (BR) scores. The use of BR scores is a distinguishing feature of the MACI and represents the conversion of raw scores into a scale based on the relative prevalence rates of syndromes and concerns in the normative sample. Briefly, scores are considered clinically significant at levels of BR ≥ 75, which signifies the *presence* of a particular trait or syndrome, and BR ≥ 85, which signifies the *prominence* of a trait or syndrome.

Once the raw score contributions of the prototypic items were identified, the raw score contributions attributed to secondary and tertiary items were combined to yield the degree to which more subtle items contribute to scale elevation. To address the first two of the proposed questions, the raw score contribution due to prototypic items and the combined secondary/tertiary items were each converted into a BR score using tables in Appendix C of the MACI manual. Since there are four conversion tables corresponding to two age groups of males (13–15-year-olds and 16–19-year-olds) and two age groups of females (13–15-year-olds and 16–19-year-olds), the four BR values for a given raw score were averaged to provide a mean BR score for the BR values reported in Table B.1.

Based on this methodology, a traditional BR cutoff of 75 was utilized to determine whether prototypic items alone could yield clinically significant elevations. Likewise, this cutoff was used to determine whether the combined secondary/tertiary items could result in a significant elevation. Results from these analyses are reported in Table B.1 and are discussed more fully in Chapter 3.

Table B.1
MACI Scale Composition and Item Weight Contributions

Scale Composition	Raw Score Contribution	Possible BR Score[a]
1. Introversive (44 items)	0–72	
6 prototypic items	18	43
16 secondary items	32	71
22 tertiary items	22	50
Secondary and tertiary items	54	114
2A. Inhibited (37 items)	0–67	
6 prototypic items	18	42
18 secondary items	36	84
13 tertiary items	13	32
Secondary and tertiary items	49	101
2B. Doleful (24 items)	0–49	
7 prototypic items	21	73
11 secondary items	22	75
6 tertiary items	6	20
Secondary and tertiary items	28	87
3. Submissive (48 items)	0–83	
7 prototypic items	21	30
21 secondary items	42	52
20 tertiary items	20	29
Secondary and tertiary items	62	79
4. Dramatizing (41 items)	0–64	
6 prototypic items	18	29
11 secondary items	22	37
24 tertiary items	24	41
Secondary and tertiary items	46	65
5. Egotistic (39 items)	0–64	
6 prototypic items	18	27
13 secondary items	26	38
20 tertiary items	20	30
Secondary and tertiary items	46	68
6A. Unruly (39 items)	0–75	
8 prototypic items	24	49
20 secondary items	40	73
11 tertiary items	11	20
Secondary and tertiary items	51	89
6B. Forceful (22 items)	0–45	
7 prototypic items	21	72
9 secondary items	18	64
6 tertiary items	6	18
Secondary and tertiary items	24	79
7. Conforming (39 items)	0–65	
7 prototypic items	21	28
12 secondary items	24	33
20 tertiary items	20	27
Secondary and tertiary items	44	55

(continued)

Table B.1 (Continued)

Scale Composition	Raw Score Contribution	Possible BR Score[a]
8A. Oppositional (43 items)	0–63	
6 prototypic items	18	50
18 secondary items	36	78
19 tertiary items	19	49
Secondary and tertiary items	55	104
8B. Self-Demeaning (44 items)	0–74	
8 prototypic items	24	56
14 secondary items	28	68
22 tertiary items	22	52
Secondary and tertiary items	50	93
9. Borderline Tendency (21 items)[b]	0–42	
N/A prototypic items	N/A	N/A
N/A secondary items	N/A	N/A
N/A tertiary items	N/A	N/A
Secondary and tertiary items	N/A	N/A
A. Identity Diffusion (32 items)	0–49	
5 prototypic items	15	46
7 secondary items	14	43
20 tertiary items	20	61
Secondary and tertiary items	34	101
B. Self-Devaluation (38 items)	0–67	
5 prototypic items	15	31
19 secondary items	38	77
14 tertiary items	14	29
Secondary and tertiary items	52	98
C. Body Disapproval (17 items)	0–32	
5 prototypic items	15	50
5 secondary items	10	33
7 tertiary items	7	23
Secondary and tertiary items	17	57
D. Sexual Discomfort (37 items)	0–57	
5 prototypic items	15	27
10 secondary items	20	36
22 tertiary items	22	40
Secondary and tertiary items	42	82
E. Peer Insecurity (19 items)	0–34	
4 prototypic items	12	64
7 secondary items	14	74
8 tertiary items	8	43
Secondary and tertiary items	22	85
F. Social Insensitivity (39 items)	0–65	
5 prototypic items	15	32
16 secondary items	32	67
18 tertiary items	18	46
Secondary and tertiary items	50	103

Table B.1 (Continued)

Scale Composition	Raw Score Contribution	Possible BR Score[a]
G. Family Discord (28 items)	0–44	
5 prototypic items	15	65
6 secondary items	12	52
17 tertiary items	17	72
Secondary and tertiary items	29	95
H. Childhood Abuse (24 items)	0–37	
5 prototypic items	15	59
3 secondary items	6	24
16 tertiary items	16	63
Secondary and tertiary items	22	80
AA. Eating Dysfunctions (20 items)	0–44	
10 prototypic items	30	66
4 secondary items	8	19
6 tertiary items	6	14
Secondary and tertiary items	14	34
BB. Substance Abuse Proneness (35 items)	0–64	
10 prototypic items	30	66
9 secondary items	18	39
16 tertiary items	16	35
Secondary and tertiary items	34	74
CC. Delinquent Predisposition (34 items)	0–52	
5 prototypic items	15	34
8 secondary items	16	36
21 tertiary items	21	48
Secondary and tertiary items	37	87
DD. Impulsive Propensity (24 items)	0–38	
5 prototypic items	15	47
4 secondary items	8	25
15 tertiary items	15	47
Secondary and tertiary items	23	72
EE. Anxious Feelings (42 items)	0–57	
5 prototypic items	15	32
5 secondary items	10	22
32 tertiary items	32	68
Secondary and tertiary items	42	97
FF. Depressive Affect (33 items)	0–56	
5 prototypic items	15	66
13 secondary items	26	87
15 tertiary items	15	66
Secondary and tertiary items	41	109
GG. Suicidal Tendency (25 items)	0–41	
5 prototypic items	15	48
6 secondary items	12	39
14 tertiary items	14	45
Secondary and tertiary items	26	78

[a] Base Rate scores are the average of the four values obtained from converting the raw score contribution to BR scores for each of the four normative groups in the MACI manual (i.e., 13–15-year-old males and females and 16–19-year-old males and females).
[b] Scale 9 (Borderline Tendency) does not have any prototypic items and is composed of mostly secondary items; therefore, analyses were not performed for this scale.

APPENDIX C

Content Scales for the MACI Personality Patterns Scales

The following content scales for each of the MACI Personality Patterns scales were derived by factor analysis, followed by refinement on theoretical and substantive grounds (Davis, 1994). Individual item responses on these scales were factor analyzed and specific items were eliminated in cases where factor loadings were marginal or individual items did not have a clear substantive connection to the apparent theme of each subscale.

Content scales are reported such that the thematic descriptor for each is followed by the internal consistency (i.e., alpha coefficient) and the individual items making up each subscale. Also listed are the keyed direction for each item on a subscale, item weight attached to each item for the overall scale, and the text of the MACI item.

These content scales are provided to offer some empirical support for the validity of each Personality Patterns scale, to assist with interpretation, and to stimulate further research.

SCALE 1: INTROVERSIVE

EXISTENTIAL AIMLESSNESS ($\alpha = 0.80$)

F 2	002.	I'm pretty sure I know who I am and what I want in life.
T 1	034.	I often feel as if I'm floating around sort of lost in life.
T 1	115.	Other people my age seem more sure than I am of who they are and what they want.
F 2	145.	I'm very mature for my age and know what I want to do in life.
T 1	147.	My future seems hopeless.
T 2	154.	I feel pretty aimless and don't know where I'm going.

ANHEDONIC AFFECT ($\alpha = 0.60$)

T 3	012.	Nothing much seems to happen to make me either happy or sad.
T 2	047.	Very few things or activities seem to give me pleasure.
T 3	061.	I don't seem to have much feeling for others.
T 3	085.	I don't seem to enjoy being with people.
T 2	091.	I rarely look forward to anything with pleasure.

SOCIAL ISOLATION ($\alpha = 0.80$)

T 1	013.	I seem to have a problem getting along with other teenagers.
T 1	024.	I seem to fit in right away with any group of new kids I meet.
T 1	035.	Most other teenagers don't seem to like me.
T 2	038.	I often feel that others do not want to be friendly to me.
T 1	069.	I feel left out of things socially.
F 2	070.	I make friends easily.
T 2	119.	Others my age never seem to call me to get together with them.
T 1	142.	Although I want to have friends I have almost none.

SEXUAL INDIFFERENCE ($\alpha = 0.50$)

T 1	051.	I don't think I have as much interest in sex as others my age.
F 2	059.	I like to flirt a lot.
T 1	116.	Thinking about sex confuses me much of the time.
F 1	143.	I am glad that feelings about sex have become a part of my life now.

SCALE 2A: INHIBITED

EXISTENTIAL SADNESS ($\alpha = 0.77$)

T 2	064.	I often feel sad and unloved.
T 2	080.	I often feel I'm not worthy of the nice things in my life.
T 2	084.	I sometimes feel very unhappy with who I am.
T 2	140.	I don't like being the person I've become.
T 2	153.	I feel lonely and empty most of the time.

PREFERRED DETACHMENT ($\alpha = 0.52$)

F 2	024.	I seem to fit in right away with any group of new kids I meet.
T 2	036.	When I have a choice I prefer to do things alone.
T 1	085.	I don't seem to enjoy being with people.
T 1	100.	Socially I'm a loner and I don't mind it.

SELF-CONSCIOUS RESTRAINT ($\alpha = 0.55$)

F 1	018.	I usually act quickly without thinking.
F 1	077.	When things get boring, I like to stir up some excitement.
F 2	117.	I do what I want without worrying about its effects on others.
F 2	149.	When I don't get my way I quickly lose my temper.

SEXUAL AVERSION ($\alpha = 0.60$)

T 1	051.	I don't think I have as much interest in sex as others my age.
F 2	059.	I like to flirt a lot.
F 1	062.	I enjoy thinking about sex.
T 1	116.	Thinking about sex confuses me much of the time.
F 2	143.	I am glad that feelings about sex have become a part of my life now.

REJECTION FEELINGS ($\alpha = 0.82$)

T 1	013.	I seem to have a problem getting along with other teenagers.
T 2	035.	Most other teenagers don't seem to like me.
T 3	038.	I often feel that others do not want to be friendly to me.
T 2	069.	I feel left out of things socially.
F 2	070.	I make friends easily.
T 3	087.	I'm very uncomfortable with people unless I'm sure they really like me.
T 3	106.	I won't get close to people because I'm afraid they may make fun of me.

T 2   119.   Others my age never seem to call me to get together with them.

T 3   142.   Although I want to have friends I have almost none.

UNATTRACTIVE SELF-IMAGE ($\alpha = 0.80$)

F 2   010.   I like the way I look.

T 1   026.   I hate the fact that I don't have the looks or brains I wish I had.

T 2   031.   Most people are better looking than I am.

F 1   068.   I think I have a good body.

T 3   071.   I'm a somewhat scared and anxious person.

T 3   099.   I don't think people see me as an attractive person.

T 3   127.   There are times I wish I was someone else.

SCALE 2B: DOLEFUL

BROODING MELANCHOLIA ($\alpha = 0.80$)

T 1   019.   I guess I'm a complainer who expects the worst to happen.

T 2   025.   So little of what I have done has been appreciated by others.

T 2   042.   I see myself as falling far short of what I'd like to be.

T 2   043.   Things in my life just go from bad to worse.

T 2   079.   I spend a lot of time worrying about my future.

T 2   084.   I sometimes feel very unhappy with who I am.

T 2   110.   Good things just don't last.

T 2   118.   Lots of things that look good today will turn out bad later.

T 3   121.   I make my life worse than it has to be.

T 1   140.   I don't like being the person I've become.

T 2   147.   My future seems hopeless.

T 1   154.   I feel pretty aimless and don't know where I'm going.

SOCIAL JOYLESSNESS ($\alpha = 0.55$)

T 3   047.   Very few things or activities seem to give me pleasure.

T 1   085.   I don't seem to enjoy being with people.

T 3   091.   I rarely look forward to anything with pleasure.

T 3   098.   I often feel lousy after something good has happened to me.

SELF-DESTRUCTIVE IDEATION (α = 0.69)

T 2   054.   I sometimes get so upset that I want to hurt myself seriously.

T 2   095.   No one really cares if I live or die.

T 2   107.   More and more often I have thought of ending my life.

ABANDONMENT FEARS (α = 0.67)

T 3   020.   It is not unusual to feel lonely and unwanted.

T 1   063.   I worry a great deal about being left alone.

T 3   064.   I often feel sad and unloved.

T 3   153.   I feel lonely and empty most of the time.

T 3   158.   There are times when nobody at home seems to care about me.

SCALE 3: SUBMISSIVE

DEFICIENT ASSERTIVENESS (α = 0.70)

F 1   018.   I usually act quickly without thinking.

F 2   021.   Punishment never stopped me from doing what I wanted.

F 1   044.   As soon as I get the impulse to do something I act on it.

F 2   092.   I'm very good at making up excuses to get out of trouble.

F 1   117.   I do what I want without worrying about its effects on others.

F 1   148.   My parents have had a hard time keeping me in line.

AUTHORITY RESPECT (α = 0.61)

T 2   006.   I can depend on my parents to be understanding of me.

T 1   093.   It is very important that children learn to obey their elders.

T 2   096.   We should respect our elders and not think we know better.

F 1   158.   There are times when nobody at home seems to care about me.

PACIFIC DISPOSITION ($\alpha = 0.75$)

F 2	028.	I sometimes scare other kids to get them to do what I want.
F 2	041.	I don't mind telling people something they won't like hearing.
F 2	052.	I don't see anything wrong with using others to get what I want.
F 2	078.	I will sometimes do something cruel to make someone unhappy.
F 2	097.	I sometimes get pleasure by hurting someone physically.
F 2	128.	I don't mind pushing people around to show my power.
F 2	157.	I enjoy starting fights.

ATTACHMENT ANXIETY ($\alpha = 0.59$)

T 3	063.	I worry a great deal about being left alone.
T 2	071.	I'm a somewhat scared and anxious person.
T 3	109.	I get frightened when I think of being all alone in the world.
T 1	132.	I often get frightened when I think of the things I have to do.

SOCIAL CORRECTNESS ($\alpha = 0.55$)

T 2	005.	I do my very best not to hurt other people's feelings.
T 2	009.	I always try to do what is proper.
T 2	023.	I like to follow instructions and do what others expect of me.
T 1	130.	I try to make everything I do as perfect as possible.

GUIDANCE SEEKING ($\alpha = 0.41$)

T 3	001.	I would rather follow someone than be the leader.
T 2	087.	I'm very uncomfortable with people unless I'm sure they really like me.
T 3	122.	I prefer being told what to do rather than having to decide for myself.
T 3	151.	I guess I depend too much on others to be helpful to me.

SCALE 4: DRAMATIZING

CONVIVIAL SOCIABILITY ($\alpha = 0.82$)

F 1	013.	I seem to have a problem getting along with other teenagers.
T 3	024.	I seem to fit in right away with any group of new kids I meet.
F 2	035.	Most other teenagers don't seem to like me.
F 1	036.	When I have a choice I prefer to do things alone.
F 2	038.	I often feel that others do not want to be friendly to me.
F 2	069.	I feel left out of things socially.
T 3	070.	I make friends easily.
F 2	085.	I don't seem to enjoy being with people.
F 1	100.	Socially I'm a loner and I don't mind it.
F 1	106.	I won't get close to people because I'm afraid they may make fun of me.
F 2	119.	Others my age never seem to call me to get together with them.
F 2	142.	Although I want to have friends I have almost none.

ATTENTION-SEEKING ($\alpha = 0.50$)

T 3	056.	I am a dramatic and showy sort of person.
T 3	059.	I like to flirt a lot.
T 3	103.	I like being the center of attention.
T 1	135.	I can charm people into giving me almost anything I want.

ATTRACTIVE SELF-IMAGE ($\alpha = 0.80$)

T 2	010.	I like the way I look.
F 1	026.	I hate the fact that I don't have the looks or brains I wish I had.
F 2	031.	Most people are better looking than I am.
F 1	084.	I sometimes feel very unhappy with who I am.
F 2	099.	I don't think people see me as an attractive person.
F 1	127.	There are times I wish I was someone else.

OPTIMISTIC OUTLOOK ($\alpha = 0.67$)

F 1	019.	I guess I'm a complainer who expects the worst to happen.
F 1	034.	I often feel as if I'm floating around sort of lost in life.
F 1	043.	Things in my life just go from bad to worse.
F 1	047.	Very few things or activities seem to give me pleasure.
F 1	110.	Good things just don't last.

BEHAVIORAL DISINHIBITION ($\alpha = 0.54$)

T 1	028.	I sometimes scare other kids to get them to do what I want.
T 3	077.	When things get boring, I like to stir up some excitement.
T 1	092.	I'm very good at making up excuses to get out of trouble.
T 1	111.	I've had a few "run-ins" with the law.
T 1	143.	I am glad that feelings about sex have become a part of my life now.
T 1	148.	My parents have had a hard time keeping me in line.

SCALE 5: EGOTISTIC

ADMIRABLE SELF-IMAGE ($\alpha = 0.84$)

T 2	010.	I like the way I look.
F 1	026.	I hate the fact that I don't have the looks or brains I wish I had.
F 2	031.	Most people are better looking than I am.
T 1	068.	I think I have a good body.
F 2	099.	I don't think people see me as an attractive person.
F 2	127.	There are times I wish I was someone else.
T 2	131.	I am pleased with the way my body has developed.

SOCIAL CONCEIT ($\alpha = 0.53$)

F 1	001.	I would rather follow someone than be the leader.
T 3	007.	Some people think of me as a bit conceited.
T 2	056.	I am a dramatic and showy sort of person.
T 1	059.	I like to flirt a lot.

T 2   103.   I like being the center of attention.

T 3   135.   I can charm people into giving me almost anything I want.

CONFIDENT PURPOSEFULNESS ($\alpha = 0.72$)

T 1   002.   I'm pretty sure I know who I am and what I want in life.

F 1   034.   I often feel as if I'm floating around sort of lost in life.

F 1   115.   Other people my age seem more sure than I am of who they are and what they want.

T 2   145.   I'm very mature for my age and know what I want to do in life.

SELF-ASSURED INDEPENDENCE ($\alpha = 0.58$)

F 1   019.   I guess I'm a complainer who expects the worst to happen.

F 1   020.   It is not unusual to feel lonely and unwanted.

F 1   025.   So little of what I have done has been appreciated by others.

F 2   063.   I worry a great deal about being left alone.

F 1   071.   I'm a somewhat scared and anxious person.

F 1   151.   I guess I depend too much on others to be helpful to me.

EMPATHIC INDIFFERENCE ($\alpha = 0.44$)

T 1   039.   I don't care much what other kids think of me.

T 1   041.   I don't mind telling people something they won't like hearing.

T 3   052.   I don't see anything wrong with using others to get what I want.

T 1   104.   If I want to do something I just do it without thinking of what might happen.

T 1   139.   I will make fun of someone in a group just to put them down.

SUPERIORITY FEELINGS ($\alpha = 0.55$)

F 2   084.   I sometimes feel very unhappy with who I am.

T 3   086.   I have talents that other kids wish they had.

T 3   101.   Almost anything I try comes easily for me.

F 2   140.   I don't like being the person I've become.

T 3   146.   In many ways I feel very superior to most people.

SCALE 6A: UNRULY

IMPULSIVE DISOBEDIENCE ($\alpha = 0.76$)

T 2   018.   I usually act quickly without thinking.

T 3   021.   Punishment never stopped me from doing what I wanted.

T 2   044.   As soon as I get the impulse to do something I act on it.

T 2   077.   When things get boring, I like to stir up some excitement.

T 2   104.   If I want to do something I just do it without thinking of what might happen.

T 3   117.   I do what I want without worrying about its effects on others.

T 3   148.   My parents have had a hard time keeping me in line.

T 2   149.   When I don't get my way I quickly lose my temper.

SOCIALIZED SUBSTANCE ABUSE ($\alpha = 0.75$)

F 2   008.   I would never use drugs no matter what.

T 2   057.   I can hold my beer or liquor better than most of my friends.

T 1   120.   There have been times when I could not get through the day without some pot.

T 1   150.   I often have fun doing certain unlawful things.

T 1   152.   When we're having a good time my friends and I can get pretty drunk.

AUTHORITY REJECTION ($\alpha = 0.64$)

F 2   005.   I do my very best not to hurt people's feelings.

F 2   009.   I always try to do what is proper.

F 2   023.   I like to follow instructions and do what others expect of me.

F 2   093.   It is very important that children learn to obey their elders.

F 1   096.   We should respect our elders and not think we know better.

T 3   155.   Telling lies is a pretty normal thing to do.

UNLAWFUL ACTIVITY ($\alpha = 0.60$)

F 2   015.   I've never done anything for which I could have been arrested.

F 2   045.   I've never been called a juvenile delinquent.

T 2   073.   I'm no different from lots of other kids who steal things now and then.

T 2   111.   I've had a few "run-ins" with the law.

CALLOUS MANIPULATION ($\alpha = 0.60$)

T 2   028.   I sometimes scare other kids to get them to do what I want.

T 2   041.   I don't mind telling people something they won't like hearing.

T 1   052.   I don't see anything wrong with using others to get what I want.

T 3   058.   Parents and teachers are too hard on kids who don't follow the rules.

T 3   076.   Too many rules get in the way of my doing what I want.

T 3   092.   I'm very good at making up excuses to get out of trouble.

T 1   135.   I can charm people into giving me almost anything I want.

SEXUAL ABSORPTION ($\alpha = 0.50$)

F 1   I don't think I have as much interest in sex as others my age.

T 1   I like to flirt a lot.

F 1   Thinking about sex confuses me much of the time.

T 2   I am glad that feelings about sex have become part of my life now.

SCALE 6B: FORCEFUL

INTIMIDATING ABRASIVENESS ($\alpha = 0.78$)

T 3   028.   I sometimes scare other kids to get them to do what I want.

T 2	052.	I don't see anything wrong with using others to get what I want.
T 3	078.	I will sometimes do something cruel to make someone unhappy.
T 3	097.	I sometimes get pleasure by hurting someone physically.
T 3	128.	I don't mind pushing people around to show my power.
T 3	139.	I will make fun of someone in a group just to put them down.
T 3	157.	I enjoy starting fights.

PRECIPITOUS ANGER ($\alpha = 0.79$)

T 1	018.	I usually act quickly without thinking.
T 2	021.	Punishment never stopped me from doing what I wanted.
T 1	074.	I prefer to act first and think about it later.
T 2	104.	If I want to do something I just do it without thinking of what might happen.
T 2	117.	I do what I want without worrying about its effects on others.
T 2	148.	My parents have had a hard time keeping me in line.
T 2	149.	When I don't get my way I quickly lose my temper.

EMPATHIC DEFICIENCY ($\alpha = 0.45$)

F 2	005.	I do my very best not to hurt other people's feelings.
T 3	041.	I don't mind telling people something they won't like hearing.
T 2	060.	To see someone suffering doesn't bother me.
F 2	081.	I sort of feel sad when I see someone who's lonely.

SCALE 7: CONFORMING

INTERPERSONAL RESTRAINT ($\alpha = 0.78$)

F 2	018.	I usually act quickly without thinking.
F 2	021.	Punishment never stopped me from doing what I wanted.
F 2	074.	I prefer to act first and think about it later.
F 1	104.	If I want to do something I just do it without thinking of what might happen.

F 2   117.   I do what I want without worrying about its effects on others.

F 1   149.   When I don't get my way I quickly lose my temper.

EMOTIONAL RIGIDITY ($\alpha = 0.80$)

F 1   019.   I guess I'm a complainer who expects the worst to happen.

F 1   034.   I often feel as if I'm floating around sort of lost in life.

F 2   042.   I see myself as falling far short of what I'd like to be.

F 1   043.   Things in my life just go from bad to worse.

F 2   107.   More and more often I have thought of ending my life.

F 1   110.   Good things just don't last.

F 1   118.   Lots of things that look good today will turn out bad later.

F 1   133.   Lately, I feel jumpy and nervous almost all the time.

T 2   145.   I'm very mature for my age and know what I want to do in life.

F 2   154.   I feel pretty aimless and don't know where I'm going.

RULE ADHERENCE ($\alpha = 0.58$)

F 1   004.   I often resent doing things others expect of me.

T 3   050.   It is good to have a routine for doing most things.

T 3   093.   It is very important that children learn to obey their elders.

T 3   096.   We should respect our elders and not think we know better.

T 3   159.   It is good to have a regular way of doing things so as to avoid mistakes.

SOCIAL CONFORMITY ($\alpha = 0.64$)

T 2   015.   I've never done anything for which I could have been arrested.

F 2   073.   I'm no different from lots of other kids who steal things now and then.

F 1   090.   Drinking really seems to help me when I'm feeling down.

F 1   148.   My parents have had a hard time keeping me in line.

F 2   150.   I often have fun doing certain unlawful things.

RESPONSIBLE CONSCIENTIOUSNESS ($\alpha = 0.51$)

T 3   009.   I always try to do what is proper.

T 3   023.   I like to follow instructions and do what others expect of me.

F 1   058.   Parents and teachers are too hard on kids who don't follow the rules.

T 3   130.   I try to make everything I do as perfect as possible.

SCALE 8A: OPPOSITIONAL

SELF-PUNITIVENESS ($\alpha = 0.74$)

T 1   016.   I think everyone would be better off if I were dead.

T 2   054.   I sometimes get so upset that I want to hurt myself seriously.

T 2   066.   I often deserve it when others put me down.

T 2   088.   Killing myself may be the easiest way of solving my problems.

T 2   095.   No one really cares if I live or die.

T 2   107.   More and more often I have thought of ending my life.

ANGRY-DOMINANCE ($\alpha = 0.74$)

T 1   028.   I sometimes scare other kids to get them to do what I want.

T 2   078.   I will sometimes do something cruel to make someone unhappy.

T 2   097.   I sometimes get pleasure by hurting someone physically.

T 1   128.   I don't mind pushing people around to show my power.

T 2   149.   When I don't get my way I quickly lose my temper.

T 2   157.   I enjoy starting fights.

RESENTFUL DISCONTENT ($\alpha = 0.77$)

T 3   004.   I often resent doing things others expect of me.

T 2   019.   I guess I'm a complainer who expects the worst to happen.

F 2	023.	I like to follow instructions and do what others expect of me.
T 3	025.	So little of what I have done has been appreciated by others.
T 1	034.	I often feel as if I'm floating around sort of lost in life.
T 3	067.	People put pressure on me to do more than is fair.
T 2	091.	I rarely look forward to anything with pleasure.
T 1	105.	I'm terribly afraid that no matter how thin I get, I will start to gain weight if I eat.
T 3	110.	Good things just don't last.
T 3	118.	Lots of things that look good today will turn out bad later.
T 1	127.	There are times I wish I was someone else.
T 3	136.	Many other kids get breaks I don't get.
T 1	158.	There are times when nobody at home seems to care about me.

Social Inconsiderateness ($\alpha = 0.52$)

F 1	005.	I do my very best not to hurt other people's feelings.
T 2	037.	Becoming involved in other people's problems is a waste of time.
T 2	039.	I don't care much what other kids think of me.
T 1	041.	I don't mind telling people something they won't like hearing.
T 1	049.	I find it hard to feel sorry for people who are always worried about things.
T 2	117.	I do what I want without worrying about its effects on others.

Contrary Conduct ($\alpha = 0.50$)

T 1	018.	I usually act quickly without thinking.
F 1	045.	I've never been called a juvenile delinquent.
F 2	073.	I'm no different from lots of other kids who steal things now and then.
T 1	148.	My parents have had a hard time keeping me in line.

SCALE 8B: SELF-DEMEANING

Self-Ruination ($\alpha = 0.73$)

F 2	002.	I'm pretty sure I know who I am and what I want in life.
T 3	019.	I guess I'm a complainer who expects the worst to happen.
T 2	034.	I often feel as if I'm floating around sort of lost in life.
T 3	046.	I'm often my own worst enemy.
T 1	121.	I make my life worse than it has to be.
T 2	140.	I don't like being the person I've become.
T 3	141.	I seem to make a mess of the good things that come my way.

Low Self-Valuation ($\alpha = 0.84$)

F 1	010.	I like the way I look.
T 1	026.	I hate the fact that I don't have the looks or brains I wish I had.
F 2	068.	I think I have a good body.
T 2	084.	I sometimes feel very unhappy with who I am.
T 2	099.	I don't think people see me as an attractive person.
T 2	112.	I'd like to trade bodies with someone else.
T 2	127.	There are times I wish I was someone else.

Undeserving Self-Image ($\alpha = 0.57$)

T 3	066.	I often deserve it when others put me down.
T 3	080.	I often feel I'm not worthy of the nice things in my life.
T 3	089.	I sometimes get confused or upset when people are nice to me.
T 3	108.	I sometimes put myself down just to make someone else feel better.
T 3	160.	I probably deserve many of the problems I have.

Hopeless Outlook ($\alpha = 0.72$)

T 2	020.	It is not unusual to feel lonely and unwanted.
T 1	025.	So little of what I have done has been appreciated by others.

T 1	064.	I often feel sad and unloved.
T 2	110.	Good things just don't last.
T 1	118.	Lots of things that look good today will turn out bad later.
T 1	136.	Many other kids get breaks I don't get.
T 1	153.	I feel lonely and empty most of the time.

SCALE 9: BORDERLINE TENDENCIES

EMPTY LONELINESS ($\alpha = 0.72$)

T 2	063.	I worry a great deal about being left alone.
T 2	064.	I often feel sad and unloved.
T 2	084.	I sometimes feel very unhappy with who I am.
T 1	121.	I make my life worse than it has to be.
T 2	141.	I seem to make a mess of the good things that come my way.
T 2	153.	I feel lonely and empty most of the time.

CAPRICIOUS REACTIVITY ($\alpha = 0.70$)

T 2	004.	I often resent doing things others expect of me.
T 2	018.	I usually act quickly without thinking.
T 2	044.	As soon as I get the impulse to do something I act on it.
T 1	078.	I will sometimes do something cruel to make someone unhappy.
T 2	104.	If I want to do something I just do it without thinking of what might happen.
T 2	117.	I do what I want without worrying about its effects on others.

UNCERTAIN SELF-IMAGE ($\alpha = 0.78$)

F 2	002.	I'm pretty sure I know who I am and what I want in life.
T 2	034.	I often feel as if I'm floating around sort of lost in life.
T 2	115.	Other people my age seem more sure than I am of who they are and what they want.
F 2	145.	I'm very mature for my age and know what I want to do in life.
T 2	154.	I feel pretty aimless and don't know where I'm going.

SUICIDAL IMPULSIVITY ($\alpha = 0.63$)

T 2	054.	I sometimes get so upset that I want to hurt myself seriously.
T 2	088.	Killing myself may be the easiest way of solving my problems.
T 2	107.	More and more often I have thought of ending my life.
T 2	149.	When I don't get my way I quickly lose my temper.

References

Acklin, M. W. (1993). Integrating the Rorschach and the MMPI in clinical assessment: Conceptual and methodological issues. *Journal of Personality Assessment, 60*, 125–131.

American Psychiatric Association. (1994). *Diagnostic and statistical manual of mental disorders* (4th ed.). Washington, DC: Author.

Andreasen, N. C. (1985). Positive vs. negative schizophrenia: A critical evaluation. *Schizophrenia Bulletin, 11*, 380–389.

Andreasen, N. C., & Flaum, M. (1991). Schizophrenia: The characteristic symptoms. *Schizophrenia Bulletin, 17*, 27–50.

Antoni, M. H. (1997). Integrating the MCMI and the MMPI. In T. Millon (Ed.), *The Millon inventories: Clinical and personality assessment* (pp. 106–123). New York: Guilford Press.

Archer, R. P., & Ball, J. D. (1988). Issues in the assessment of adolescent psychopathology. In R. L. Greene (Ed.), *The MMPI: Use with specific populations* (pp. 259–277). Philadelphia: Grune & Stratton.

Archer, R. P., & Kristnamurthy, R. (1993). Combining the Rorschach and the MMPI in the assessment of adolescents. *Journal of Personality Assessment, 60*, 132–140.

Archer, R. P., Maruish, M., Imhof, E. A., & Piotrowski, C. (1991). Psychological test usage with adolescent clients: 1990 survey findings. *Professional Psychology: Research and Practice, 22*, 247–252.

Atkinson, L. (1986). The comparative validities of the Rorschach and MMPI: A meta-analysis. *Canadian Psychology, 27*, 238–247.

Bagby, R. M., Gillis, J. R., & Rogers, R. (1991). Effectiveness of the Millon clinical multiaxial inventory validity index in the detection of random responding. *Psychological Assessment, 3*, 285–287.

Beck, A. T., & Steer, R. A. (1987). *Beck depression inventory manual.* San Antonio, TX: Psychological Corporation.

Beck, A. T., & Steer, R. A. (1988). *Beck hopelessness scale manual.* San Antonio, TX: Psychological Corporation.

Beck A. T., & Steer, R. A. (1990). *Beck anxiety scale manual.* San Antonio, TX: Psychological Corporation.

Berman, A. L., & Jobes, D. A. (1991). *Adolescent suicide: Assessment and intervention.* Washington, DC: American Psychological Association.

Briere, J. (1992). *Child abuse trauma: Theory and treatment of the lasting effects.* Newbury Park, CA: Sage.

Briere, J. (1996). *Trauma symptom checklist for children (TSCC): Professional manual.* Odessa, FL: Psychological Assessment Resources.

Brown, D. T. (1985). Review of the Millon adolescent personality inventory. In J. V. Mitchell (Ed.), *Ninth mental measurement yearbook* (pp. 978–979). Lincoln, NE: Buros Institute.

Butcher, J. N., Williams, C. L., Graham, J. R., Archer, R. P., Tellegen, A., Ben-Porath, Y. S., & Kaemmer, B. (1992). *MMPI-A manual for administration, scoring, and interpretation.* Minneapolis: University of Minnesota Press.

Coleman, J. C. (1992). The nature of adolescence. In J. C. Coleman & C. Warren-Adamson (Eds.), *Youth policy in the 1990's: The way forward* (pp. 8–27). London: Routledge and Kegan Paul.

Cook, L. D. (1979). The adolescent with a learning disability: A developmental perspective. *Adolescence, 14,* 697–707.

Davis, R. D. (1994). *The development of content scales for the Millon adolescent clinical inventory.* Unpublished master's thesis.

Dorr, D. (1997). Clinical integration of the MCMI-III and the comprehensive system Rorschach. In T. Millon (Ed.), *The Millon inventories: Clinical and personality assessment* (pp. 75–105). New York: Guilford Press.

Dyer, F. J. (1985). Millon adolescent personality inventory. In D. J. Keyser & R. C. Sweetland (Eds.), *Test critiques* (Vol. 4, pp. 425–433). Kansas City, MO: Test Corporation of America.

Elliott, D. M., & Briere, J. (1995). Posttraumatic stress associated with delayed recall of sexual abuse: A general population study. *Journal of Traumatic Stress, 8,* 629–647.

Erikson, E. G. (1968). *Identity: Youth and crisis.* New York: Norton.

Everly, G. S. (1995). Domain-oriented personality theory. In P. D. Retzlaff (Ed.), *Tactical psychotherapy of the personality disorders: An MCMI-III-based approach* (pp. 24–39). Needham Heights, MA: Allyn & Bacon.

Exner, J. E. (1993). *The Rorschach: A comprehensive system* (Vol. 1, 3rd ed.). New York: Wiley.

Federal Bureau of Investigation. (1993). *Uniform crime reports: 1993.* Washington, DC: U.S. Department of Justice.

Finkelhor, D., Hotaling, G., Lewis, I. A., & Smith, C. (1989). Sexual abuse and its relationship to later sexual satisfaction, marital status, religion, and attitudes. *Journal of Interpersonal Violence, 4,* 279–299.

Ganellen, R. J. (1996). *Integrating the Rorschach and the MMPI-2 in personality assessment.* Mahwah, NJ: Erlbaum.

Garfield, S. L. (Ed.). (1995). *Psychotherapy: An eclectic-integrative approach* (2nd ed.). New York: Wiley.

Garner, D. M. (1991). *Eating disorders inventory–2: Professional manual.* Odessa, FL: Psychological Assessment Resources.

Greenbaum, P. E., Prange, M. E., Friedman, R. M., & Silver, S. E. (1991). Substance abuse prevalence and comorbidity with other psychiatric disorders among adolescents with severe emotional disturbances. *Journal of the American Academy of Child and Adolescent Psychiatry, 30,* 575–583.

Grilo, C. M., Fehon, D. C., Walker, M., & Martino, S. (1996). A comparison of adolescent inpatients with and without substance abuse using the Millon adolescent clinical inventory. *Journal of Youth and Adolescence, 25,* 379–388.

Hart, L. R. (1991). The egocentricity index as a measure of self-esteem and egocentric personality style for inpatient adolescents. *Perceptual and Motor Skills, 73,* 907–914.

Hase, H. E., & Goldberg, L. R. (1967). Comparative validity of different strategies of deriving personality inventory scales. *Psychological Bulletin, 67,* 231–248.

Ihilevich, D., & Gleser, G. C. (1986). *Defense mechanisms: Their classification, correlates, and measurement with the defense mechanisms inventory.* Owosso, MI: DMI Associates.

Jackson, D. N. (1970). A sequential system for personality scale development. In C. D. Spielberger (Ed.), *Current topics in clinical and community psychology* (Vol. 2, pp. 61–92). New York: Academic Press.

Johnson, B. A., Brent, D. A., Connolly, J., Bridge, J., Matta, J., Constantine, D., Rather, C., & White, T. (1995). Familial aggregation of adolescent personality disorders. *Journal of the American Academy of Child and Adolescent Psychiatry, 34,* 798–804.

Knoff, H. M., & Paez, D. (1992). Investigating the relationship between the Millon adolescent personality inventory and the personality inventory for children with a sample of learning disabled adolescents. *Psychological Reports, 70,* 775–785.

Loevinger, J. (1957). Objective tests or instruments of psychological theory. *Psychological Reports, 3,* 635–694.

Marton, P., Korenblum, M., Kutchner, S., Stein, B., Kennedy, B., & Pakes, J. (1989). Personality dysfunction in depressed adolescents. *Canadian Journal of Psychiatry, 34,* 810–813.

Mattanah, J. J. F., Becker, D. F., Levy, K. N., Edell, W. S., & McGlashan, T. H. (1995). Diagnostic stability in adolescents followed up 2 years after hospitalization. *American Journal of Psychiatry, 152,* 889–894.

McCann, J. T. (1990). A multitrait-multimethod analysis of the MCMI-II clinical syndrome scales. *Journal of Personality Assessment, 55,* 465–476.

McCann, J. T. (1991). Convergent and discriminant validity of the MCMI-II and MMPI personality disorder scales. *Psychological Assessment, 3,* 9–18.

McCann, J. T. (1997). The MACI: Composition and clinical applications. In T. Millon (Ed.), *The Millon inventories: Clinical and personality assessment* (pp. 363–388). New York: Guilford Press.

McCann, J. T. (1998). *Malingering and deception in adolescents: Assessing credibility in clinical and forensic settings.* Washington, DC: American Psychological Association.

McCann, J. T., & Dyer, F. J. (1996). *Forensic assessment with the Millon inventories.* New York: Guilford Press.

McCann, J. T., & Gergelis, R. E. (1990). Utility of the MCMI-II in assessing suicide risk. *Journal of Clinical Psychology, 46,* 764–770.

Millon, T. (1969). *Modern psychopathology: A biosocial approach.* Philadelphia: Saunders.

Millon, T. (1981). *Disorders of personality: DSM-III: Axis II.* New York: Wiley.

Millon, T. (1990). *Toward a new personology: An evolutionary model.* New York: Wiley.

Millon, T. (1994). *Manual for the Millon clinical multiaxial inventory–III.* Minneapolis, MN: National Computer Systems.

Millon, T., & Davis, R. D. (1993). The Millon adolescent personality inventory and the Millon adolescent clinical inventory. *Journal of Counseling & Development, 71,* 570–574.

Millon, T., & Davis, R. D. (1994). *Disorders of personality: DSM-IV and beyond.* New York: Wiley.

Millon, T., Davis, R., & Millon, C. (1997). *MCMI-III manual.* Minneapolis, MN: National Computer Systems.

Millon, T., Green, C. J., & Meagher, R. B. (1982). *Millon adolescent personality inventory manual.* Minneapolis, MN: National Computer Systems.

Millon, T., Millon, C., & Davis, R. (1993). *Millon adolescent clinical inventory manual.* Minneapolis, MN: National Computer Systems.

Moffitt, T. (1993). Adolescence-limited and life-course-persistent antisocial behavior: A developmental taxonomy. *Psychological Review, 100,* 674–701.

National Institute on Drug Abuse. (1991). *The adolescent assessment/referral system manual* (DHHS Pub. No. ADM 91-1735). Washington, DC: U.S. Government Printing Office.

Norcross, J. C., & Goldfried, M. R. (Eds.). (1992). *Handbook of psychotherapy integration.* New York: Basic Books.

Parker, K. C. H., Hanson, R. K., & Hunsley, J. (1998). MMPI, Rorschach, and WAIS: A meta-analytic comparison of reliability, stability, and validity. *Psychological Bulletin, 103,* 367–373.

Petersen, A. C. (1988). Adolescent development. *Annual Review of Psychology, 39,* 583–607.

Reinherz, H. Z., Giaconia, R. M., Lefkowitz, E. S., Padis, B., & Frost, A. K. (1993). Prevalence of psychiatric disorders in a community population of older adolescents. *Journal of the American Academy of Child and Adolescent Psychiatry, 32,* 369–377.

Retzlaff, P. D. (Ed.). (1995). *Tactical psychotherapy of the personality disorders: An MCMI-III-based approach.* Needham Heights, MA: Allyn & Bacon.

Retzlaff, P. D., Sheehan, E., & Lorr, M. (1990). MCMI-II scoring: Weighted and unweighted algorithms. *Journal of Personality Assessment, 55,* 219–223.

Rey, J. M., Morris-Yates, A., Singh, M., Andrews, G., & Stewart, G. W. (1995). Continuities between psychiatric disorders in adolescents and personality disorders in young adults. *American Journal of Psychiatry, 152,* 895–900.

Rogers, R. (1995). *Diagnostic and structured interviewing: A handbook for psychologists.* Odessa, FL: Psychological Assessment Resources.

Rogers, R. (1997). *Clinical assessment of malingering and deception* (2nd ed.). New York: Guilford Press.

Rogers, R., Bagby, R. M., & Dickens, S. E. (1992). *Structured interview of reported symptoms: Professional manual.* Odessa, FL: Psychological Assessment Resources.

Rubenzer, S. (1992). A comparison of traditional and computer-generated psychological reports in an adolescent inpatient setting. *Journal of Clinical Psychology, 48,* 817–827.

Schiraldi, V. (1998). Making sense of juvenile homicides in America. *Criminal Justice, 13*(2), 63–64.

Singer, M. I., Anglin, T. M., Song, L. Y., & Lunghofer, L. (1995). Adolescents' exposure to violence and associated symptoms of psychological trauma. *Journal of the American Medical Association, 273*, 477–482.

Timmons-Mitchell, J., Brown, C., Schulz, S. C., Webster, S. E., Underwood, L. A., & Semple, W. E. (1997). Comparing the mental health needs of female and male incarcerated juvenile delinquents. *Behavioral Sciences & the Law, 15*, 195–202.

Timmons-Mitchell, J., Brown, C., Underwood, L. A., Johnston, C., & Schulz, S. C. (1996). *Assessing the mental health of adolescents in the mental health and juvenile justice systems.* Paper presented at the 8th Annual Research and Training Center Conference of the Florida Mental Health Institute, University of South Florida, Tampa, FL.

Trenerry, M. R., & Pantle, M. (1990). MAPI code types in an inpatient crisis unit sample. *Journal of Personality Assessment, 55*, 683–691.

Watson, R. A., & Pantle, J. L. (1993). Reflection on the Rorschach and the Millon adolescent personality inventory. *Perceptual and Motor Skills, 77*, 1138.

Weiner, I. B. (1993). Clinical consideration in the conjoint use of the Rorschach and the MMPI. *Journal of Personality Assessment, 60*, 148–152.

Widiger, T. A. (1985). Review of the Millon adolescent personality inventory. In J. V. Mitchell (Ed.), *Ninth mental measurements yearbook* (pp. 979–981). Lincoln, NE: Buros Institute.

Widiger, T. A., Mangine, S., Corbitt, E. M., Ellis, C. G., & Thomas, G. V. (1995). *Personality disorder interview-IV: A semi-structured interview for the assessment of personality disorders.* Odessa, FL: Psychological Assessment Resources.

Author Index

Subject Index